CABELA'S – THE FIRST HALF CENTURY

CELEBRATING 50 YEARS AS THE WORLD'S FOREMOST OUTFITTER

Editor

Joe Arterburn

Content Advisor

Sharon Robison

50th Anniversary Book Committee
Tom Rosdail
Tim Joseph
Sharon Robison
Brenda Appelhans
Joe Arterburn
Larry Brown
Mark Mazour
Casey Smith

Design and Layout
Tim Hackleman
Katherine Dayton

Editorial Contributors
Kristin Lauver
Chuck Smock
Kent Walton

Cover and Feature Photography
by Luke Fasoldt and Torrey Morrison

Publication Consultants
InterMedia Outdoors, Inc.
Dick Metcalf
Jim Bequette

Printing
Printed in the USA by Quad Graphics

Published by:
Cabela's Inc.,
One Cabela Drive
Sidney, NE 69160

ISBN: 978-0-615-44785-8

WORLDSFOREMOSTOUTFITTER
Cabela's
OUTDOOR GEAR
SINCE 1961

Contents

Dedication

The list of people we would like to thank for helping us live this American dream includes thousands – friends, employees, friends who became employees, employees who became friends; vendors and other business associates; shareholders who put their faith in us; and our dear loyal customers.

When we started out, we never thought of becoming a multibillion-dollar company with thousands of employees and exciting retail stores across the United States and Canada. It was just a lot of hard work and long days, but it also was fun – because we were selling fun. We were joined by like-minded employees and we grew, a phenomenon that continues to this day.

When asked if someone could now duplicate our success, we say, "Certainly." Find something you love and pour your heart and soul into it. Take small steps, but always move forward. If you stumble, pick yourself up and go again. The only ones who never fail are those who never try.

As you will read, we come from a long line of business entrepreneurs. So, for us it is virtually impossible to explain the sense of pride we feel when we see the Cabela name on stores, catalogs, products and our website and, especially, when our customers tell us how much they love our company. Believe us, the feeling is mutual.

We have been blessed with wonderful employees and customers, and it is to all of them – the Cabela's family of employees and customers – we dedicate this book, this chronicle of our first 50 years. To that dedication we would like to add our thanks to our parents and grandparents for instilling in us the importance of hard work, honesty, integrity and a fair deal.

It has been an extraordinary experience, one we never could have hoped to dream.

Thank you, and God bless you all.

Sincerely,

Jim Cabela Mary Cabela Dick Cabela

Preface: A Moment of Clarity

The Miracle Mile of the North Platte River near Casper, Wyoming.

Dick Cabela looked upstream at fishermen casting into the North Platte River's famed Miracle Mile near Casper, Wyoming. Then he looked at fishermen lining the downstream banks.

It was April 1961. President Kennedy took office, created the Peace Corps and challenged Americans to be the first to put a man on the moon. Alan Shepherd became the first American in space. To Kill a Mockingbird was published; and moviegoers lined up to see West Side Story and Breakfast at Tiffany's.

Dick had been pondering a predicament he was in back home in Chappell, Nebraska. The previous January he had impulsively purchased 2,880 fishing flies at a bargain price while in Chicago with his father on a buying trip for the family furniture and hardware store. He had planned to sell them through the store's small sporting-goods display. But they weren't selling.

Contemplating this on the crowded Platte riverbank, he had a moment of clarity. Instead of waiting for fishermen to happen into Cabela's furniture store to buy the flies, he would take the flies to the fishermen.

After all, how many fishermen live in or around Chappell? How many passed through town, and of those, how many were likely to come into the store looking for flies? If any – and there hadn't been one since his fly purchase – it would be a fraction of the total number of fishermen outside this Midwest farm community.

And how many fishermen loved to fish, but, like himself, didn't live near a well-stocked sporting-goods supplier?

Dick Cabela's mother, Marian, often said when Dick and his younger brother, Jim, were growing up, they would rather fish or hunt than eat. So it was no surprise that while Dick and his wife, Mary, were visiting family in her hometown of Casper, he found time to fish.

Driving home to Chappell, he told Mary he had decided to start a fishing supply company and try to sell the flies through classified ads in publications read by fishermen. That was 50 years ago. After an adjustment in ad strategy, the flies began to sell. The business, and sales, began to grow.

Dick approached his brother, Jim, with a surprising proposal. If Jim would resign his banking job in Denver, return to Chappell and take over day-to-day operation of the fledgling company, Dick would give him half-ownership in Cabela's Distributing Company. Jim accepted, and joined Cabela's in early 1963.

Two years apart in age, Dick and Jim had grown up as companions, roaming the grassy hills around Chappell with, first, a BB gun and later an old .22-caliber pump rifle they shared. They camped during all four seasons, if not outside town, then in the backyard; they learned to fish on nearby Lodgepole Creek. The outdoors was more than boyhood recreation. It would be their lifetime passion.

It was a leap of faith, for both of them, yet it seemed reasonable to two young men with an idea and a deep love of the outdoors.

From the brothers' shared passion grew what is today universally recognized as the World's Foremost Outfitter, a global phenomenon that in 2009 tallied more than $2.6 billion in revenues from mail-order-catalog, telephone and online sales, and a growing number of strategically placed retail stores.

Cabela's has revolutionized the outdoor marketplace and, in so doing, became a worldwide consumer business model. Cabela's methods and impact will be studied and imitated by future generations of entrepreneurs.

Cabela's unprecedented success is the result of the unwavering business ethics and acumen of its founders, combined with the dedication and hard work of loyal, like-minded employees. This diverse, but dedicated family came together to nurture a fledgling business against odds they did not pause to consider. First a handful of employees, and now thousands, have signed on to this living, growing example of the American Dream.

Today's employees live and breathe the company's core business values and unique standard of service, with an underlying and deep passion for the outdoor lifestyle. They carry on Dick and Jim's vision 50 years after that day in Chicago when Dick stopped to examine a small display of fishing flies.

Dick and Jim never miss an opportunity to credit their success to their family of employees, from the first multitasking employees who joined the company in its early days and helped fuel its meteoric growth to those joining the growing enterprise today.

The Cabela's story is the story of people, the story of these employees.

CATALOG
1968
Cabela's
SIDNEY, NEBR.

Chapter 1

Laying the Foundation

– The 1960s –

In January 1961, Dick Cabela was working as sales and advertising manager for his father's furniture store in Chappell, Nebraska, population 1,200. A fishing enthusiast since childhood and a 25-year-old father of four, he and his dad, A.C. Cabela, were on a buying trip that had taken them first to Kansas City, then on to trade shows at the Chicago Furniture Mart and Merchandise Mart.

The trip had been long — 1,000 miles in about 24 hours on snow-slick two-lane highways, with the two taking turns driving and sleeping in the family car. After making purchases at the furniture shows, they moved on to a housewares show at Chicago's Navy Pier, looking for small goods and gift items to add to their stock. The Cabela's store offered not only furniture, but also general household and hardware items, and a selection of sporting goods.

Walking the back aisles of the Navy Pier's International Exposition Center with his dad, Dick encountered something unexpected. In a remote corner was a small booth occupied by a company called Walker International, whose merchandise consisted primarily of fishing equipment. Among their offerings were assorted hand-tied fishing flies, priced at $2.25 per gross. Like most fly-fishermen, Dick was a fly aficionado, and he was pleasantly surprised by their quality and price. At a penny and a half apiece, they were an incredible bargain compared to the retail price for flies he bought for himself, and he thought there might be a nice profit potential for the sporting-goods section of the Cabela's store. He proposed buying the whole stock on hand: 2,880 for $45.

His father was dubious, thinking they weren't likely to sell 2,880 fishing flies to local residents of the High Plains of western Nebraska. But Dick was persuasive, and the assortment of flies went back to Chappell with father and son, into the store's display case. Months passed, and not a single fly moved off the counter —except those Dick used for himself.

Then, in April, Dick was fishing the Miracle Mile on the North

In 1932, A.C. Cabela and his brother Louis acquired this building in Chappell and opened a furniture and hardware store. The furniture store remains open to this day and is still in the Cabela family. *Photo by Dale Graham.*

Platte River near Casper, Wyoming, when he was struck with the idea of offering his stock of flies by mail order. Thinking the Casper area was certainly a place fishermen congregated, he placed a small classified ad in the Casper Tribune, offering "12 hand-tied fishing flies for $1, postage paid." Three months passed, and the ad generated one order, from Mrs. Ernest Lindahl of Casper. But Dick Cabela was nothing if not tenacious, having learned perseverance from his father's approach to small-town business management. He had been struck by the many pages of classified ads in the back of one of his favorite magazines, Sports Afield, while sipping coffee and reading at Wieland's Drug Store in Chappell. In fact, his awareness of those ads had helped form the idea for selling flies by mail order that day on the banks of the Platte.

The Sports Afield issue that carried Dick's first ad.

So, having no wish to be stuck with more than 2,800 flies and what he suspected his wife and father thought of his impulse buy, he decided to go national — "Plan B," as he now refers to it. Figuring classified ads in Sports Afield and other magazines had to be working or there wouldn't be pages and pages of them month after month, he placed a small ad in Sports Afield's October 1961 issue. It read: "FREE introductory offer!!! 5 popular Grade A hand tied flies. Send 25¢ for postage and handling."

Dick returned with his father to Chicago for the fall 1961 furniture and housewares shows. Calling home one afternoon from the Navy Pier to check on his family, he listened to Mary's excited report. She had received 23 orders in their household mail that morning. They quickly did the math. Each fly had cost them a cent and a half, for a total of seven and a half cents per order. The envelopes were a half-cent, and postage was six cents. Their total cost (since their labor was free) was 14 cents, leaving a net profit of 11 cents on each order — $2.53 profit in one day!

Dick surmised these people would be interested in more fishing equipment. So he again sought out the Walker International booth where he made his original purchase nine months before. He bought as many bamboo fly rods, reels, hooks and lures as he thought he and Mary could afford. When he got back home, he and Mary created a mimeographed flyer listing the new fishing items and a few other sporting goods, including a $9.95 pellet rifle. They sent the flyer to each new customer along with the fishing flies they'd ordered. At the end of that first three-page

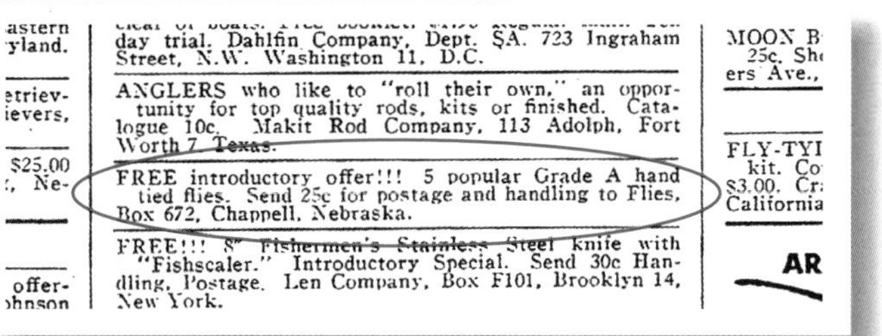
day trial. Dahlfin Company, Dept. SA. 723 Ingraham Street, N.W. Washington 11, D.C.

ANGLERS who like to "roll their own," an opportunity for top quality rods, kits or finished. Catalogue 10c. Makit Rod Company, 113 Adolph, Fort Worth 7, Texas.

FREE introductory offer!!! 5 popular Grade A hand tied flies. Send 25c for postage and handling to Flies, Box 672, Chappell, Nebraska.

FREE!!! 8" Fishermen's Stainless Steel knife with "Fishscaler." Introductory Special. Send 30c Handling, Postage. Len Company, Box F101, Brooklyn 14, New York.

Cabela's Time Line

1960s

1961

- Dick purchases fishing flies from Walker International in Chicago.
- First ad in Casper Tribune.
- First sale to Mrs. Ernest Lindahl.
- First ad in Sports Afield.
- First mimeographed three-page product list sent with orders.
- 100 percent satisfaction guarantee introduced.
- Total revenue: $627.

1962

- Backyard warehouse built, a 10- x 10-foot shed.
- Hired part-time typist Susie Gerber, a high-school girl.
- Total revenue: $5,236.

1963

- Jim Cabela joins Cabela's when Dick offers him half-ownership to help run the growing business.
- First catalog mailed to customer list.
- Total revenue: $24,326.

In the early '60s, it was virtually unheard of for any company, no matter how large or small, to make such a commitment to unconditional customer service.

Cabela's price list was a promise: "...Satisfaction Guaranteed. All items listed carry our money-back guarantee. If you are not completely satisfied, simply return the merchandise and your money will be promptly refunded."

In the early '60s, it was virtually unheard of for any company, no matter how large or small, to make such a commitment to unconditional customer service. Refund or replacement of defective or damaged goods, yes. Exchange with a restocking fee for returned goods, perhaps. A partial refund or replacement after lengthy correspondence and phone calls, more likely. But a simple, no-questions-asked full refund on request? Unprecedented, particularly for a young couple getting started by essentially giving away product for 25¢ and the hope of future business. Any business professional or professor would have scoffed at the notion.

But from the outset, the Cabelas had a clear sense that the vast majority of American consumers, particularly those interested in products for outdoor recreation, were straightforward and honest and would give as they got — in spite of many who warned them that customer abuse of such generosity would ruin them. Dick Cabela says the number of customers who have taken advantage of their legendary guarantee over the years is relatively insignificant.

He also notes two other key elements in their approach from the outset. First, they offered only proven, good-quality merchandise he knew worked, which was easy for an experienced and passionate fisherman and hunter. Second, they were willing to accept a low profit margin on what they sold, both to provide their customers with high value and to compete with the same types of items offered elsewhere.

1961

CABELA DISTRIBUTING
BOX 672
CHAPPELL, NEBRASKA

WHOLESALE PRICE

ORDER NOS.	ITEMS
217	Hooks—6 hooks to folder. Barbed shank, nylo hand forged, tied with monofilament nylon, 7" with 3/4" loop. Sizes #4, #6, #8, or # 10. (30 hooks)*........
231	Hooks—6 hooks to folder. Plain shank, nyl above. Sizes #4, & #6. 5 folders (30hooks
228	Leaders—Nylon coated wire leaders with st snaps. 35 lb. test. Assorted lengths....
384	Snaps—Ball bearing swivel snaps. Specia design. Brass, nickel plated. Sizes #7
393	Snaps—Ball bearing swivel snaps complet steel snaps. Packed 7 assorted sizes i
027	Eyelets—No knot eyelet for fly line. So fly fisherman. 2 sizes on a card. $ .25........
046	Flies—Finest quality, grade A, wet o flies. 12 assorted patterns........
041	Flies—Highest quality hand tied fli lastic box........ Ketchum, th

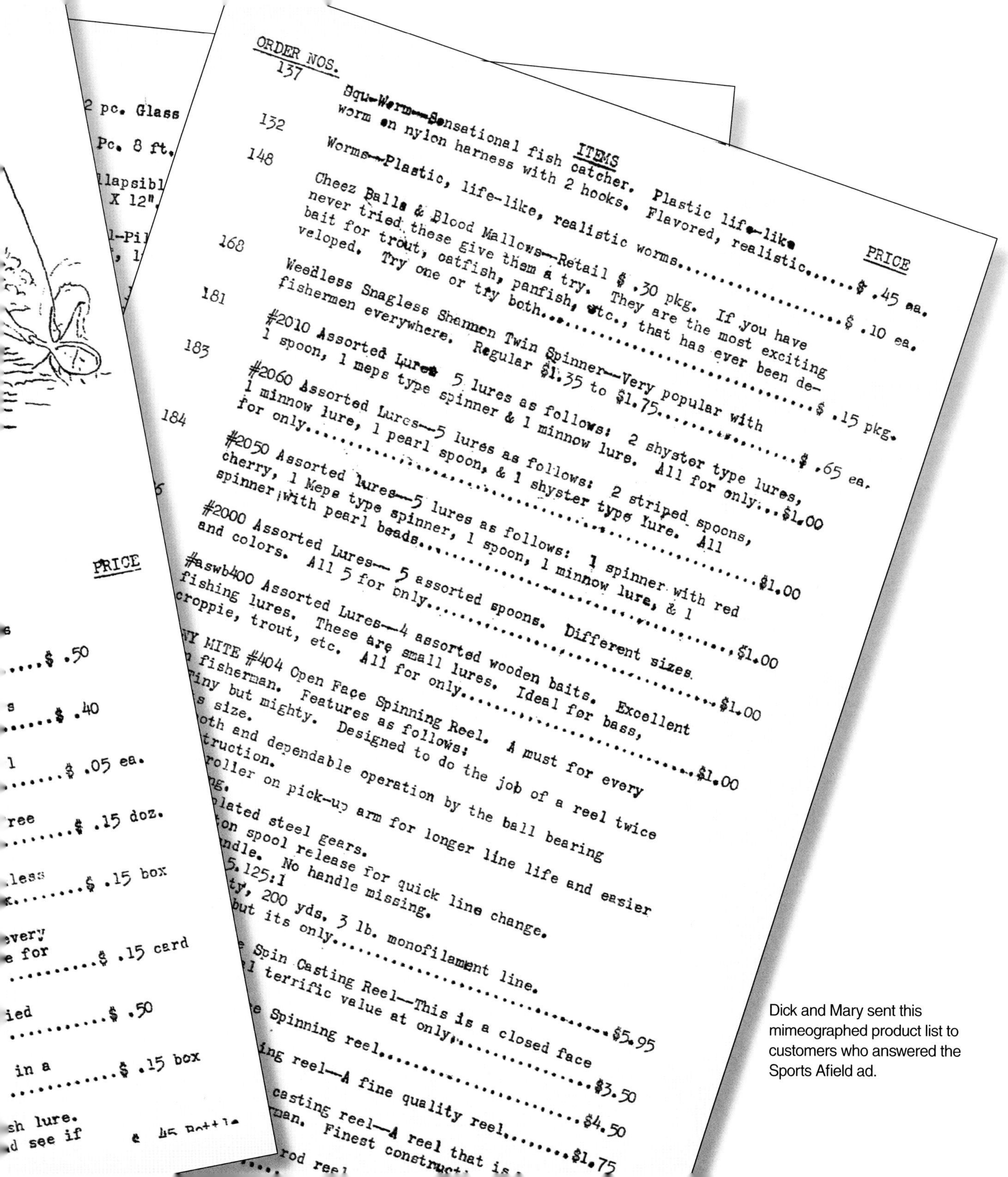

ORDER NOS. | ITEMS | PRICE

137 Squ-Worm—Sensational fish catcher. Plastic life-like worm on nylon harness with 2 hooks. Flavored, realistic......$ .45 ea.

132 Worms—Plastic, life-like, realistic worms..................$ .10 ea.

148 Cheez Balls & Blood Mallows—Retail $ .30 pkg. If you have never tried these give them a try. They are the most exciting bait for trout, catfish, panfish, etc., that has ever been developed. Try one or try both...........................$ .15 pkg.

168 Weedless Snagless Shannon Twin Spinner—Very popular with fishermen everywhere. Regular $1.35 to $1.75...............$ .65 ea.

181 #2010 Assorted Lures 5 lures as follows: 2 shyster type lures, 1 spoon, 1 meps type spinner & 1 minnow lure. All for only...$1.00

183 #2060 Assorted Lures—5 lures as follows: 2 striped spoons, 1 minnow lure, 1 pearl spoon, & 1 shyster type lure. All for only..$1.00

184 #2050 Assorted lures—5 lures as follows: 1 spinner with red cherry, 1 Meps type spinner, 1 spoon, 1 minnow lure, & 1 spinner with pearl beads..........................$1.00

#2000 Assorted Lures— 5 assorted spoons. Different sizes and colors. All 5 for only...............................$1.00

#aswb400 Assorted Lures—4 assorted wooden baits. Excellent fishing lures. These are small lures. Ideal for bass, croppie, trout, etc. All for only.......................$1.00

...Y MITE #404 Open Face Spinning Reel. A must for every ...n fisherman. Features as follows: ...iny but mighty. Designed to do the job of a reel twice ...s size. ...oth and dependable operation by the ball bearing ...truction. ...roller on pick-up arm for longer line life and easier ...ng. ...lated steel gears. ...on spool release for quick line change. ...ndle. No handle missing. ...5.125:1 ...ty, 200 yds. 3 lb. monofilament line. ...but its only.....................................$5.95

...e Spin Casting Reel—This is a closed face ...l terrific value at only.........................$3.50

...e Spinning reel...................................$4.50

...ing reel—A fine quality reel.....................$1.75

... casting reel—A reel that is ... ...man. Finest construct...

... rod reel ...

Dick and Mary sent this mimeographed product list to customers who answered the Sports Afield ad.

1964

- Business moves to basement of family furniture store.
- First Garcia products purchased.
- Total revenue: $92,365.

1965

- Housewares catalog attempted to make up for slow time in fall and winter, but is a failure.
- First security system: Burt, a 90-pound German shepherd.
- First full-time employee is hired: Sharon Robison
- Four additional manufacturers come on board as vendors.
- Total revenue: $156,419.

1966

- Added golf balls, umbrellas, and pool tables to merchandise offering.
- First fall catalog compiled and mailed, a huge risk.
- Total revenue: $273,962.

"High-quality merchandise at a fair price with a 100 percent satisfaction guarantee. Seemed pretty simple to me," says Dick. It was pretty simple to him, perhaps, but apparently not so simple for the mainstream business world, which raises the question: In a small town on the plains of Nebraska, where did such insight necessary for eventual worldwide business success come from?

Pioneer Heritage, Small-Town Values

Anyone seeking to understand the foundation of Cabela's success, and the loyalty of the millions of customers it has attracted and maintained for five decades, needs to look closely at the small-town roots and pioneer heritage of its founding family, a heritage embodied today in Cabela's Core Values.

The Cabelas' ancestors were Nebraska pioneers. Dick and Jim Cabela's grandfather, James Cabela, was born in 1869 in the village of Zvikov, north of Prague in what is now the Czech Republic. He came to America in 1884 at age 14 with his older sister, during a time when it was common for costs of poor immigrants' passage from Europe to be underwritten in exchange for labor on farms and businesses in the recently settled Great Plains. In the 1880s one such area was Butler County in eastern Nebraska, bordering the Platte River and populated by many Czech settlers. One of the small towns in the region is even named Prague.

Young James Cabela spent 10 years working off his debt on the farm of William Mickelwaite near the community of Brainard. At age 24, he moved into town where he worked first in a lumberyard and then clerked in a hardware store, saving what he could of his salary. By 1900 he had a hardware business of his own and was able to build his own brick building on a main corner in town, complete with an elevator to the basement for heavy goods, with the name "James Cabela" cast into the cornice. He eventually became mayor and also served on local school and church boards.

Dick and Jim's grandparents Barbara Tuma-Cabela and James Cabela. Before moving to America, James Cabela's family resided in a small village north of Prague.

A.C. Cabela and his older brother Louis.

James Cabela, grandfather of Cabela's founders Dick and Jim Cabela, had his name placed prominently on the exterior of his hardware store in Brainard, Nebraska. The store was well stocked with products necessary for living in Nebraska at the turn of the 20th century.

1967

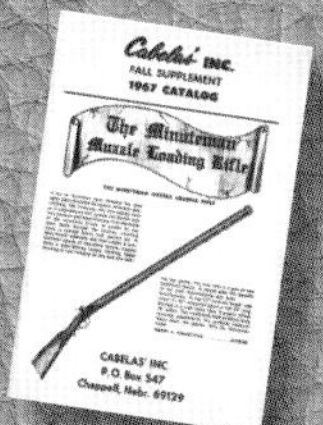

- Cabela's moves to former American Legion Hall in Chappell.
- First discontinued items: golf items and pool tables.
- Total revenue: $523,713.

1968

- Dick quit his job at the furniture store.
- First salaries paid to Dick and Jim Cabela.
- Three-story, 50,000-square-foot former John Deere building purchased in Sidney (after ground had been purchased and plans drawn to construct a new building near Chappell exit off of I-80.
- Total revenue: $862,025.

1969

- Cabela's moves to John Deere building in Sidney.
- Total revenue: $1,178,535.

A.C. Cabela had a firm sense of business and personal values, which he and his wife, Marian, instilled in their children.

Cabela's Rule No. 1 of mid-American small-town business: Treat customers like family.

James' life was a classic American success story in all respects. He passed on his standards of business integrity and public service to his sons Louis and Albin Charles (A.C.) Cabela, who worked in their father's store as youngsters, then moved west to Chappell, Nebraska, in 1932 to open Cabela Brother's Furniture and Hardware Store. A.C. bought out his brother's interest in 1942. He and his wife, Marian, raised six children, the oldest of whom were Dick and his business-partner-to-be, Jim. Like their father, both boys worked at the family store as youngsters, learning Cabela's Rule No. 1 of mid-American small-town business: Treat customers like family. The Cabela's Furniture Store in Chappell is still in business, operated by Dick and Jim's younger brother Jerry.

Pioneer roots on Dick and Jim's mother's side stretch back even further. Their maternal great-grandfather, Michael Casey, first came to Nebraska with his parents by covered wagon in 1859, settling near Lincoln. His older brothers moved farther west. One, Patrick Casey, became an Army officer and helped in the construction of Fort Sedgwick (made famous in the movie Dances With Wolves). The fort was located on the South Platte River just west of Julesburg, Colorado, along Lodgepole Creek, which flows through present-day Chappell. The other brother, Martin Casey, opened a butcher shop in Julesburg, which was burned down in 1865 when Cheyenne and Sioux warriors attacked the town in retribution for the Sand Creek Massacre in southern Colorado. Local history claims Martin's business was the first in town to be rebuilt after the fighting. Dick and Jim's great-grandfather Michael Casey eventually followed his brothers west and, according to family history, as a boy, worked for the Pony Express at stations along the run from Julesburg to Mud Springs near present-day Bridgeport, Nebraska, the route passing through Chappell.

All this history and small-town business heritage was soaked up by brothers Dick and Jim Cabela at their parents', A.C. and Marian's, knees. As Dick Cabela says, "For us, operating our own business is the normal thing to do, and all the rest of our family and ancestors have felt the same way. It is probably in our family genes. My father had a business, his father had a business; we're from a whole family of merchants."

Considering Dick and his brother Jim's life-long passion for fishing and hunting, he also observes, "An amazing thing about the Cabela's story is our dad didn't really hunt or fish. He did a little fishing later on in his life, but he never hunted. But he always supported our interests and ideas. When my brother and I finally got guns as youngsters, he would go with us, and he could shoot, but it wasn't one of his personal interests in life. He played a little golf, but he mostly just worked. He was a hard worker, and we got that from him."

The Cabela's company name itself reflects its small-town business origins. Its earliest legal name was actually Cabela's Distribution Company. Today, its full legal name is still simple and unpretentious: Cabela's Inc. In this it was the same as thousands of small-town grocery, hardware, furniture and general stores across America proudly carrying their proprietors' names. "It seemed like the natural thing to do," Dick said. "Our grandpa named his store Cabela's, our dad named his Cabela's; and that's what we wanted to name our business."

The foundation of Cabela's business approach is outlined in its Core Values: Superior Customer Service, Quality Products and Services, Integrity and Honesty, Respect for Individuals, and Excellence in Performance.

Cabela's family left to right: Dianne, A.C., Dick (standing), Jerry, Marian, Jim. (Two other siblings, Jane and Tom, were born after this photo was taken.)

Dick Cabela

Dick and Jim fishing with their father, A.C.

Dick, center, and Jim, right, and a neighborhood friend show off their day's catch.

Jim Cabela

Jim and Dick grew up as buddies in small-town America, sharing childhood adventures, including all sorts of outdoor activities.

Jim and Dick with their mother Marian.

A.C. Cabela with sons, Jim, left, and Dick at a Rocky Mountain lake.

Dick fishing at an early age.

Dick with a nice stringer of Lake McConaughy fish.

Jim on Dick's shoulders at their boyhood home in Chappell, Nebra

Dick and Jim in costume.

Dick with Grandpa Bill Little at Lake McConaughy.

Dick, an Eagle Scout, with his merit badges.

Left to right: Jim, A.C., Dick, Bob Casey and Grandpa Bill Little pack for a fishing excursion at Lake McConaughy.

Dick Cabela and Mary Kerns were married in 1955. Left to right are Dick, Mary, Jim (best man) and Mary's sister, Rita (maid of honor).

Dick and Mary's first home in Chappell where the kitchen table was the hub of early company operations.

Dick and Mary with children, in 1985 family photo. Back row: Joe, Chaz, Dan, Rich, David, and Nancy Front row: Geri, Mary, Cari, Dick and Teri

Not a Dream, Not a Plan, Just a Process

Another key ingredient in turning the tiny business started on Dick and Mary Cabela's kitchen table into the powerhouse it is today has been the notable absence of grandiose dreams, inflexible models or rigid business-school textbook outlines. Instead, the Cabela's management attitude was from the outset always an open-minded, step-by-step approach, an attitude free of preconceptions and a willingness to shrug off mistakes and move on. Mary Cabela remembers, "Dick always said, 'Take baby steps. Just baby steps.'"

Dick concurs. "We really didn't have a game plan, it just sort of happened." He goes on: "Everybody thinks we sat down and made this big plan, saying, 'This is how we're going to do business.' Nothing like that happened. I just said to Mary, 'We are going to play it by ear.'"

"Did we dream or plan that someday we were going to be a billion-dollar company? Nothing like that ever by any stretch of the imagination, believe me. If you do the right thing, I think anyone can grow a business. You just have to mind your P's and Q's and take care of your customers and employees, and be honest. Then your business can keep growing."

Dick Cabela also realized early the importance of keeping a clear sense of who his customers were. At one point during Cabela's early years, he decided to try to generate revenue during the slack fall and winter seasons when fishermen weren't making many purchases by mailing a housewares flyer to his customer list. Completely different from the regular product categories, it contained such novelty items as doorknob covers with faces on them, diaper pins, imitation-leather drink coasters and serving spoons with thermometers. "I forgot who I was," he says. "I hunt, and I'd rather go fishing than eat. Most of our customers are the same kind of people. I have no patience for gimmicks, and neither do they. What was I thinking?" The housewares flyer was a miserable failure, never to be repeated. "There might still be some exploding golf balls down in our basement," he grumbles.

But he learned from the experience and shrugged it off. "You have to keep your options open so you can go a different direction if something doesn't work out," he said.

Cabela's tried selling household goods in 1965, but quickly realized sales for outdoor-related gear was where they should focus their attention.

"There are always other things you can try. If you just take one step at a time and don't overcommit or get too wedded to a bad idea, each step can lead to another step and you may eventually find yourself down a road you never anticipated."

The Beginnings of Growth

By the end of 1961, three months after those first orders, Dick and Mary's grand total of sales was $627. They were happy they had succeeded in recovering the expense of those first fishing flies, but with expenditures made for additional products and their own unpaid labor, there was certainly no true overall profit yet. On the other hand, orders were continuing to come in, the spring fishing season was coming, new potential customers were requesting product lists, and Dick was gearing up for another trip to the winter trade shows in Chicago.

This 10- x 10-foot storage shed in Dick and Mary's backyard was Cabela's first warehouse.

"We didn't know what we were doing," says Mary. "And I had no idea of the time this was going to take in my life. None at all. We had four little kids, all less than school age, and Dick still worked at the furniture store." Mary worked at the kitchen table during the day, typing names and addresses, keeping customer information on recipe cards in a shoe box in the pantry alongside their inventory. "I would make labels, with four copies for each name that came in. Somehow or other we kept track of every name, and Dick bought more merchandise from the same company, and we were making these little mimeographed flyers and stapling them together. That was our first catalog."

Dick now shakes his head. "It's certainly not like we were getting rich. I'd figured it out. With a cent and a half in each fly, plus postage and all, I suppose by the time we got all done if we didn't figure any labor at all, we maybe made a dime on each order. If you figured labor, we lost. But we were getting enough response to pay expenses, and what is kind of shocking when you think about it, we thought it was great! I mean, we were sending out this little mimeographed flyer in the mail, and people responded to it. Think about that today — it's crazy."

Dick came home from the Chicago shows in January 1962 with still more inventory and a growing problem: storage. The pantry simply couldn't hold everything anymore, and it wasn't long before his wife's sidelong looks persuaded him it was time for Cabela's to invest in its first warehouse. So, when the weather warmed, Dick and Mary assembled a 10- x 10-foot metal storage shed in the backyard, just outside the kitchen door.

They both sighed in relief, Mary because she had her pantry back, Dick because Mary was happy — and they had room for more merchandise.

As an increased volume of orders and flyer requests came rolling in during the spring, Mary's relief was even more pronounced when Dick hired a neighborhood high-school girl, Susie Gerber, for part-time typing and office help. Historians take note: Miss Gerber thus holds the distinction of being the first person ever to be paid actual wages by Cabela's. She would come across the street from her parents' house after school and work for a few hours, typing the ever-expanding product-list flyers and helping with package labeling. She also doubled as babysitter.

The year ended with total sales of $5,236. This was 1962, remember, so that was not exactly small change for a fledgling home-based business (about $37,900 in 2010 dollars), but it wasn't enough to support a family. Expenses were being paid, but everything that came in was being put back into the business, and the young couple was taking no salary. Dick couldn't afford to quit his job in his dad's store. On the other hand, the new business couldn't be considered a hobby any longer. Dick and Mary were by then routinely staying up as late as 2 to 3 a.m. on a near-daily basis filling orders. If the enterprise was going to continue at all, they needed full-time help. It was a make-or-break moment.

Along Comes Jim

Just before 1962 ended, Dick approached his brother Jim with his now-famous proposal. If Jim would take over full-time, day-to-day management of Cabela's Distributing Company, Dick and Mary would give him half-ownership, with no buy-in or other strings attached. Of course, the company was still not making a true overall profit, as all revenues were going right back into expenses and growth, and the owners weren't drawing a salary, but, hey, ownership is something. Besides, the desire to have his own business was also in Jim Cabela's genes. "I always knew I wanted to work for myself," Jim says.

In the late '60s, Jim and Dick were poised to lead their company through decades of steady growth.

"I think they were good partners for two reasons. First, they always got along just fine, just great. Second, because Dick is an optimist and Jim is more cautious, they would offset each other." – Mary Cabela

History does not record, and the participants have never shared, the details of that discussion, but the result was definitive. Jim accepted the offer.

In January 1963, James William Cabela was 24 years old and living in Denver, where he had just taken a job on the first rung of a career ladder in the banking business. Like his older brother Dick, he had grown up helping in the family furniture store and attended Regis College in Denver. He was also serving in the National Guard. The arrangement worked out within the close-knit Cabela family was that Jim would stay with parents A.C. and Marian and live off his small National Guard stipend while managing the new business. Nobody would yet take any salary from the business. It was not as big a risk for Jim as it might appear, as he was unmarried with no family to support and would be able to live in the home in which he grew up. Plus, the shared passion for hunting, fishing and the outdoor life he and Dick developed together as youngsters had persisted into adulthood. So the prospect of a start-from-scratch business partnership with his brother devoted to serving outdoor customers was an attractive alternative to a career inside the offices of an urban bank. Within a short time Jim resigned his position at the Denver bank and returned to Chappell.

The two brothers had always been close, in spite of the fact that, by all accounts, they were near-opposites in personality. Dick, gregarious and outgoing, is a natural leader and automatic center of attention, always comfortable with people and charmingly effective at the front of a room. By contrast, Jim is quiet and soft-spoken, yet strong-willed and determined, a man of few words who in social gatherings is most comfortable standing on the periphery, quietly observing and learning — never missing a trick.

Looking back, Mary Cabela observes, "I think they were good partners for two reasons. First, they always got along just fine, just great. Second, because Dick is an optimist and Jim is more cautious, they would offset each other. Dick would always be gung-ho to do whatever, and Jim would be, 'Well, let's think this through.'"

With Jim on board and back in Chappell full-time, the Cabelas now had the human resources necessary to take yet another significant step and replace their mimeographed product flyers with a real printed catalog. Fronted with a drawing of a fly-fisherman reeling in a jumping trout, it contained 55 pages dedicated to fishing equipment and supplies. The catalog was produced, labeled and inserted in envelopes by hand. Hauled to the post office in the family's old green van, the catalogs were mailed to all previous Cabela's customers in the early spring of 1963. The first catalog was a significant success, and it needed to be, since Dick was bringing back larger and larger loads of merchandise from his twice-annual trade show visits. Total sales for 1963 reached $24,326.

Dick (left) and Jim manned the dock at the former American Legion building in Chappell. As business continued to grow they started looking for a larger facility, which ultimately led to the company moving to Sidney in 1969.

CABELA'S
WHOLESALE CATALOG

Fishing Equipment and Supplies

CABELA DISTRIBUTING

BOX 41 CHAPPELL, NEBRASKA

THE FIRST NAME IN DISTINCTIVE FISHING REELS
AMERICAN MADE BRONSON REELS

NEW BRONSON 902 SCOUT
Order No. 111

west priced spin-casting reel. Once again ilds the lowest priced spinning reel avail- dy undersells Cabela's on this reel. Check nced features normally found only on reels, 4-point pickup to distribute line table drag, anti reverse drag, anti re- black high impact moulded frame, ano- num cover, all metal gears. Complete test monofilament line. List $3.75, **HOLESALE PRICE** **$2.50**

BRONSON 910 SAVAGE
Order No. 112

A handsome rugged buy from Bronson. The Savage features new radical type adjustable drag. New lever-type line pickup device. Polystyrene push-button and handle grips. Die cast aluminum pinion gear and drive gear. Rich bronze finish. Positive anti-reverse crank. Comes with 100 yards 8 lb. test monofilament line. Lists for $9.95. Cabela's have this one priced at rock bottom. **CABELA'S WHOLESALE $6.50**

NSON 905 DART
rder No. 113

cost. The DART has the exclusive s adjustable. Its many selling line twist at any time and an ll metal gears. Finished in rich minum frame cover, complete nonofilament line. List $5.75. **W WHOLESALE PRICE $3.75**

BRONSON 907 COMET
Order No. 114

The COMET is a big seller with the forward looking design, has pre-set drag, yet its adjustable. Features no line twist at any time and anti-reserve crank. All metal gears. Sturdy black frame with red anodized aluminum cover. Complete with 10 lb. test monofilament line. List $7.95. Check our price on this one. Cabela's will not be undersold. **WHOLESALE $4.95**

uth Bend—The Exciting No. 63
RAG SPIN CASTING REEL
Order No. 121

drag spincast reel . . . is priced so an can afford to be without one. northerns, crappies and larger pan enamel and cone in Aqua-Therm grip handle and comfortable are Forest Green tenite. Diamond ratio gear. A truly great Star Drag spin-cast value that has already proven to be a best seller with 90 yards 8 lb. test monofilament line. List $9.95.
CABELA'S WHOLESALE PRICE **$6.95**

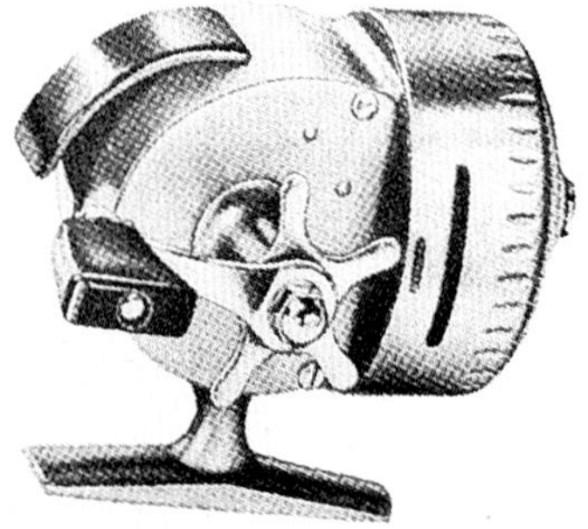

3

"After doing this for a few days, I think to myself: I've got to get a different job; this one is going nowhere. But I like the dog, so I stay."

– Sharon Robison

Sharon went to work on the first day of October, right in the middle of preparation of the doomed housewares flyer. "First day, I'm given my instructions. I have a stack of 8½ x 14 flyers to which I'm affixing mailing labels. The flyer is red and black on white paper folded twice. It's offering clown-faced doorknob covers, genuine fake imitation-leather coasters, a soup spoon with a built-in thermometer, egg slicers, etcetera. The gummed labels are 33 or so to a perforated sheet. I tear them apart and run a damp sponge over them, stick them to the mail piece. After doing this for a few days, I think to myself: I've got to get a different job; this one is going nowhere. But I like the dog, so I stay."

Sharon remembers that the day she was hired, there were already three young local girls working part-time after school who would do baby sitting and then come down to the shop to work. The part-time job had evolved into her becoming the first full-time employee. Sharon's first duties included going to the post office, getting the mail, opening the mail, removing the payment, making the bank deposit, filling the order, checking the order, packing the order and taking it to the post office. She also dealt with complaints, "which were always handled very seriously," she emphasized, "by usually writing a formal letter of response." Duties included all the day-to-day office functions, she said. "You cleaned the bathrooms, made the coffee, cleaned out the refrigerator, fed the dog, watered the dog, dewatered the dog and scrubbed the toilets." Everything was typed or written by hand, no computers, no databases. Label sheets were quadruplicate carbons, so they would have three spare label sets for future mailings from a single typing. Orders were still kept on recipe cards, just like they had been in Mary's kitchen. Sharon remembers, "Mary Cabela would sometimes come in and type the customer labels if I got behind, and she could type like the wind; really fast."

In the early days, Cabela's hired local residents to handle orders and shipping. Pictured is the operation in the former American Legion building, with Sharon Robison seated.

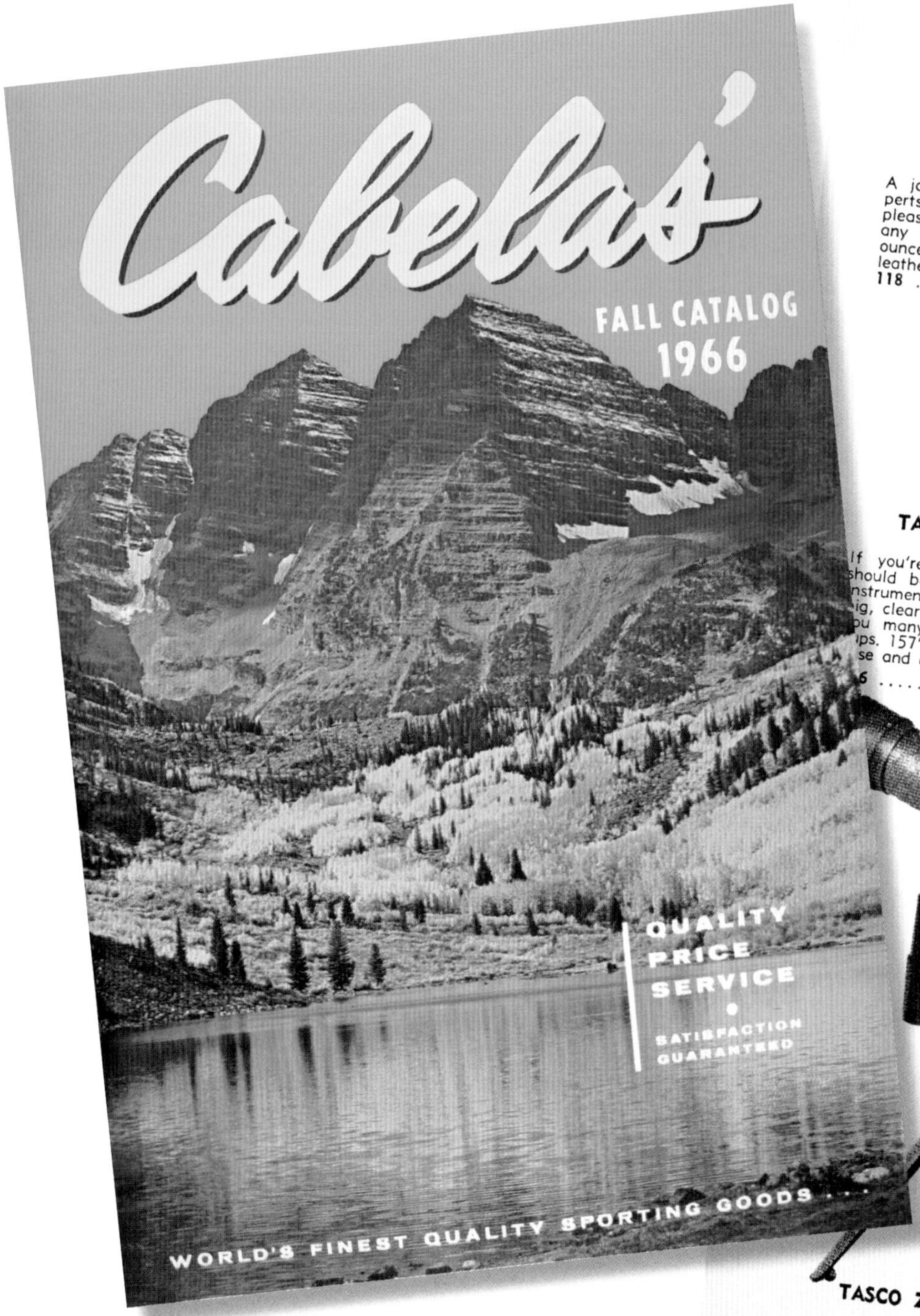

$28.75

TASCO ATTACHE WIDE ANGLE 7X35mm BINOCULARS

A jack-of-all-trades—rated best in its field by experts. The 578' wide field of view will give you added pleasure in watching sporting events, in hunting, or any other outdoor activity. Light weight. Only 27 ounces. 578' field of view at 1000 yds. Genuine leather case and carrying strap included.
118 . . . . $28.75

$17.95

TASCO SEA PILOT 7X35mm BINOCULA

Fast, easy center focusing at a touch. Sharp, cl clear images for sportsmen, bird-watchers, and docrsmen! Large 35mm lens lets you see objects brightness and clarity, even under adverse ligh conditions! 358' field of view at 1000 yds. Li weight; weighs only 22 ounces. Complete with lea case and carrying strap.
304 . . . . $17

$44.95

TASCO SUPER SPOTTER 20X60mm BINOCULARS

If you're looking for distance, the Super Spotter should be your choice. This is a strong 20-power nstrument, that will show you a far-off object in a ig, clear, sharp-to-the-edge image. It's built to give ou many years of viewing thrills. Retractive eyeps. 157' field of view at 1000 yds. Genuine leather se and carrying strap included.
6 . . . . $44.95

$22.95

TASCO SEA DOG 7X50mm BINOCULARS

Fast center focusing for bright-at-night viewing! You'll use these anywhere and everywhere—day or night! Boating, hunting, racing or vacationing, you'll always see a clear, bright image. 372' field of view at 1000 yds. Genuine leather case and carrying strap included.
306 . . . . $22.95

$39.99

TASCO ZOOM SPOTTING SCOPE 20-60 POWER

Zoom from 20 to 60X with just a twist of the wrist. 60mm objective lens for bright images. Micro-fine altitude and asimuth adjustments. Sturdy metal table top tripod and built-in camera tripod adapter. Resolves 1 second at 100 yds.
8TOZ . . . .

EAGLE CLAW TIE FOCAL

Now, you can leave your bi-focals and flashlight at home when you go fishing. Poor light and tedious tying and attaching of small hooks, flies and leaders is no longer a problem with the New Eagle Claw "Tie Focal." Magnifies and provides light so you can see —pins to your fishing jacket and leaves both hands free. Its 2 power glass gives a long focal range for seeing up close. For use in the dark . . . merely switch on the light. You have just the right light and magnification to tie the tiniest flies, hooks and lures. The "Tie Focal" is the perfect answer for fishing after dark, or anytime. Handy for desk and work bench. Stands upright. Easy and convenient to use. 3¼" high, 2¼" wide, ¾" thick (folded ...

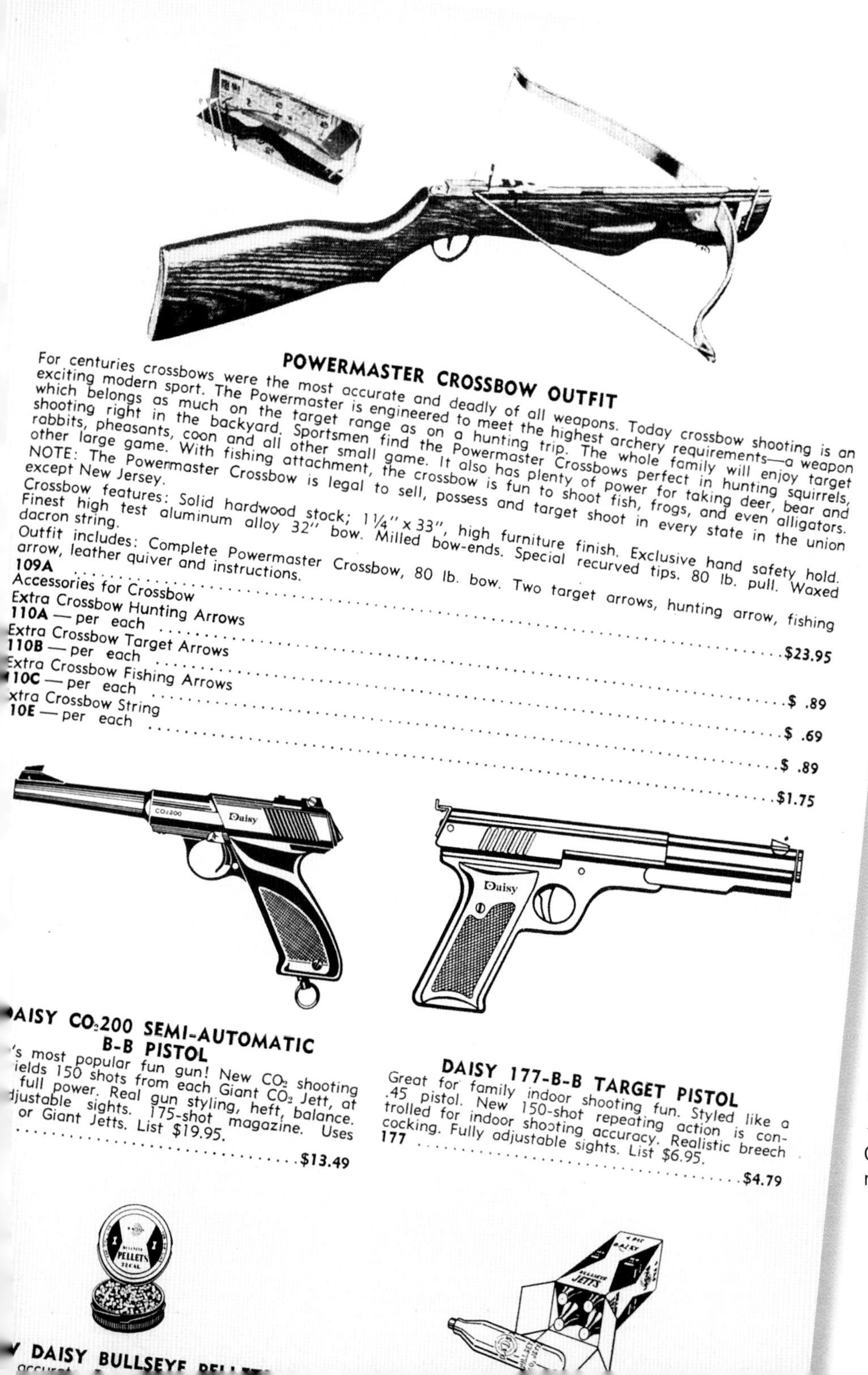

Sharon and Jim Cabela had hit it off right away — maybe because she liked Burt — and her long service with the three Cabela's founders adds additional understanding to the success of Dick and Jim's partnership. "They each naturally took on different roles within the corporation," she said. "Dick was the public face of Cabela's; he was the leader of the parade, very obvious wherever there was a gathering. If there was a trade show or meeting where Cabela's needed a presence, he and Mary were there. They were very much the showmen. Jim was the quiet one, happy if no one realized who he was. But in spite of that difference, or, more accurately, because of it, they made this thing a success."

The year 1965 ended with total sales of $160,946, in spite of the housewares flyer everyone wanted to forget, and the company's archives note this was the first year the books showed an actual formal net profit. But Jim, Dick and Mary were still not taking salaries. They didn't think it was quite time yet. So they continued to put all their resources into growth and expansion.

On the Threshold of Success

In 1966 the spring catalog grew even more, to 86 pages, and two more full-time employees were added, Alene Stutzman in January and Pearl Kayton in June. Both would work for Cabela's for more than 20 years. Dick and Jim were still concerned about the same slack order period in fall and winter that had prompted the housewares experiment the year before. This time, however, they stuck with what they knew. The spring catalog was almost entirely fishing equipment, but Dick and Jim were also hunters and they knew hunting equipment just as well. So the first 33-page version of what would become Cabela's signature fall catalog devoted more than half its space to the outdoor activities of autumn: seven pages of archery gear, then 10 pages of hunting knives, optics, sleeping bags, tents, hunting clothing, compasses and other hunting and camping accessories.

Cabela's first fall catalog was produced in 1966 and expanded the merchandise offering into hunting goods.

Pearl Kayton (foreground), Doris Earnhardt and other employees at work in the American Legion building in Chappell.

Dick and Jim acquired the American Legion Hall in Chappell in 1967, which afforded them more space for storage and the growing number of employees.

It worked. The autumn sales slump vanished, and sales for 1966 nearly doubled from the previous year, to $273,962. Eventually, sales from Cabela's fall catalog would surpass the spring catalog.

The continued growth in sales volume and attendant inventory increase had other consequences as well. Space had been an ongoing problem since 1962, and Dick and Jim had realized even when they first moved into the USDA building that it would be merely another temporary solution, if things went as hoped. So in early 1967 they made arrangements with the owner of the former Chappell American Legion Hall that included swapping their smaller building for the larger building, and moved Cabela's for the third time in three years. The new structure offered enough space for warehousing and a retail counter at the foot of the stairs where walk-in customers could select items from catalogs that would be brought directly to them off the shelves. Even so, an extension to the rear of

American Legion Hall Sold To Cabela Brothers for Mail Order Warehouse

Arrangements have been completed by the Chappell American Legion and Auxiliary to sell the Legion Hall to Cabelas, Inc., and, as part of the sale, establish a new meeting place in the Cabela building on Matlock.

A spokesman for Clinton McAuliffe Post said Legionaires and Auxiliary members figured the thirty year-old Legion Hall had served its purpose as a meeting place for large gatherings and was no longer necessary since the new high school auditorium had been built.

A smaller building was all that was needed at this time for a meeting place for service men and their auxiliaries, they felt, and would save them considerable expense as far as heating and the like were concerned.

The Cabela brothers, Dick, Jim and Jerry, will use their new building to house their expanding mail order business for fishing equipment, gift items and notions which they ship to major portions of the United Sates and many foreign countries.

They have already begun work on the building and expect to move in within the next thirty days.

Considerable remodeling will also take place at the new Legion Hall. This includes kitchen facilities and some minor changes to the inside of the building.

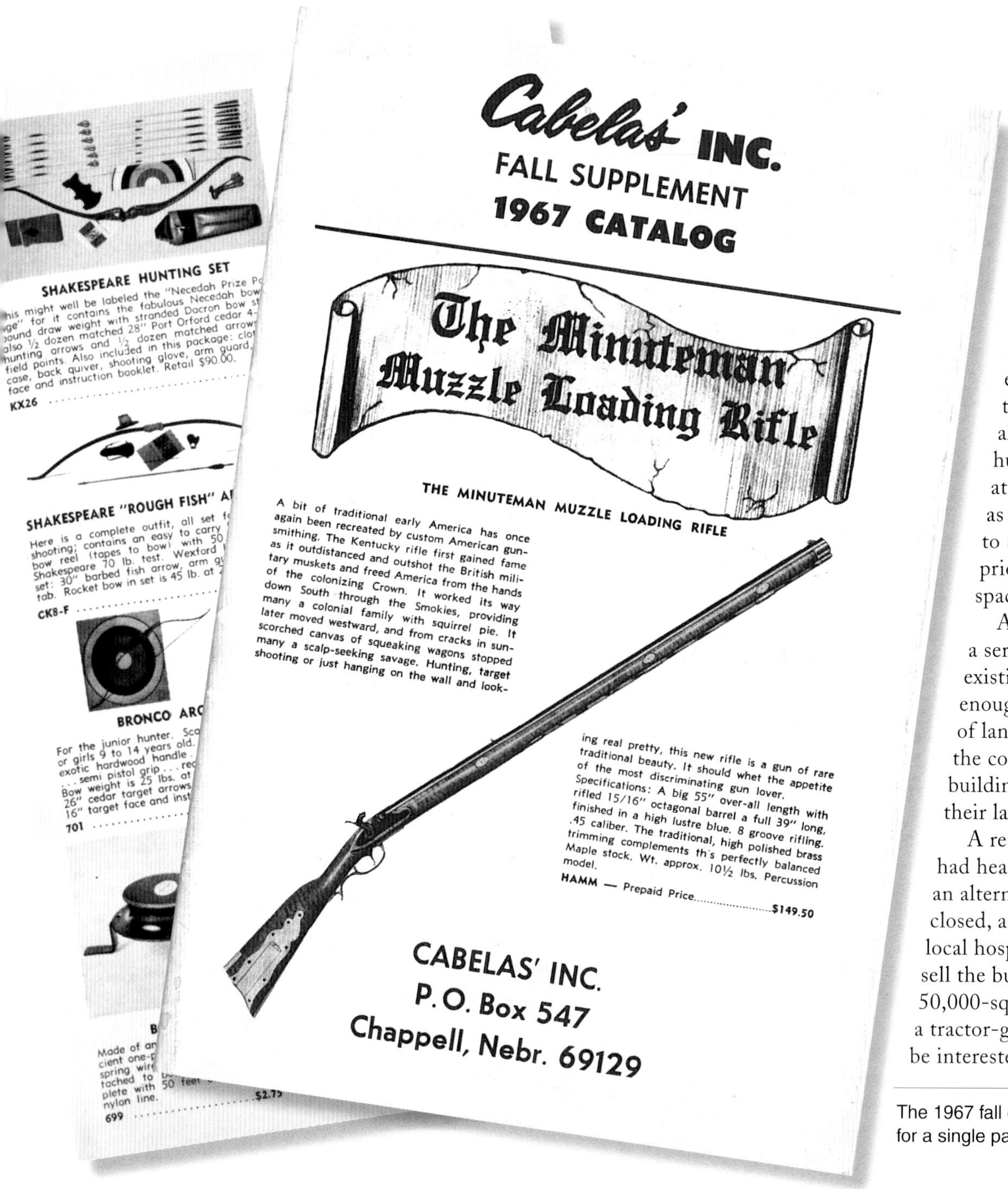

the building was built for additional storage before a year had passed to accommodate larger items being added to the catalogs and to free room in the main building for additional personnel being hired to handle the growth in orders and catalog mailings.

Also in 1967, Dick and Jim eliminated fishing equipment from the greatly expanded fall catalog except for a single page of ice-fishing gear, and for the first time they included muzzleloading firearms along with a more varied and extensive line of other hunting items. Requests for this catalog swarmed in at an unanticipated rate. Hunters were apparently as eager for Cabela's service as fishermen. Sales rose to $541,037, and the partners decided their top priority for 1968 needed to be a real solution to the space problem.

Accordingly, as the new year began, they initiated a serious search for new quarters. It was apparent no existing building in Chappell was suitable or sizable enough for their needs, so they purchased a six-acre tract of land just south of town, near the surveyed route for the coming Interstate 80, and had plans drawn for a new building. Then an unexpected opportunity dropped in their laps.

A real estate broker from nearby Sidney, 25 miles west, had heard the Cabelas were planning to build. He proposed an alternative. A Sidney John Deere distributorship had closed, and the company had donated its facility to the local hospital as a tax write-off. The hospital wanted to sell the building before property taxes came due. It was a 50,000-square-foot, three-story, solid-brick structure with a tractor-grade elevator and full basement. Would Cabela's be interested?

The 1967 fall catalog featured only hunting merchandise, except for a single page of ice-fishing gear.

A few aisles of gear-laden shelves in the former John Deere building in Sidney.

At one time, this building in downtown Sidney housed a John Deere dealership. The Cabela brothers moved their growing operation into the building in 1969. The building served as headquarters through decades of rapid growth until 1998, when corporate offices moved to a new building near Interstate 80. The old corporate headquarters building, a local landmark, is still in use as storage space.

Cabela's in Sidney was along U.S. Highway 30 and this sign was the guidepost for many traveling outdoor enthusiasts.

DICK CABELA

JIM CABELA

Cabela Sporting Goods Set[s] Opening Event This Weeken[d]

The grand opening of Cabela's Sporting Goods store is scheduled for this week--Thursday, Friday and Saturday.

Rated as one of the largest mail order sporting goods dealers in the west, Cabela's also has a huge stock of merchandise f…

pushe… until… job o… ney l… C… Chap… last… the… buil… nes… Ca… th… be…

perly organized that the re… department opening was dela… until now. However, Cabe… intends to be an aggres… merchandiser of sporting go… and this is expected to attract business from the entire Nebraska Panhandle, eastern Wyoming and northeastern Colo…

Fishing Big Business With Chappell Firm; Catalogs Go Out To 50 States

New industry in Chappell has been a topic of much discussion … of Chappell's fairly … a's In… nd op… a and …

plies, boating equipment, clothing and boots, stocking over 4000 di… ferent items and maki… two warehouses … ing on Th…

…the Third St. …he Legion … Goo… …wenty-four … sporting …e State of …ding area. …ods of all …ll types of …ping equip… …unting sup…

the … reas… Offic… every … iron cu… 90% of … side of … Expens… sidered i… volumn o… year.

Dick and Jim Cabela pose in retail shop of Cabela's Inc.

Omaha World-He[rald]
Midlands News—Nebrask[a]
OMAHA, NEBR., THURSDAY, AUG. 29, 1968

Sidney to Get New Industry

World-Herald News Service.

Sidney, Neb. — Cabela's Inc. of Chappell, a mail-orde[r] business dealing in fishing ta[c]kle and related products, h[as] purchased the former Jo[hn] Deere Company building h[ere] and will move its operations [to] Sidney.

Richard and James C[abela] signed a contract for purchase Monday night… company employs abo[ut] … persons.

The building was ow[ned by] the Cheyenne County … Association and was giv[en the] association by the Jo[hn Deere] Company last year. J[ohn Deere] closed its assembly, d… and wholesale parts … Sidney several year[s ago and] the building has b[een vacant] since.

The Cabela bu[siness] started in the ba… home. It outgrew… quarters and was … downtown busine… Chappell, which … come inadequat[e] … ing volume.

Negotiations … and …

Sporting Goods Firm Now Located Here Circulates Its Sales Story Thruout U. S. And Foreign Lands

Cabela's Inc., a catalog and retail sporting goods firm, is the most recent addition to t… Sidney business commu… Start…

About …

SCOTTSBLUFF (NEBRASKA) DAILY STAR-HERALD SUNDAY, NOVEMBER 17, 1968

F…st-Growing Cabela's Moves to Sidney Plant

… business was … Much of the equipment the … sell is for the fisher…

Dick, Mary and Jim knew Sidney well, having graduated from St. Patrick's Parochial Academy there. The Sidney community of 8,000 (according to the 1960 census) had a much better potential employment base than Chappell, and the building was centrally located downtown. The three toured the building in September 1968 and listened to the hospital's offer: $1 per square foot, no down payment, a 15-year payoff at 6 percent interest. Sold. "It was an offer we couldn't refuse," Dick said.

Back in Chappell, the three Cabelas immediately began making plans to move their entire operation to the new quarters the following year. And with ever-growing sales that would reach $897,154 by the end of 1968, Jim, Dick and Mary also decided the time had finally come to draw some pay of their own. Dick took a deep breath and went to his father to tell him the long-hoped-for, anticipated and yet dreaded day had finally come for him to resign his job in the family furniture business and leave its future in the hands of younger brother Jerry. Like their grandfathers and father before them, Dick and Jim Cabela were moving west to a new life and their own enterprise in a new town.

The move to Sidney was complete by the middle of 1969, with business uninterrupted and sales continuing their unbroken steady growth, topping the million-dollar mark at $1,178,535 by the end of that year. Along for the ride went Burt and Sharon Robison and a handful of others who had tied their futures to the Cabelas' dream. They would soon be joined by many new faces.

Mary Cabela now looks back and thinks, "We were pretty sure it was all working by the time we moved to Sidney. But when we were inside and looking around that big building on main street, we said, 'We will never fill this building.' But it didn't take long, and it was full."

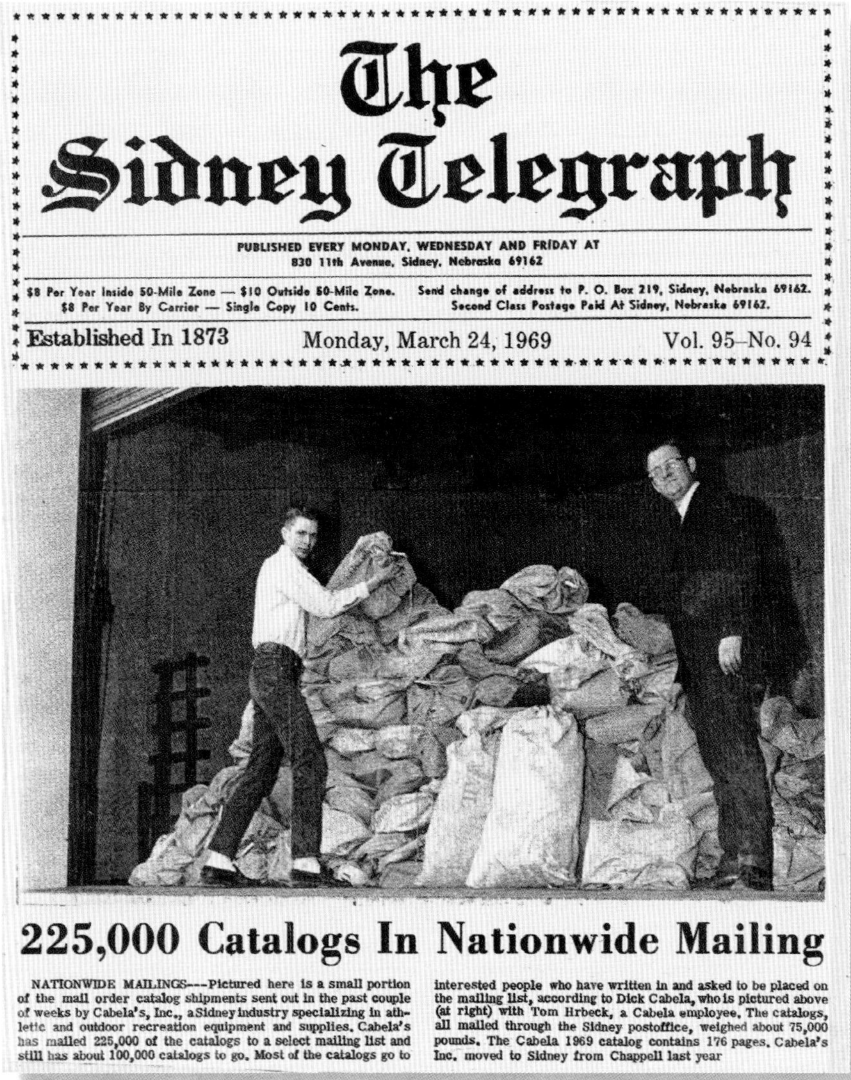

The Sidney Telegraph

PUBLISHED EVERY MONDAY, WEDNESDAY AND FRIDAY AT
830 11th Avenue, Sidney, Nebraska 69162

$8 Per Year Inside 50-Mile Zone — $10 Outside 50-Mile Zone.
$8 Per Year By Carrier — Single Copy 10 Cents.

Send change of address to P. O. Box 219, Sidney, Nebraska 69162.
Second Class Postage Paid At Sidney, Nebraska 69162.

Established In 1873 — Monday, March 24, 1969 — Vol. 95–No. 94

225,000 Catalogs In Nationwide Mailing

NATIONWIDE MAILINGS---Pictured here is a small portion of the mail order catalog shipments sent out in the past couple of weeks by Cabela's, Inc., a Sidney industry specializing in athletic and outdoor recreation equipment and supplies. Cabela's has mailed 225,000 of the catalogs to a select mailing list and still has about 100,000 catalogs to go. Most of the catalogs go to interested people who have written in and asked to be placed on the mailing list, according to Dick Cabela, who is pictured above (at right) with Tom Hrbeck, a Cabela employee. The catalogs, all mailed through the Sidney postoffice, weighed about 75,000 pounds. The Cabela 1969 catalog contains 176 pages. Cabela's Inc. moved to Sidney from Chappell last year

Left (page 34): Newspaper clippings tell the story of the rapid rise and expansion of Cabela's and the move to Sidney, Nebraska. This page: Sidney Telegraph article announcing 225,000 Cabela's catalogs were being mailed nationwide – a tremendous jump from the first mailing of mimeographed flyers just nine years earlier.

WORLD'S FINEST QUALITY SPORTING GOODS
Cabela's
1977
FALL-WINTER CATALOG
QUALITY / PRICE / SERVICE / SATISFACTION GUARANTEED

Chapter 2

Settling In Sidney

– The 1970s –

Cabela's early letterhead design.

After preparing their new three-story headquarters in Sidney with essentials such as electricity, phone service and workspace layout, the Cabela's core staff made the move from the old American Legion Hall in Chappell in just one day. Jim Cabela insisted there be no interruption in service to customers. Trucking inventory to the new building took a few days longer.

Initially, they used only the first floor of the 50,000-square-foot former John Deere building for operations – offices, merchandise receiving, warehousing, order fulfillment, packing, shipping, everything. Burt, the German shepherd security system, was given free run of the second floor, and Dick and Jim set up an archery practice/testing range on the third floor. The basement remained mostly unused.

A retail counter on the first floor was added almost immediately to accommodate the growing number of walk-in customers, at first, mostly residents from western Nebraska, then Cabela's customers passing by on the newly opened Interstate 80.

Further, the rapid growth in sales that had marked their beginnings in Chappell continued at an accelerating rate in Sidney, and it was not long before the receiving department was moved

Cabela's store in Sidney, early 1970s.

The former John Deere building in Sidney became Cabela's headquarters.

to the basement, along with backstock, returns and discontinued items. Warehousing and shipping were moved to the second floor, then spread to fill the third floor as well. Everybody was glad to have access to the industrial-grade elevator to avoid carrying heavy boxes up and down the stairs. By the end of 1970, sales had reached a total of $1.8 million. That samc ycar Cabela's received its first national recognition when the U.S. Small Business Administration named Dick and Jim Cabela jointly as "Man of the Year" for the growth Cabela's had achieved in just eight years.

Cabela's Time Line

1970s

1970

- Dick and Jim Cabela jointly named U.S. Small Business Administration's "Man of the Year".
- Total revenue: $1,785,265.

1971

- Cabela's begins accepting credit cards.
- Total revenue: $2,713,057.

1972

- Dot Kruse, long-time Customer Service manager, joins staff.
- Total revenue: $1,924,489.

1973

- Purchased warehouse next to the downtown Sidney building.
- Total revenue: $3,780,301.

Cabela's store interior and retail operation in downtown Sidney in the early '70s was pretty simple compared to Cabela's current stores.

The Good Old Days

Growth required additional help, and the Cabela brothers began adding more full-time staff almost as soon as they arrived in their new location, capitalizing on Sidney's larger population base. Initially, nearly all new employees were women, typical of small-town businesses needing administrative workers. Many of these first new hires would go on to work for Cabela's for 20 years and more. Some are working there still. They were the backbone of Cabela's early success. Their memories of the good old days in the old brick building downtown paint a picture of how the World's Foremost Outfitter took shape and developed.

Alice Needham started in 1969, as soon as the Sidney operation opened. She would go on to serve for 40 years, ending her career as a customer service supervisor. "When I first heard about Cabela's, they were based in Chappell. We were in Mount Shasta, California, visiting a friend, and he told my husband he had found this great place to get fishing tackle. My husband asked, 'Where?' He said, 'A place in Chappell, Nebraska,' and my husband said, 'Why, that's just 25 miles from us.' We didn't even know about it. I was working at a local restaurant in Sidney and waited on Dick Cabela and the guy who sold them the John Deere building while they were talking about it. I decided to work at Cabela's when I read in the paper they were moving to Sidney. Dick hired me."

Alice remembers, "When I started, I had assorted duties – including preparing catalogs for mailing; overseeing in-bound mail and freight; and creating a manual inventory-control system."

Monica Martinosky began in 1970 and stayed 35 years. "When I first started, the majority of employees were women and we did most of the labor, including the cleaning. We looked like chimney sweeps after we got through cleaning out the back storage room. Back then, Dick and Jim sponsored a women's Wednesday-night bowling team, and Jim and some of the other guys would usually

Dick and Jim pose for a newspaper photo in the first Cabela's retail location in Sidney.

1974
- Steve Treinen hired for MIS (retired 2009, after 34 years).
- Total revenue: $4,625,153.

1975
- Cabela's first computer system replaces recipe-card filing system.
- Total revenue: $5,165,123.

1976
- Dennis Highby joins company as 40th employee; first full-time, salaried employee.
- Total revenue: $5,167,126.

1977
- Total revenue: $6,341,542

1978
- Telemarketing department implemented.
- Total revenue: $9,016,470.

1979
- First Sioux Army Depot building near Sidney acquired for distribution center.
- Total revenue: $13,253,632.

Cabela's early handwritten system of tracking sales.

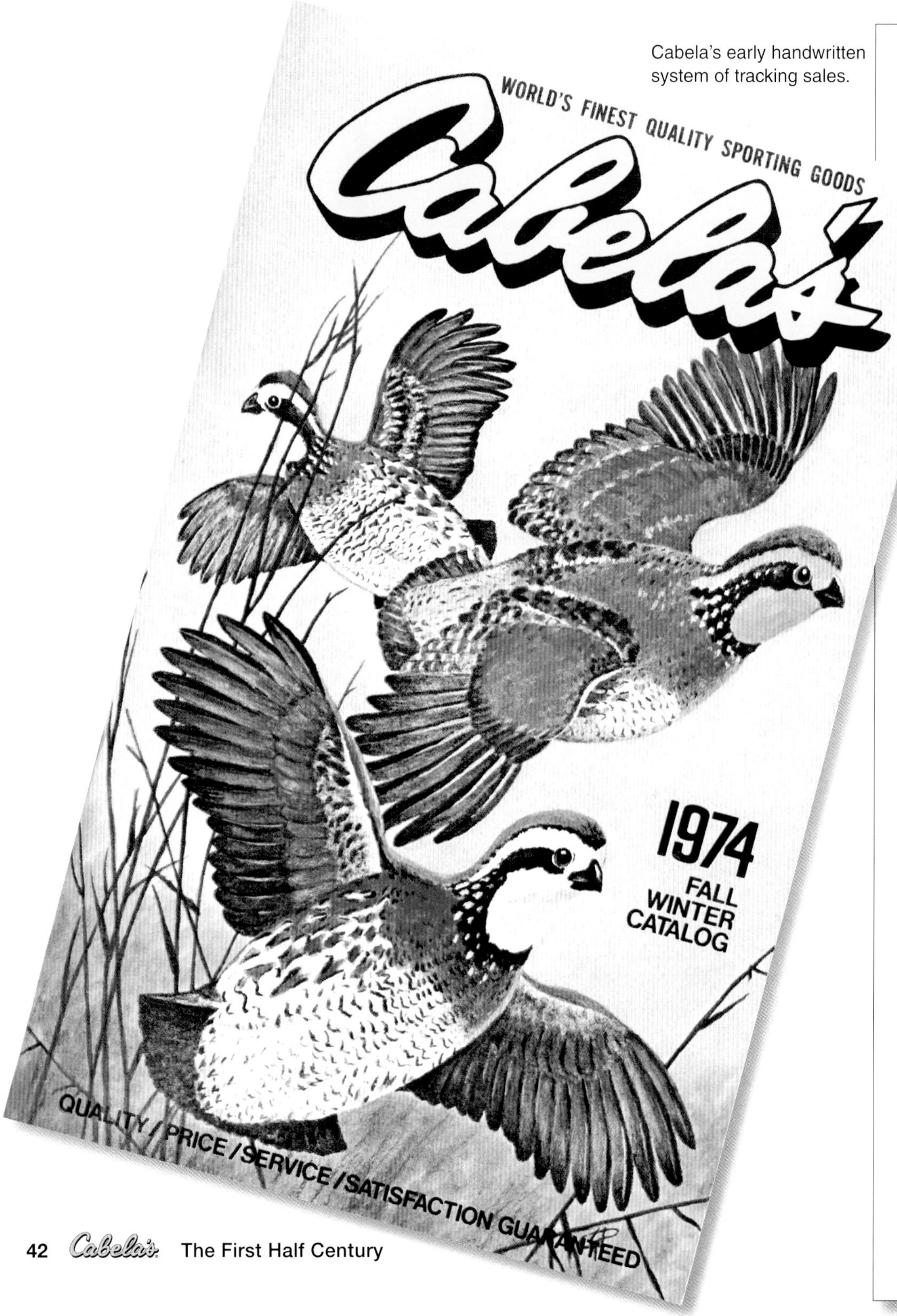

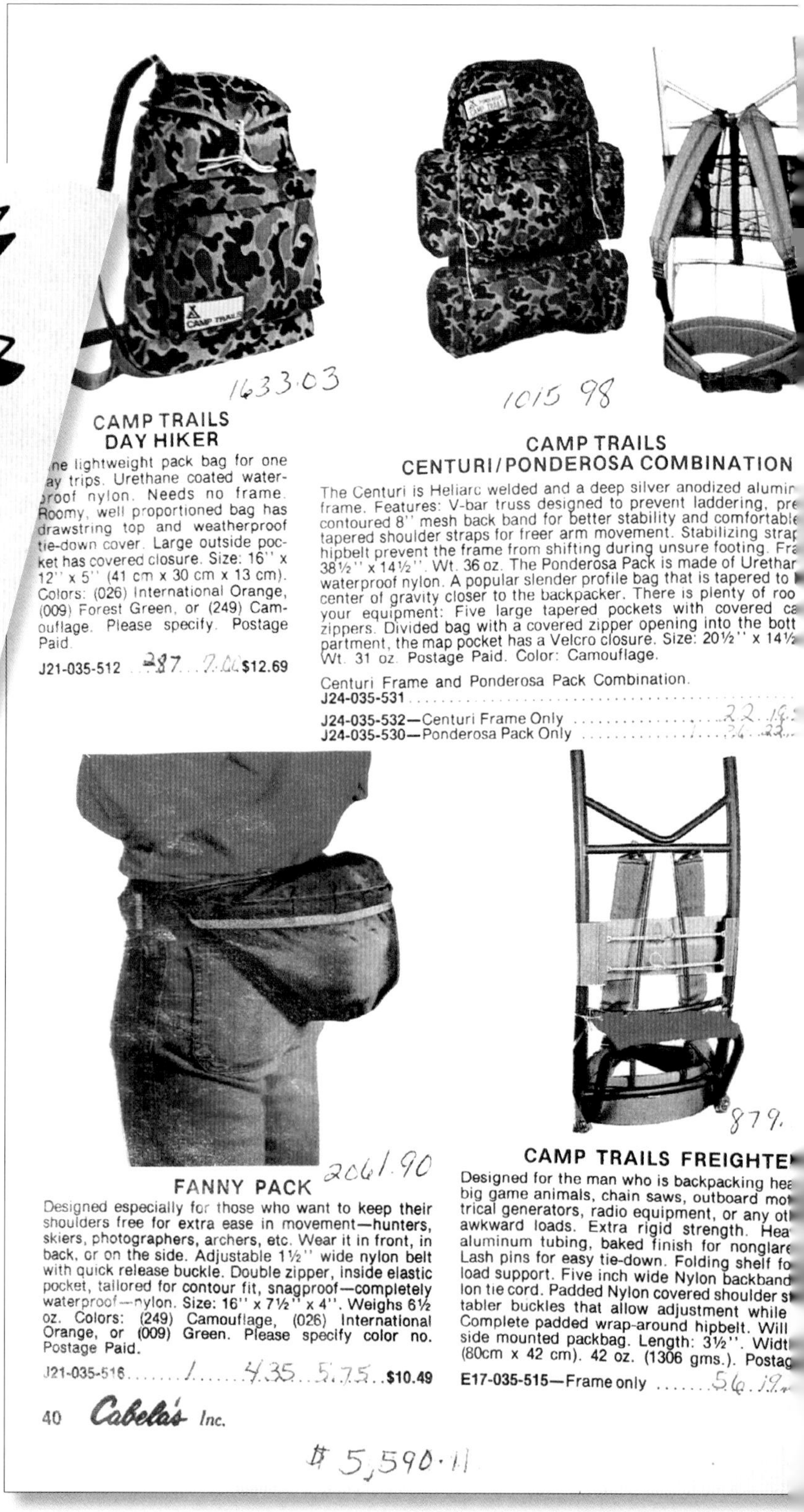

1633.03

CAMP TRAILS
DAY HIKER

...ne lightweight pack bag for one ...ay trips. Urethane coated waterproof nylon. Needs no frame. Roomy, well proportioned bag has drawstring top and weatherproof tie-down cover. Large outside pocket has covered closure. Size: 16'' x 12'' x 5'' (41 cm x 30 cm x 13 cm). Colors: (026) International Orange, (009) Forest Green, or (249) Camouflage. Please specify. Postage Paid.

J21-035-512 ...287...7.00 $12.69

1015 98

CAMP TRAILS
CENTURI / PONDEROSA COMBINATION

The Centuri is Heliarc welded and a deep silver anodized alumin... frame. Features: V-bar truss designed to prevent laddering, pre... contoured 8'' mesh back band for better stability and comfortable... tapered shoulder straps for freer arm movement. Stabilizing strap... hipbelt prevent the frame from shifting during unsure footing. Fra... 38½'' x 14½''. Wt. 36 oz. The Ponderosa Pack is made of Urethan... waterproof nylon. A popular slender profile bag that is tapered to ... center of gravity closer to the backpacker. There is plenty of roo... your equipment: Five large tapered pockets with covered ca... zippers. Divided bag with a covered zipper opening into the bott... partment, the map pocket has a Velcro closure. Size: 20½'' x 14½... Wt. 31 oz. Postage Paid. Color: Camouflage.

Centuri Frame and Ponderosa Pack Combination.
J24-035-531 ...

J24-035-532—Centuri Frame Only ...22.19...
J24-035-530—Ponderosa Pack Only ...1...36...22...

2061.90

FANNY PACK

Designed especially for those who want to keep their shoulders free for extra ease in movement—hunters, skiers, photographers, archers, etc. Wear it in front, in back, or on the side. Adjustable 1½'' wide nylon belt with quick release buckle. Double zipper, inside elastic pocket, tailored for contour fit, snagproof—completely waterproof—nylon. Size: 16'' x 7½'' x 4''. Weighs 6½ oz. Colors: (249) Camouflage, (026) International Orange, or (009) Green. Please specify color no. Postage Paid.

J21-035-516 ......1......4.35..5.75..$10.49

879.

CAMP TRAILS FREIGHTE...

Designed for the man who is backpacking hea... big game animals, chain saws, outboard mo... trical generators, radio equipment, or any ot... awkward loads. Extra rigid strength. Hea... aluminum tubing, baked finish for nonglare... Lash pins for easy tie-down. Folding shelf fo... load support. Five inch wide Nylon backband... lon tie cord. Padded Nylon covered shoulder s... tabler buckles that allow adjustment while ... Complete padded wrap-around hipbelt. Will ... side mounted packbag. Length: 3½''. Widt... (80cm x 42 cm). 42 oz. (1306 gms.). Postag...

E17-035-515—Frame only ......56.19...

40 Cabela's Inc.

$5,590.11

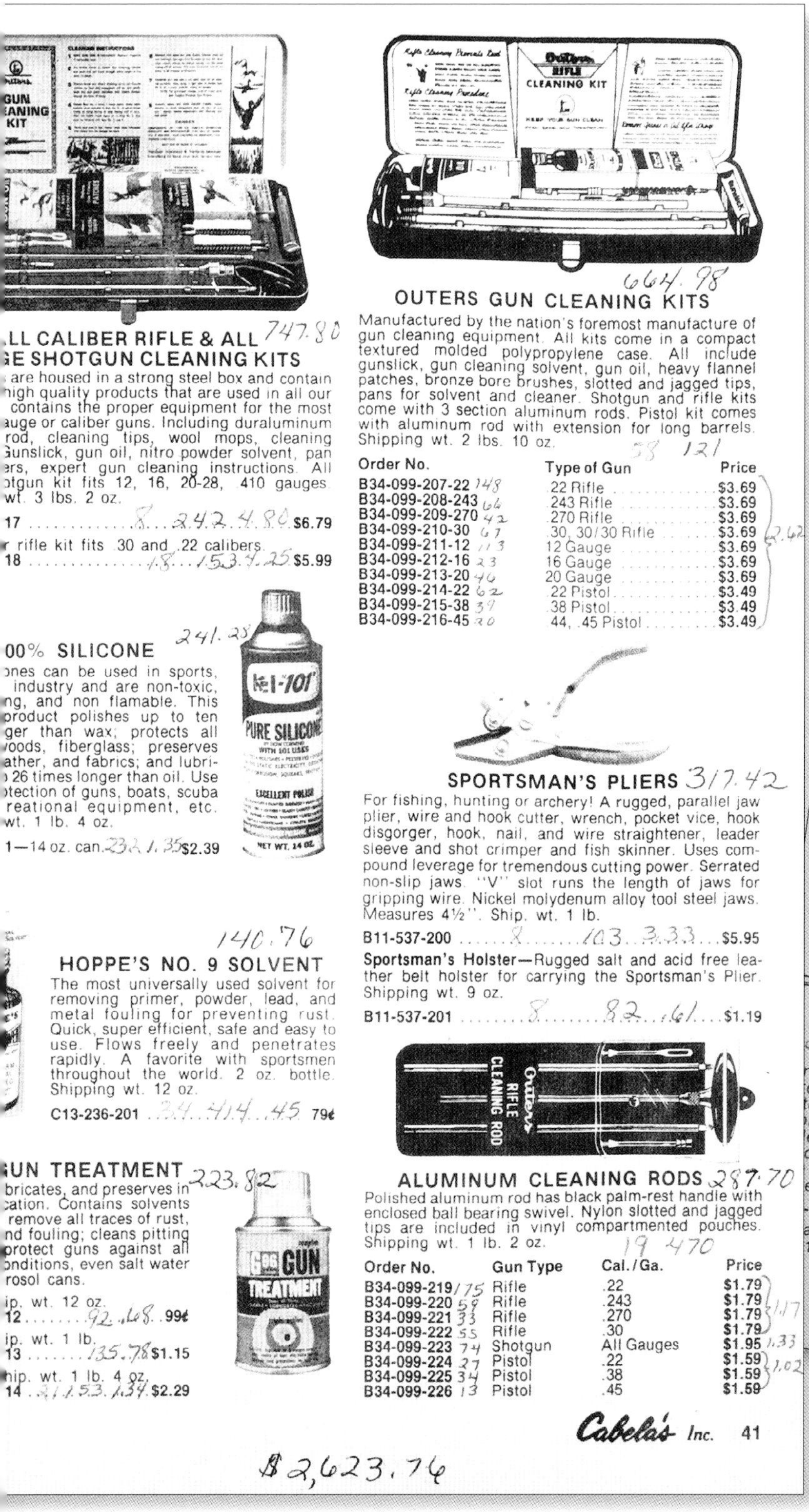

...LL CALIBER RIFLE & ALL ...E SHOTGUN CLEANING KITS

...are housed in a strong steel box and contain ...high quality products that are used in all our ...contains the proper equipment for the most ...auge or caliber guns. Including duraluminum ...rod, cleaning tips, wool mops, cleaning ...Gunslick, gun oil, nitro powder solvent, pan ...ers, expert gun cleaning instructions. All ...otgun kit fits 12, 16, 20-28, .410 gauges. ...wt. 3 lbs. 2 oz.

...17 .... $6.79

...rifle kit fits .30 and .22 calibers.

...18 .... $5.99

OUTERS GUN CLEANING KITS

Manufactured by the nation's foremost manufacture of gun cleaning equipment. All kits come in a compact textured molded polypropylene case. All include gunslick, gun cleaning solvent, gun oil, heavy flannel patches, bronze bore brushes, slotted and jagged tips, pans for solvent and cleaner. Shotgun and rifle kits come with 3 section aluminum rods. Pistol kit comes with aluminum rod with extension for long barrels. Shipping wt. 2 lbs. 10 oz.

Order No.	Type of Gun	Price
B34-099-207-22	.22 Rifle	$3.69
B34-099-208-243	.243 Rifle	$3.69
B34-099-209-270	.270 Rifle	$3.69
B34-099-210-30	.30, 30/30 Rifle	$3.69
B34-099-211-12	12 Gauge	$3.69
B34-099-212-16	16 Gauge	$3.69
B34-099-213-20	20 Gauge	$3.69
B34-099-214-22	.22 Pistol	$3.49
B34-099-215-38	.38 Pistol	$3.49
B34-099-216-45	.44, .45 Pistol	$3.49

...00% SILICONE

...ones can be used in sports, ...industry and are non-toxic, ...ng, and non flamable. This ...product polishes up to ten ...ger than wax; protects all ...oods, fiberglass; preserves ...ather, and fabrics; and lubri... ...26 times longer than oil. Use ...tection of guns, boats, scuba ...reational equipment, etc. ...wt. 1 lb. 4 oz.

...1—14 oz. can. $2.39

SPORTSMAN'S PLIERS

For fishing, hunting or archery! A rugged, parallel jaw plier, wire and hook cutter, wrench, pocket vice, hook disgorger, hook, nail, and wire straightener, leader sleeve and shot crimper and fish skinner. Uses compound leverage for tremendous cutting power. Serrated non-slip jaws. "V" slot runs the length of jaws for gripping wire. Nickel molydenum alloy tool steel jaws. Measures 4½". Ship. wt. 1 lb.

B11-537-200 .... $5.95

Sportsman's Holster—Rugged salt and acid free leather belt holster for carrying the Sportsman's Plier. Shipping wt. 9 oz.

B11-537-201 .... $1.19

HOPPE'S NO. 9 SOLVENT

The most universally used solvent for removing primer, powder, lead, and metal fouling for preventing rust. Quick, super efficient, safe and easy to use. Flows freely and penetrates rapidly. A favorite with sportsmen throughout the world. 2 oz. bottle. Shipping wt. 12 oz.

C13-236-201 .... 79¢

...UN TREATMENT

...bricates, and preserves in... ...cation. Contains solvents ...remove all traces of rust, ...nd fouling; cleans pitting ...protect guns against all ...onditions, even salt water ...rosol cans.

...ip. wt. 12 oz.

...12 .... 99¢

...ip. wt. 1 lb.

...13 .... $1.15

...hip. wt. 1 lb. 4 oz.

...14 .... $2.29

ALUMINUM CLEANING RODS

Polished aluminum rod has black palm-rest handle with enclosed ball bearing swivel. Nylon slotted and jagged tips are included in vinyl compartmented pouches. Shipping wt. 1 lb. 2 oz.

Order No.	Gun Type	Cal./Ga.	Price
B34-099-219	Rifle	.22	$1.79
B34-099-220	Rifle	.243	$1.79
B34-099-221	Rifle	.270	$1.79
B34-099-222	Rifle	.30	$1.79
B34-099-223	Shotgun	All Gauges	$1.95
B34-099-224	Pistol	.22	$1.59
B34-099-225	Pistol	.38	$1.59
B34-099-226	Pistol	.45	$1.59

Cabela's Inc. 41

$2,623.76

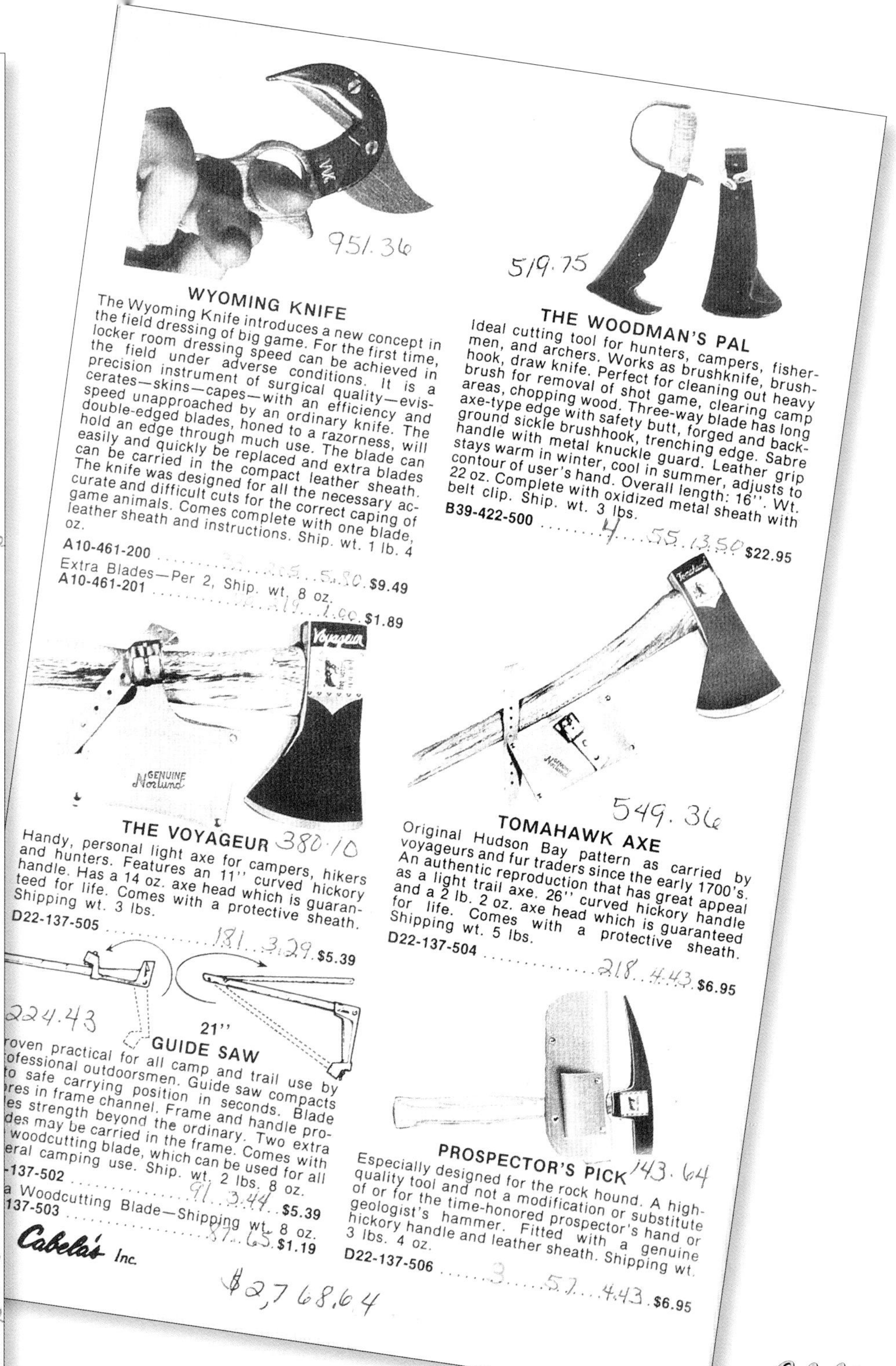

WYOMING KNIFE

The Wyoming Knife introduces a new concept in the field dressing of big game. For the first time, locker room dressing speed can be achieved in the field under adverse conditions. It is a precision instrument of surgical quality—eviscerates—skins—capes—with an efficiency and speed unapproached by an ordinary knife. The double-edged blades, honed to a razorness, will hold an edge through much use. The blade can easily and quickly be replaced and extra blades can be carried in the compact leather sheath. The knife was designed for all the necessary accurate and difficult cuts for the correct caping of game animals. Comes complete with one blade, leather sheath and instructions. Ship. wt. 1 lb. 4 oz.

A10-461-200 .... $9.49

Extra Blades—Per 2, Ship. wt. 8 oz.

A10-461-201 .... $1.89

THE WOODMAN'S PAL

Ideal cutting tool for hunters, campers, fishermen, and archers. Works as brushknife, brushhook, draw knife. Perfect for cleaning out heavy brush for removal of shot game, clearing camp areas, chopping wood. Three-way blade has long axe-type edge with safety butt, forged and background sickle brushhook, trenching edge. Sabre handle with metal knuckle guard. Leather grip stays warm in winter, cool in summer, adjusts to contour of user's hand. Overall length: 16". Wt. 22 oz. Complete with oxidized metal sheath with belt clip. Ship. wt. 3 lbs.

B39-422-500 .... $22.95

THE VOYAGEUR

Handy, personal light axe for campers, hikers and hunters. Features an 11" curved hickory handle. Has a 14 oz. axe head which is guaranteed for life. Comes with a protective sheath. Shipping wt. 3 lbs.

D22-137-505 .... $5.39

TOMAHAWK AXE

Original Hudson Bay pattern as carried by voyageurs and fur traders since the early 1700's. An authentic reproduction that has great appeal as a light trail axe. 26" curved hickory handle and a 2 lb. 2 oz. axe head which is guaranteed for life. Comes with a protective sheath. Shipping wt. 5 lbs.

D22-137-504 .... $6.95

21" GUIDE SAW

...roven practical for all camp and trail use by ...ofessional outdoorsmen. Guide saw compacts ...to safe carrying position in seconds. Blade ...ores in frame channel. Frame and handle pro... ...es strength beyond the ordinary. Two extra ...des may be carried in the frame. Comes with ...woodcutting blade, which can be used for all ...eral camping use. Ship. wt. 2 lbs. 8 oz.

...-137-502 .... $5.39

...a Woodcutting Blade—Shipping wt. 8 oz.

...137-503 .... $1.19

PROSPECTOR'S PICK

Especially designed for the rock hound. A high-quality tool and not a modification or substitute of or for the time-honored prospector's hand or geologist's hammer. Fitted with a genuine hickory handle and leather sheath. Shipping wt. 3 lbs. 4 oz.

D22-137-506 .... $6.95

Cabela's Inc.

$2,768.64

Cabela's company-sponsored women's bowling teams in the '70s and '80s. Above, left to right: Monica Martinosky, Judy Mitchell, Darlene Bondegard, Maggie Bartlett, Roxie Bartling. And the '83 team, left to right: Debbie Dolan, Maggie Bartlett, Roxie Bartling, Darlene Bondegard, Julie Herrera.

come out and cheer us on," she said. "It was fun and made us feel like we were part of a big family."

Marietta Leypoldt also began in 1970 and stayed with Cabela's for 21 years. "I went to work in shipping on the second floor. I got my nickname when this gal came up to me, and said she couldn't remember my name so she was just going to call me 'George.' And to this day, Dick, Jim, everybody calls me George."

Another of the early-years veterans is Judy Bayne, who spent 21 years with Cabela's. She remembers how catalog requests and order forms were color-coded to avoid confusion. "I remember around the holidays, from the first of November until after Christmas, the yellow catalog request cards got shoved into huge totes, stacked

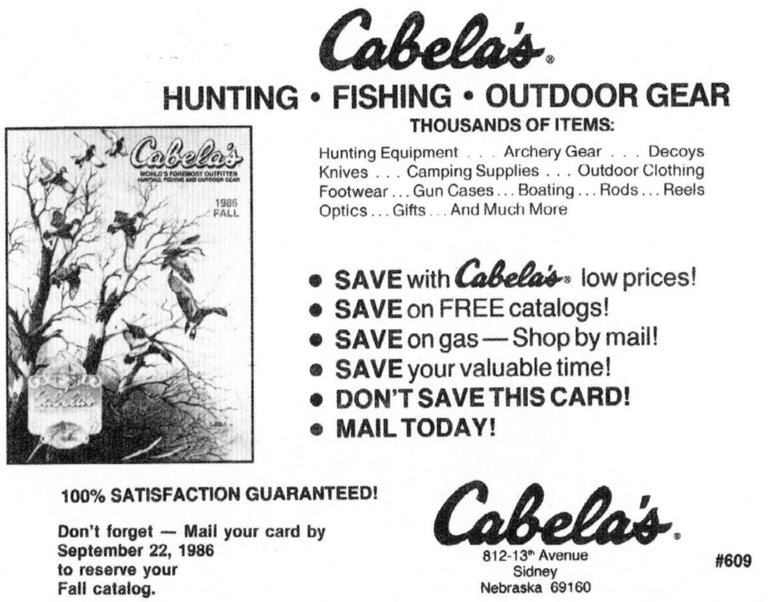

> "The yellow cards, that was our customer acquisition strategy at that point."
> – Sharon Robison

clear to the ceiling, because nobody had time to deal with them, everybody was doing the orders." Sharon Robison adds, "The yellow cards, that was our customer acquisition strategy at that point. I would dive into our old customer base to see if we could reactivate customers. We would send out yellow double-sided postal cards perforated in the middle. It would say, 'Are you still interested in receiving a Cabela's catalog?' Or, 'Would you like to receive a Cabela's catalog?' We would get those back by the buckets full." She also notes, "Sometimes customers would write comments at the bottom, like, 'I would love to continue to get your catalog, but I am 84 years old and am no longer able to stand, so I don't go hunting any more.' Some were little stories by themselves."

The small retail department on the first floor was an early harbinger of things to come, but in those days it was only a tiny part of the operation. Mike Wieser began working there part-time in 1972 when he was 20 and became Cabela's 25th full-time employee the following year and retired in 2009 as Senior Director of Merchandising.

He remembers an opening in the ceiling above the retail area, open to the second floor where merchandise was warehoused. When customers wanted merchandise not on a retail shelf, the retail person would holler up through the hole what they needed, and whoever was working on the second floor would drop the items down through the opening. After several near misses, and a few total misses, a nylon net was put under the opening to catch the goods before they crashed to the floor or onto the clerk's head.

Throughout the years, Cabela's promoted family and community programs, such as youth fishing events. Jim and Dick were usually on hand to help stock ponds and congratulate participants.

Steve Treinen works with an early IBM computer.

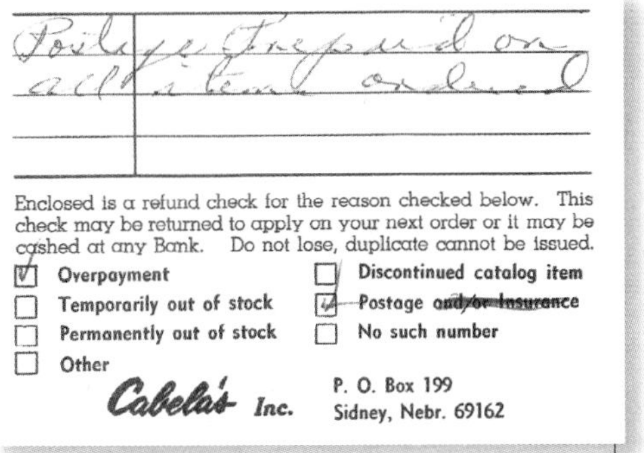

Postage Prepaid on all items ordered

Enclosed is a refund check for the reason checked below. This check may be returned to apply on your next order or it may be cashed at any Bank. Do not lose, duplicate cannot be issued.

- [x] Overpayment
- [ ] Temporarily out of stock
- [ ] Permanently out of stock
- [ ] Other
- [ ] Discontinued catalog item
- [x] Postage ~~and/or Insurance~~
- [ ] No such number

Cabela's Inc.
P. O. Box 199
Sidney, Nebr. 69162

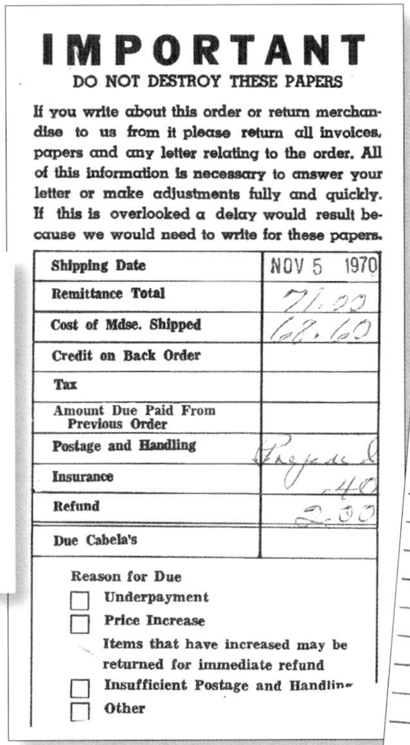

IMPORTANT
DO NOT DESTROY THESE PAPERS

If you write about this order or return merchandise to us from it please return all invoices, papers and any letter relating to the order. All of this information is necessary to answer your letter or make adjustments fully and quickly. If this is overlooked a delay would result because we would need to write for these papers.

Shipping Date	NOV 5 1970
Remittance Total	71.00
Cost of Mdse. Shipped	68.60
Credit on Back Order	
Tax	
Amount Due Paid From Previous Order	
Postage and Handling	Prepaid
Insurance	.40
Refund	2.00
Due Cabela's	

Reason for Due
- [ ] Underpayment
- [ ] Price Increase

Items that have increased may be returned for immediate refund
- [ ] Insufficient Postage and Handlin–
- [ ] Other

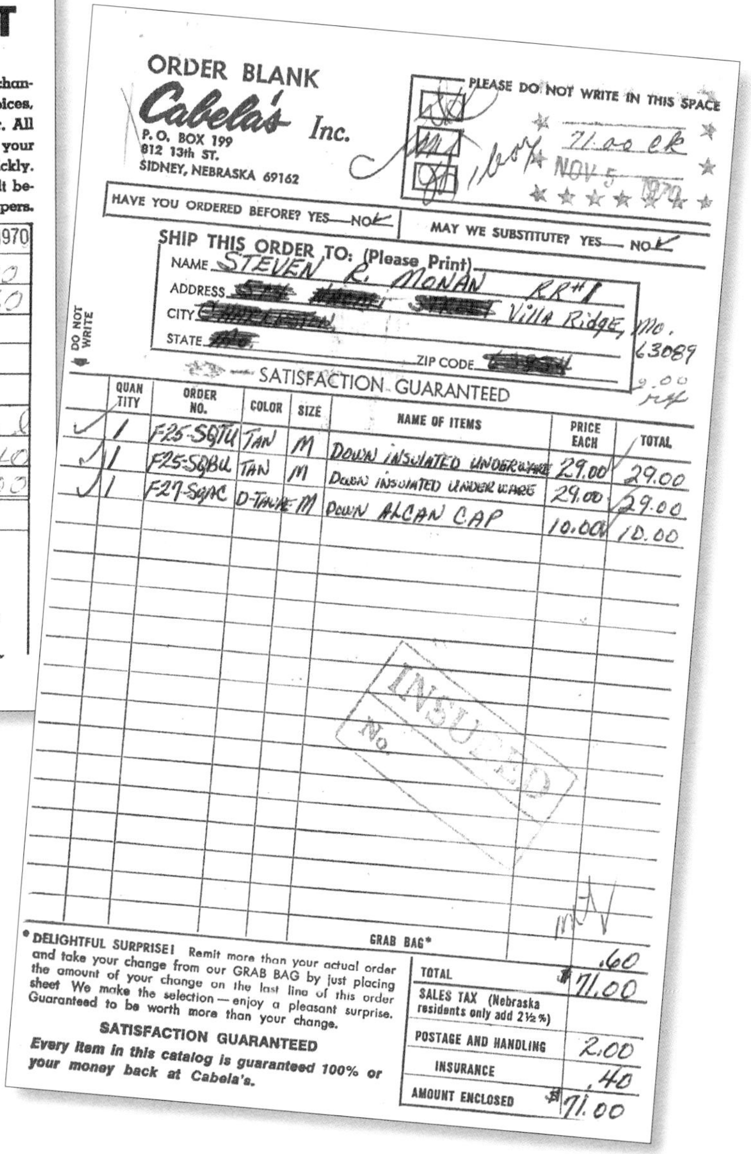

ORDER BLANK
Cabela's Inc.
P. O. BOX 199
812 13th ST.
SIDNEY, NEBRASKA 69162

PLEASE DO NOT WRITE IN THIS SPACE
71.00 ck
NOV 5 1970

HAVE YOU ORDERED BEFORE? YES— NO ✓
MAY WE SUBSTITUTE? YES— NO ✓

SHIP THIS ORDER TO: (Please Print)
NAME STEVEN R. MONAN
ADDRESS [redacted] RR#1
CITY [redacted] Villa Ridge, Mo.
STATE [redacted] ZIP CODE [redacted] 63089

DO NOT WRITE

SATISFACTION GUARANTEED

QUANTITY	ORDER NO.	COLOR	SIZE	NAME OF ITEMS	PRICE EACH	TOTAL
1	F25-SQTU	TAN	M	DOWN INSULATED UNDERWARE	29.00	29.00
1	F25-SQBU	TAN	M	DOWN INSULATED UNDERWARE	29.00	29.00
1	F27-SQAC	D-TAN	M	DOWN ALCAN CAP	10.00	10.00
				GRAB BAG*		.60

INSURED
No.

*DELIGHTFUL SURPRISE! Remit more than your actual order and take your change from our GRAB BAG by just placing the amount of your change on the last line of this order sheet. We make the selection — enjoy a pleasant surprise. Guaranteed to be worth more than your change.

SATISFACTION GUARANTEED
Every item in this catalog is guaranteed 100% or your money back at Cabela's.

TOTAL	$71.00
SALES TAX (Nebraska residents only add 2½%)	
POSTAGE AND HANDLING	2.00
INSURANCE	.40
AMOUNT ENCLOSED	$71.00

Customer paperwork from an order in 1970.

"We Probably Need a Computer"

When Mary Cabela first looked at the building in Sidney, she believed Cabela's would never fill it. But after three years it was full, with no room for the archery range anymore, and in 1973 the company purchased a 14,000-square-foot storage building next door. By then annual sales had more than doubled from when Cabela's arrived in Sidney, to $3.78 million.

It also became obvious the recipe-card customer record system and growing stacks of file-card boxes for inventory records could not keep up. Dick and Jim decided to install a computer. It's easy to forget that

"This was a huge turn in the road. Having statistics allowed us to make systematic decisions on purchases for the first time."

– Sharon Robison

computers then were monstrous devices, requiring large numbers of punch cards, and there was no commercial general-business software as there is today. Everything had to be programmed for individual businesses' needs and continually modified and updated every time procedures changed even slightly.

Cabela's first IBM computer system was purchased in early 1974, and Marietta "George" Leypoldt's son, Bruce, was hired to install it. Another fresh-from-college local boy with training in computer programming, Steve Treinen, was also looking for a job. When he heard Cabela's was computerizing, he drove to Dick and Mary's house and knocked on the door. "I got Dick out of the shower," he remembers, "and I asked him if he needed a computer programmer." Dick asked him how much money he wanted, and Steve said, "Five dollars an hour." Dick muttered, "Nobody is worth that," then asked how long it would take to get a payroll system up and running. Steve answered, "Thirty days." Thirty days later, Steve had the payroll system in place, and Dick asked him how long it would take to add accounts payable to the system. "Another 30 days," said Steve. When that task was completed, Dick told him they next needed a general ledger and simply commented, "I bet it will take 30 days to get that done, too." Thirty-four years later Steve retired from Cabela's management information system department.

Cabela's first big, blue IBM mainframe computer was fully online by 1975. In addition to basic internal accounting, it replaced the old recipe-card order file system and handwritten inventory records, plus it also systemized shipping. It was a major transition for the women working on the first and second floors, none of whom had any experience with computers. Sharon Robison remembers, "This was a huge turn in the road. Having statistics allowed us to make systematic decisions on purchases for the first time."

According to Alice Needham, "It was a huge undertaking to convert from color-coded file cards to the computerized system."

Like all early mainframe punch-card systems, the computer required around-the-clock attention. Steve Treinen remembers one particular maintenance session that for him typifies the dedication of Cabela's owners. "Bruce Leypoldt and I were working late at night doing a computer system upgrade. At that time, the computer room was on the first floor. We were sure we were the only people in the building, but about 1 a.m. we heard a thump from either the second or third floor. We were talking to an IBM person in Denver, so I stayed on the phone while Bruce slowly went up the back stairs. I told the IBM person if there was no activity on the line after 10 minutes to call the Sidney police. When Bruce crept around the landing between the second and third floors, he was suddenly face to face with Jim Cabela. Jim had made the noise we'd heard, and he was sneaking down the stairs to investigate the noise Bruce had made closing the stairwell door." Jim had also been working into the wee hours.

> "Hunting and fishing were my passion, so I was like a kid in a candy store."
> – Mike Wieser

Building the Employee Family

As the Cabela's employee family continued to grow with managerial staff for merchandising and product selection, the Cabela brothers actively sought people from small-town backgrounds throughout the Midwest who shared their passion for the outdoors, understood their commitment to customer service and enjoyed the same lifestyle as Cabela's customers. Dick Cabela remembers, "We wanted our employees to hunt and fish. I told them, 'We sell fun; so have fun selling.' A lot of people already had good jobs but wanted to come work with us."

Mike Wieser fit right in. "Hunting and fishing were my passion," he says. "So I was like a kid in a candy store, when I started working at the retail counter after high school."

"Dick and Jim didn't go looking to hire Harvard MBA graduates," he says. "What it really boils down to, you have all these people who are passionate for hunting and fishing," he says. "These common values and lifestyle passions created a closely bonded atmosphere from the very beginning. Dick and Jim always made our families feel like

Jim and Dick would often be in charge of the grill during summer picnics.

they were part of the Cabela's family. We always had company picnics and other events that our wives and children participated in."

That sense is shared by all Cabela's long-term employees, active and retired alike. Marietta "George" Leypoldt says, "What I miss most are the people. We were like one happy family. We had big Cabela's picnics every summer, and everybody's family would come. Jim and Dick would be grilling."

Clockwise from left: Marietta "George" Leypoldt, 21 years, Shipping and Customer Service; Monica Martinosky, 35 years, Shipping; Roxie Bartling, 33 years, Shipping; Sharon Robison, 45 years as of 2010; Alice Needham, 40 years, Customer Service Supervisor; Judy Bayne, 21 years, Executive Assistant; Julie Herrera, Shipping, 37 years as of 2010; Steve Treinen, 34 years, Computers/MIS.

Julie Herrera, who is still working in the Shipping Department after 37 years, remembers, "I started in 1972. Then in 1975 I told Jim I was going to quit and work at a grocery store because I thought it was going to be better there. He said, 'You're going to be sorry. You'll be back.' Sure enough, about 11 months later I went back, and they were still hiring, and Jim says, 'I told you you'd be back.' He was very nice about it, giving me my job back. And I'm still here."

Today, if you ask the Cabela's retirement group what it was about Cabela's that made them stay their entire careers, their answers come in a chorus: "It was a family." "Dick and Jim were good bosses." "They were down-to-earth, and no matter what, they would come and work things out with us and always had time for us." "They never, ever turned us away." "It was the best-paying job in town, and it was good working conditions and everybody got along." "We're very proud of it." "We still call Cabela's ours."

Monica Martinosky remembers that Jim Cabela was everywhere and knew everything, but he was never overbearing. "Roxie and I often volunteered on Saturdays to work inventory on the second floor, and one day Jim calls up on the intercom and wants a particular arrow." So she and Roxie looked through a wall of shelves full of arrows but couldn't find it. "We were panicking because we thought he was going to be upset. Pretty soon, the door opens and Jim steps in, says, 'Having trouble?' and walks right over and picks up the arrow off the shelf, then turns around and walks right out. We couldn't find it, but he went right to it. Like it was no big deal."

Mike Wieser sums up the Cabela brothers' approach to building a family of committed, passionate employees: "They always gave us the latitude and respect to do business as we saw fit for our specific areas. If they thought you were getting off course a little, they would get you back on track. Jim would bring something to you and say, 'Don't you think maybe you should have tried this?'" Mike says, "What a neat way to work. For being here for almost 36 years, I enjoyed coming to work every single day and that's something. I don't think a lot of people can say."

"...George Herter called me at home and asked me to stay. I just said, 'Sorry, George.' I guess the rest is history."

– Dennis Highby

The Smartest Hire

By 1976 with sales reaching $5 million, the Cabela brothers decided they needed experienced management help, which was not readily available in Sidney. As luck would have it, Dennis Highby's résumé landed on their desks at about the same time. He had been working at a senior position with Herter's, which was then the only other powerhouse company in the catalog-order business for outdoorsmen. Using a small original investment and his background of military organizational experience, founder George Herter built a company that sold hunting, fishing, camping, shooting and reloading supplies through a chain of six stores and a mail-order operation. Concentrating on salesmanship and service, Herter's unique writing style also spread from his catalogs to a long list of popular outdoor books. Eventually, Herter sold the business and ownership changed hands a couple times. In 2002, Cabela's purchased the company and the rights to manufacture Herter's brand products, which are still sold by Cabela's.

Dennis Highby and his son, Matt with trophy deer.

Dennis Highby
in Africa with a kudu.

BOAT
HERTER'S
HERTER'S
World famous Morning Dove and White Wing Dove
FOR the serious Dovehunter
FAMOUS
HERTER'S
SINCE 1893
MANUFACTURERS, IMPORTERS, EXPORTERS
THE AUTHENTIC WORLD SOURCE FOR HUNTERS,
FISHERMEN, GUIDES, GUNSMITHS, LAW ENFORCEMENT
OFFICERS, TACKLE MAKERS, FOREST RANGERS,
COMMERCIAL FISHERMEN, TRAPPERS AND EXPLORERS
MARQUE DEPOSEE
TENACIOUS FOR QUALITY

Dennis Highby with an elk.

Dennis, who would eventually retire as President and Chief Executive Officer of Cabela's in 2009, tells the story:

"I started working at Herter's in 1969. It was my first job. I'd gone to college for two years, couldn't figure out what I wanted to do, so I went to work for Herter's." He says his first awareness of Cabela's was when "George Herter came in my office one day in 1972, dropped a Cabela's catalog on my desk and said, 'Here's a competitor you'd better pay attention to.' I had never heard of Cabela's."

Not long after, business at Herter's began to suffer, and Dennis started sending out résumés. He got a response from Cabela's, so he chartered a small plane to Sidney from Mitchell, South Dakota, in the early spring of 1976. "Jim Cabela picked me up at the local airport," he remembers. Looking back at his initial conversations with the Cabela brothers, Dennis says, "The biggest hurdle was convincing Dick and Jim that Herter's was having financial difficulties and I couldn't stand not sleeping at night, worrying about vendors not getting paid. I just told them it was time to get out of there. I had to reassure them I wasn't out there to spy on their company."

Cabela's first Christmas catalog

Dennis Highby with a walleye.

"Sometimes Jim and Dick thought my copy was a little bit strong, but I reassured them it would sell."

– Dennis Highby

OUTDOORSMAN'S SOFT CANVAS TRAVEL BAGS

Designed to combine the height of fashion with the ultimate in dependability. This exclusive line of soft luggage is crafted from the **heaviest** 21.28 ounce tightweave luggage grade canvas with a water repellent exterior that actually allows the bags to float when empty. Man-sized cotton web handles completely encircle the bag, forming loops that are perfect for carrying things that, because of their length, won't ordinarily fit in luggage. Heavy nylon coil zippers go across the entire top and down each side. Permanent name cards conform to airline regulations, and heavy 'D' ring permits padlocking the zipper. These bags were designed to hold a lot, yet they don't take up a lot of space when full.

Mini-Duffle—20'' x 10'', 3 compartments.
110-800-000 . . . . **$24.95**
Overnighter—21'' x 7'' x 13''
110-801-000 . . . . **$29.95**
Weekender—24'' x 6'' x 18''
110-802-000 . . . . **$33.95**
Pullman—26'' x 7'' x 20''
110-803-000 . . . . **$39.95**

MONEY BELTS

e handsome belts look like a regular belt yet are the safest way to carry extra cash or valuable documents. The zippered compartment in the will hold currency without wrinkles or bulges. Made from the finest ty tanned cowhide, leather lined. A perfect gift for that hard to buy for 1 3/8'' wide belt. Even waist sizes 30 thru 46. Please specify size.

00-0—Brown $9.95
01-0—Black $9.95

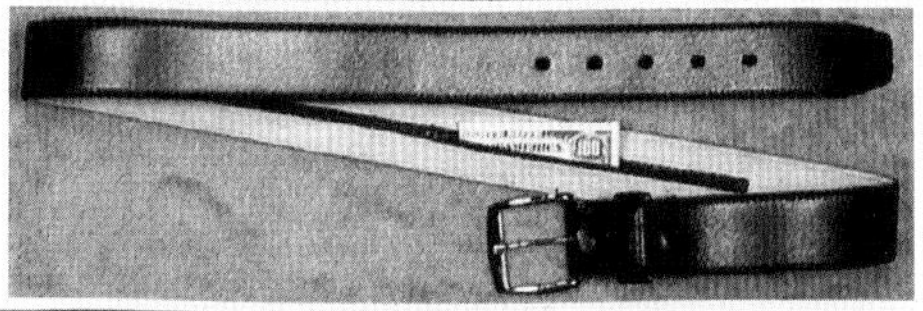

DYNALITE 93,000 CANDLE POWER

ynalite was engineered for the outdoorsmen. Switch glides from dim to bright. Drop it or jump on it, you simply can't damage the Marlex con-on. Perfect balance. Only 10'' long. Takes six standard batteries. ete with nylon carrying strap. Can't rust or corrode. Dynalite is nteed waterproof, weatherproof. Will float if dropped in water and g parts will stay dry. Black body with luminous lens.

0-000 . . . . $8.69

Charger—Recharges batteries right in your Dynalight! Dyna-Charger harge your batteries up to 50 times per set.

1-000 . . . . $5.95

Q-BEAM® SUPER SPOT LIGHT

The amazing 200,000 candlepower ''Super Spot'' illuminates objects over one mile away. Slices through murky weather conditions. It truly lights up the night. Made of rugged ABS Cycolac® plastic to withstand up to 5 G's impact, without affecting the lights operation. It floats! The sealed beam will continue to operate when submerged underwater. All hardware is stainless steel and non-corrosive. Super Spot operates on any 12-volt, DC, automotive or marine power source. A comfortable pistol grip makes handling easy. Other features include a built-in hanger, recessed switch, extended lens guard and an 8-foot coil cord.

425-101-000 . . . . **$19.95**

Cabela's

LADIES DOWN FILLED ALASKIMO PARKA

Soft, warm and luxurious! That is the only way to describe this beautiful ''man-made fur'' coat. It has the look trappers once risked their lives for. Sleek man-made seal with black tipped white trim on the hood. Because it is man-made, it gives off no offensive odor when wet, and less than half the weight of natural fur, and far more economical than natural fur. The two-way aluminum zipper has a convenient pull ring. Insulated with luxurious prime Northern Silver Grey® Goosedown. The perfect companion for those needing cold weather protection who also want styling and good looks.

Sizes: [001] Petite 6 - 8, [002] Small 8 - 10, [003] Medium 12 - 14, or [005] Large 16 - 18. Please specify size number.

180-954- **$96.95**

MEN'S DOWN-FILLED ALASKIMO PARKA

By using man-made ''fur'', this parka has eliminated all the draw backs associated with animal fur . . . without affecting the smart look that fur radiates. The man-made fur takes on the look of tan and brown wolf pelts, and the hood is trimmed in man-made white wolf. Because the Alaskimo is man-made ''fur'', it is economical . . . less than half the cost of natural fur! 100% moth and vermin proof. It features concealed storm flap, roomy slash pockets, heavy duty 2-way zipper, man-made fur lining in hood, and hidden storm cuff. The heavy duty lining resists tears. For real luxury these coats are insulated with prime Northern Silver Grey® Goosedown—the superlative natural protection against cold.

Sizes: [002] Small 36 - 38, [003] Medium 40 - 42, [005] Large 44 - 46 or [006] Extra Large 48 - 50. Please specify size number.

180-953- **$96.95**

ARCTIC CASUAL DOWN INSULATED JACKET

This tanker length all purpose jacket is insulated with Prime Everlive Northern Goose Down in both the body and sleeves. The 60/40 Sierra cloth is Zepel treated to be water repellent. The lining is matching 1.9 oz. beige rip stop nylon. A knit insert in the collar adds warmth and reduces wear and grime in this area. Extra long body with knit bottom gives protection from the cold and wind. Features two large flapped cargo pockets with handwarmers, raglan style sleeves, and heavy duty zipper. The detachable drawstring hood is also down insulated.

Sizes: [002] Small 36 - 38, [003] Medium 40 - 42, [005] Large 44 - 46 or [006] Extra Large 48 - 50. Please specify size number.

337-915- **$69.95**

PACIFIC CREST DACRON II INSULATED PARKA

9 oz. Dacron II enclosed in rip stop nylon (a total of 25 oz. of insulation) provides a warm shelter even in bone-chilling northwest rain. Dacron II is only 10% heavier than down for comparable loft and retains loft and warmth when wet. This beautiful navy parka features two way hand-warmer/cargo pockets with Velcro tab flaps. Also features extra large, heavy duty two-way zipper with a snap-closed insulated storm flap. Insulated stand up collar; snaps on collar for attaching hood. Elastic wristlets, drawstring bottom. Color: Navy.

Sizes: [002] Small, [003] Medium, [005] Large or [006] Extra Large. Please specify size number. Color: Navy.

481-911- **$43.95**
481-912-000—Matching Hood **$7.95**

Cabela's 7

"We have always listened to our customers and given them what they actually want instead of what we think they should want."

– Dennis Highby

He was impressed by the Cabela brothers' down-to-earth approach to things. "At lunch I remember Jim took me out to a little burger place downtown, very simple. After I made it back to Mitchell, Jim called me up, we talked, he hired me. I was their 40th employee, and first full-time salaried employee. My wife and two children had never been to Sidney. I will never forget, when the moving van was there, George Herter called me at home and asked me to stay. I just said, 'Sorry, George.' I guess the rest is history."

Looking back, Dennis says, "I was comfortable in my ability to do what I knew how to do. I was trained in writing copy and trained in selecting merchandise." He recalls, "At Herter's, I had a lot of good support staff. Cabela's was still small by comparison. I'd started at Herter's in customer service. Then I was merchandise manager for several categories. He emphasizes that a lot of what he'd learned at Herter's was valuable at Cabela's. "A good example is catalog copy. The Herter's catalog had pretty juicy copy. I used to write copy there, learned how to write catalog copy that made you want to buy something, told you what you needed to know, in the voice of somebody who'd actually used it and knew what it was for. Sometimes Jim and Dick thought my copy was a little bit strong, but I reassured them it would sell."

In the spring of 1977, Dennis suggested to Jim and Dick that Cabela's should have a Christmas catalog in addition to the spring and fall catalogs. They were initially dubious, but Dennis just said, "Trust me. It would be a good thing to do." They approved the idea and it proved successful.

Dennis has this to say: "Dick and Jim are good partners, people you really trust. They basically never swear, always go to church, never say a harsh word to you. They may say, 'I wish that would have worked out differently,' or even, 'Maybe we should try it this way next time.' But they mostly just let you do what you need to do."

He points with pride to the system he instituted for figuring catalog profit by square inch instead of profit by page. "To track merchandise profitability, Jim would review each catalog and write total sales on each page. I convinced them that every square inch of catalog space is so precious, we need to measure profit by the square inch," he explained. "That would really let us see what the customers were buying and not buying, which products worked and didn't. They thought that was a good idea." Dennis is emphatic, "We have always listened to our customers and given them what they actually want instead of what we think they should want."

Switchboard Stories

During the mid-1970s, telephone orders were becoming a problem. Dealing with ever-increasing mail orders was load enough, but as more customers wanted to order by phone, and have conversations with people who knew about the products, the interruption to normal workflow was becoming acute. But Dick and Jim realized it could be a viable growth channel.

Mike Wieser got the nod to supervise a system to handle the growing phone problem. "We started with two employees and me. We had no idea how many lines we needed, no idea how many employees we needed. We found out quickly, though. I'm thinking, 'What have we done?' We didn't have enough employees; we didn't have enough incoming lines. We kept adding incoming lines, then pretty soon we maxed out the local system and couldn't put in any more incoming trunk lines."

Judy Bayne was one of the first staffers in the new telemarketing department, which was formalized in 1978. "When I applied at Cabela's, they said they had an opening on the switchboard. I am visualizing this gal with headphones and thinking that sounds like fun." She found out differently in a hurry. "The gal running the switchboard was a nervous wreck. I soon found out why because that switchboard was a major challenge."

She explains, "There was no 800 number then, and we only had so many lines. Every call that came into Cabela's came through that one switchboard, whether it was an employee's wife or kids calling their mother or customer service or normal business calls. When all these calls came in, the board would light up like a Christmas tree."

Judy remembers working furiously to get callers passed to whomever they needed to talk to because there were less than 20 people in customer service to handle calls. "Someone would call in," says Judy, "and I wouldn't be able to transfer the call because the customer service lines were tied up. Understand, these customers were calling on their dime and would automatically go on hold

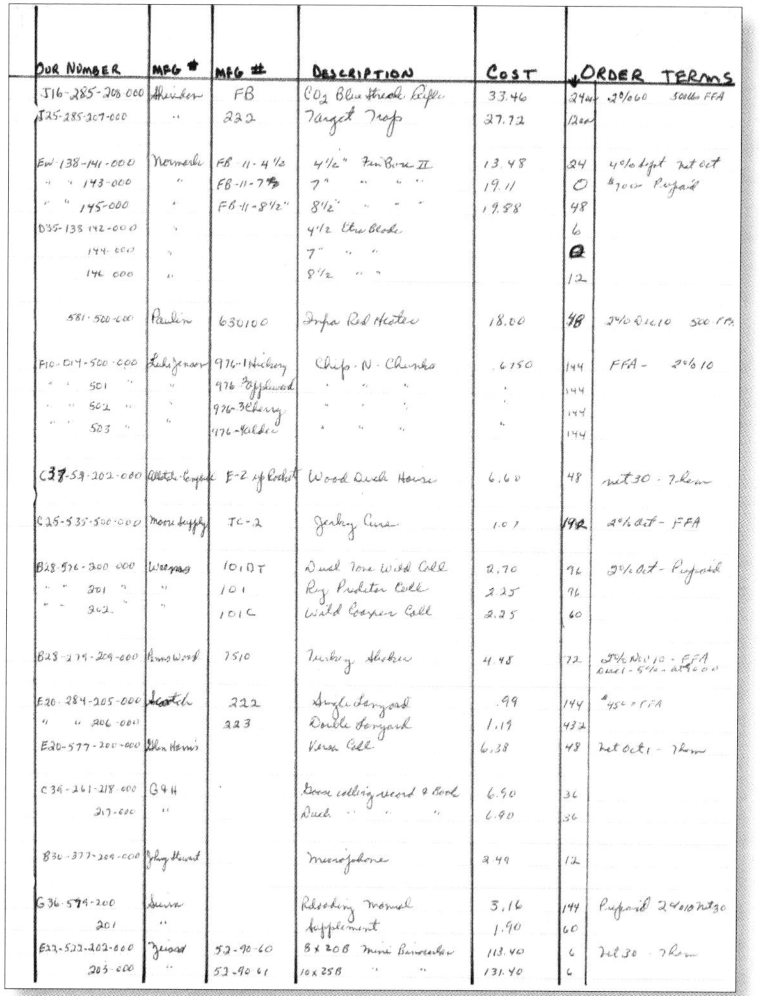

Our Number	MFG	MFG #	Description	Cost		Order Terms
J16-285-208 000	[illegible]	FB	CO_2 Blue Streak Rifle	33.46	24	2%60 [illegible] FFA
J25-285-207-000	"	222	Target Trap	27.72	12	
EW-138-141-000	Normark	FB 11-4 1/2	4 1/2" Fin Bone II	13.48	24	4% [illegible] net oct
" " 143-000	"	FB-11-7	7" " " "	19.11	0	$700 Prepaid
" " 145-000	"	FB-11-8 1/2"	8 1/2" " " "	19.88	48	
D35-138 142-000	"		4 1/2 Ultra Blade		6	
144-000	"		7" " "		[illegible]	
146 000	"		8 1/2 " "		12	
581-500-000	Paulin	630100	Infra Red Heater	18.00	48	2% Dec 10 500 FFA
F10-014-500-000	Luhr Jensen	976-1 Hickory	Chips-N-Chunks	.6150	144	FFA - 2% 10
" " 501 "	"	976-2 Applewood	" " "	"	144	
" " 502 "	"	976-3 Cherry	" " "	"	144	
" " 503 "	"	976-4 Alder	" " "	"	144	
C37-59-202-000	[illegible]	E-2 [illegible]	Wood Duck House	6.60	48	net 30 - 7 [illegible]
C25-535-500-000	Moore Supply	JC-2	Jerky Cure	1.07	192	2% Oct - FFA
B28-576-200 000	[illegible]	101 DT	Dual Tone Wild Call	2.70	96	2% Oct - Prepaid
" " 201 "	"	101	Reg Predator Call	2.25	96	
" " 202 "	"	101 C	Wild Cooper Call	2.25	60	
B28-279-209-000	Penns Woods	7510	Turkey Shaker	4.48	72	2% Nov 10 - FFA [illegible]
E20-284-205-000	Scotch	222	Single Lanyard	.99	144	$45 = FFA
" " 206-000		223	Double Lanyard	1.19	432	
E20-577-200-000	Glen Harris		Versa Call	6.38	48	Net Oct 1 - 7 [illegible]
C39-261-218-000	G&H		Goose calling record & Book	6.90	36	
217-000	"		Duck " " "	6.90	36	
B30-377-209-000	[illegible]		Microphone	2.49	12	
G36-579-200	Sierra		Reloading manual	3.16	144	Prepaid 2% 10 Net 30
201	"		Supplement	1.90	60	
E22-522-202-000	Zeiss	52-90-60	8 x 20B Mini Binoculars	113.40	6	Net 30 - 7 [illegible]
203-000	"	52-90-61	10 x 25B " "	131.40	6	

Example of a 1979 Merchandise Order Sheet.

Outstanding Purchase Order File Maintenance

Instructions for completing:

To add a record: enter the P/O number, their number, field 01 and Add in 20-22

To delete a record: either change the status field (#16) to "d' or enter field 01 , the key, and the word DELETE in 20-25

To change any field: find the field number from the list, enter the key (P/O number, their number), the field number, change type of C, and the data you want to appear in the field. Care must be taken to ensure the data is in the proper postitions on the input sheet.

FIELD LIST:

number	description	length	alpha/numeric	positions on input
01	key	17	a	1-17
02	order date	6	n	21-27
03	need date	6	n	21-27
04	terms	16	a	21-36
05	ship via	13	a	21-33
06	f. o b.	11	a	21-31
07	requestor	15	a	21-35
08	ship-to name	25	a	21-45
09	ship-to address	20	a	21-40
10	ship-to city, state, zip	25	a	21-45
11	vendor number	3	a	21-23
12	cabela number	12	a	21-32
13	quantity	7.0	n	21-27
14	cost of item	7.0	n	21-27
15	description of item	20	a	21-40
16	status of record	1	a	21-21
17	package flag for inventory	1	a	21-21
18	less description 1	4	a	21-24
19	less percentage 1(10.5%=1050)	4.2	n	21-24
20	less descriotion 2	4	a	21-24
21	less percentage 2	4.2	n	21-24
22	less cescription 3	4	a	21-24
23	less percentage 3	4.2	n	21-24

1979 Purchase Order File Maintenance computer instructions form.

while I tried to find an order-taker who wasn't already on another call." Her solution? "I'd stand up, look over the wall, try to figure out who was about to finish a call and just shove the next one to them. It was hectic, to say the least."

Eventually, Cabela's installed a dedicated routing system to separate incoming calls by department, as well as an 800-number system so customers could call toll-free.

The Challenges of Growth

As growth accelerated, Cabela's catalogs continued to be the foundation of the company. Three catalogs were published every year by then, each growing in size and complexity with every new edition. There was as yet no separate catalog department. So in the Cabela's tradition, everybody pitched in during catalog time – Dick, Jim and Dennis included – doing everything right down to cutting and pasting copy during design and layout.

Mike Wieser remembers, "Prior to having our own studio, a large portion of our photography was done by LaVern Draper at his local family photo studio in Sidney. There were shots during the 1970s and early '80s where the sizes on clothing and footwear didn't match the model very well. If a model was needed, you might be called with a minute's notice to go to Draper's studio. If you look at those catalogs today, you will see many pictures utilizing employees as models."

Judy Bayne says, "I eventually moved to catalog production where we selected merchandise and laid out pages. We had to make print deadlines, and there were lots of times when we were there till nine o'clock or later. We would lay out pages; paste copy and photos; make sure everything fit and was correct. Everyone would pitch in to make that deadline. We were devoted to the company because Dick and Jim appreciated everything you did."

"Everyone would pitch in to make that deadline. We were devoted to the company because Dick and Jim appreciated everything you did."

– Judy Bayne

She remembers, "One time it was the day before deadline and we had just a few pages left. It was pretty late at night, and I was proofing pages and suddenly realized we had the same product on two different pages. We desperately needed to find something to switch for one of the duplicate entries. I called Jim, who was also working late, and he came upstairs to help."

At that time, inventory of older samples for previous catalog photography was stored in locked cubicles along the back wall, and nobody there that night had a key. However, there were small gaps at the top of the cubicle walls below the ceiling rafters. "So," says Judy, "the only way Jim had to get in was to climb over the wall. He clambered up and over and rummaged around and crawled back out with an owl decoy that hadn't been listed in the catalog for years. Jim said, 'Let's put this back in.' So the owl decoy went back into the catalog. Must have sold because it stayed in the catalog for quite a while."

By 1979 even the additional warehouse next door had filled to overflowing, and Sidney was out of available storage space. Fortunately, there was a nearby solution. About 10 miles northwest of town was the former Sioux Army Depot, consisting of several warehouses that once stored military ammunition and equipment. They were run down and needed roof repairs, but at 90,000 square feet per building, they promised a solution to an ongoing storage problem. Cabela's bought one of the buildings and moved the majority of warehousing to the new site. It would be big enough for only three more years.

As the 1970s ended, Cabela's had been transformed in many significant ways from its arrival in Sidney just 10 years before. Its operation had been successfully computerized. The beginnings of a professional telemarketing department had been established. The core Cabela's philosophies of passion for the outdoors and customer service were being reinforced by a growing family of like-minded employees.

Dennis Highby says, "Growing the company in those days was hard, a lot of work. It was come in early and work late at night. Go in on Saturday and go back after church on Sunday. When something is growing that fast, with 30 percent more catalog pages, 30 percent more merchandise and new employees added all the time, it was quite a learning experience for a lot of people here. When I started in 1976, Jim told me the company was doing $4 million in business. At the end of 1979, it was more than $13 million. That's a lot of growth in an old brick building in a little country town."

Western
SUPER
Cabela's
WORLD'S FOREMOST OUTFITTER
HUNTING, FISHING AND OUTDOOR GEAR

Chapter 3

Building Cabela's Brand

– The 1980s –

By 1980, Cabela's had become a success. In fact, it had become a spectacular success. From $627 in orders received at Dick and Mary's kitchen table in 1961, it had grown to gross sales of $13.3 million by the end of 1979. It had been accomplished by making decisions based on small-town business experience and using small-town employee resources. Many companies and their founders would have been content to continue at that level, basking in the success and accomplishment already achieved. But it was not in Dick and Jim Cabela's makeup to rest on their laurels, especially when it was obvious their potential customer base was not close to being fully tapped.

It was a critical moment. They could stay the same size, operating with the same management organization and personnel resources they had in place, or they could push the envelope and aggressively pursue additional sales growth. But to grow even larger, to become a truly national-scale enterprise, they would need to reorganize and recruit talent to help them reach the next level.

Their solution, foreshadowed by the success of hiring Dennis Highby, was to cast a wider net, looking for outdoor and business-minded applicants who would maintain Cabela's core principles. It worked better than expected.

Seeding the Management Team

Many key hires were made by the Cabela brothers in the early 1980s; some who moved up the corporate ladder and represent the core of the management team. A unifying thread connecting the new hires was that they came from the same basic cultural background and values as the founders, and they were already Cabela's customers. When asked today about the criteria he applied when seeking those first key outside employees, Jim Cabela's answer is simple: "You just knew." Dick Cabela echoes Jim's sentiments. "You looked them in the eye, got a feel for them, and in five minutes you knew whether you wanted them to work for you."

"I told them I would sweep floors. I would do whatever. I just wanted to work for Cabela's." – Tom Rosdail

Most of the Cabela's senior managers hired in the 1980s share a similar memory: Their initial interview with the Cabela brothers or Dennis Highby lasted about five minutes. Tom Rosdail, Cabela's Vice President of Brand Marketing and Licensing, recalls his experience searching for a job in the outdoor industry. "When I came out here to Sidney in 1980, I was an unemployed college graduate looking for a job."

Tom had been making the rounds in the outdoor industry. He had hitchhiked to L.L. Bean in Freeport, Maine, had visited Herter's in Minnesota. He'd sent a letter to Coleman and he was typing a letter to Cabela's when he decided to drive to Sidney.

Tom recalls, "I told them I would sweep floors. I would do whatever. I just wanted to work for Cabela's. I told them I wanted to open my own sporting-goods store and I wanted to come here and learn the business side of the outdoor industry. I suppose it was kind of silly of me to tell Cabela's I wanted to be in direct competition with them. But, obviously, they didn't feel very threatened."

Tom was hired to work on the loading dock at $3.20 an hour. "I came in, and they issued me a pair of coveralls because the back of the building wasn't heated," he says.

Like all Cabela's new hires, Tom got a quick, all-facets introduction to the business. "I started in January, and by the middle of February I was working Saturdays on the phone giving product information, helping take customer calls. In April, they gave me a job working full-time with Dennis Highby, who was the merchandise

Tom Rosdail, Vice President of Brand Marketing and Licensing, is an avid outdoorsman who doesn't just spend time behind a desk at Cabela's corporate headquarters in Sidney. Cabela's encourages employees to spend as much time in the field as possible.

Cabela's Time Line

1980s

1980

- Tom Rosdail hired, now Vice President of Brand Marketing and Licensing.
- Total revenue: $15,705,491.

1981

- Pat Snyder hired, now Executive VP and Chief Marketing Officer.
- Doug Zingula hired; now VP of Merchandising Support Services.
- New automatic call-distribution system.
- Total revenue: $19,236,770.

1982

- Cris Hoehn hired, now manages telecommunication operations.
- Total revenue: $28,795,576.

1983

- Cabela's 800 phone system initiated.
- Purchased two more buildings at former Sioux Army Depot.
- USPS assigns Cabela's its own zip code.
- Total revenue: $43,694,607.

manager, and Paul Ringleman, of purchasing. You wore every hat there was, and Jim and Dick were involved in every detail."

Doug Zingula and Pat Snyder were hired a year later, and as Tom recounts, "We split into three departments. I had fishing; Doug took hunting; Pat took clothing. Everything from there on developed from that split." Today, Doug is Vice President of Merchandising Support Services. Pat is Executive Vice President and Chief Marketing Officer.

"Dennis was very involved in providing guidance at work and when work was done he would take us fishing and hunting," Tom said. "He even helped me shoulder-mount a deer. We did the whole job in his garage. The point being, Dennis took new employees under his wing. We all learned from that and in turn, helped new people move into their houses, got them hunting and fishing as quickly as we could, and got wives together for social events. The Cabela's approach was always very family oriented."

But even as the company expanded and became increasingly systematized, the hands-on intimacy of the operation continued. "Of course," says Tom, "there were budgets. But if you wanted to do something, you went into Jim's office and asked him. Or you would just scribble your proposal on a piece of paper. It didn't matter if it was $500 or $40,000 or even in those days sometimes $400,000. If you wanted to do a purchase order, you would just go in and Jim would give you a yes or no. Tom emphasizes that at the end of the day, "You were responsible, of course, but there has always been a lot of confidence in letting employees make their own decisions." Doug and Pat recall how the company mailed black-and-white sales flyers that also included ads for employment opportunities at Cabela's. "That's how I got here," Doug notes. He also points out that a high percentage of the 1980s employee groups came from smaller-town backgrounds in the central Midwest, and he believes Dick, Jim and Dennis specifically looked for people from that region. "It takes a certain type to live in Sidney and work at Cabela's, and I think we are still very Midwestern-value oriented," he says.

Doug Zingula, Vice President of Merchandising Support Services, with a mule deer in Mexico.

Pat believes that is the primary reason people who come to work for Cabela's tend not to leave. "I remember the first time I flew to Sidney from Minnesota, where I went to college. It was August, very hot, and everything was burnt brown. I flew back to Minnesota after the interview, and everything was green. I thought, 'Man, I don't know if I can live in western Nebraska.' Monday morning they called and offered a job, and I made the move."

He also underlines the family quality of the Cabela's business. "We are very close, a very close-knit group. In the early days we did everything together on the weekends with our families. We would go fishing or camping or take hunting trips together. We spent a lot of

Pat Snyder, Executive Vice President and Chief Marketing Officer, fishing in Alaska.

1984

- Shipping, receiving, warehousing moved to Sioux Army Depot.
- Gregg Severinson hired, now Director of Cabela's Outdoor Adventures.
- Jeff Johnson hired, now Merchandising Director for Footwear.
- Fred Neal hired, now Merchandising Director for Firearms/Shooting.
- Total revenue: $63,848,297.

1985

- Cabela's Outdoor Adventures launched.
- Total revenue: $83,965,891.

1986

- Cabela's acquires Rockwell plant in Kearney, for telemarketing operation.
- Total revenue: $98,596,239.

1987

- Kearney, Nebraska store opens in October.
- Dick Cabela elected to Direct Marketing Association's Board of Directors.
- Dick and Mary Cabela's first trip to Africa.
- Total revenue: $110,504,188.

1988

- Total revenue: $135,472,867.

1989

- Total revenue: $156,212,665.

Cris Hoehn, Multi-Site Telecommunications Manager, at a black powder product training event near Kearney, Nebraska.

time getting to know each other. All the people I came into the organization with 28 years ago, like Cris Hoehn or Fred Neal — and I think you could even include people who have been here 10 years — they very much feel they are part of the Cabela's family."

Cris Hoehn, who joined the company in 1982 and today manages Cabela's telecommunication operations, certainly agrees. "I have never wanted to work anyplace else. I always felt like Cabela's was partly mine. The quality of people and the sense of values just seem to be a part of our culture. I have always been treated well. I have always felt like I could contribute, my ideas would be listened to. When I look around the call centers today, I see a lot of people I hired in 1986. It's amazing that you started with a work relationship that melded into a family atmosphere."

Customer Service and More Customer Service

From the beginning, Cabela's motto had been "100 Percent Customer Satisfaction Guaranteed." Many other companies have made that same claim, and some have been committed to it. It's an easy promise to make, particularly when starting out, but once a company grows past a certain size, it is common for the personal touch regarding customer relations to evaporate. Cabela's is different. Customer satisfaction and customer service have always been — and continue to be — Cabela's focus in conducting business and building long-term customer relationships.

Merchandising Director for Footwear Jeff Johnson, who joined the company in 1984, observes that in every policy meeting he ever sat in, "We always looked at everything from the consumer's point of view first. That came from Jim, Dick and Dennis. They would always ask, 'What is our customer going to think about this?' about everything we would do."

The key element that sets apart Cabela's customer service from nearly any other company is that it is a two-sided approach to providing legendary service in delivering the customer's order and in dealing with any problems or questions after the order is delivered.

Ron Spath, who joined Cabela's in 1995 and is currently Vice President of Customer Experience, believes the return policy is the soul of customer service, because it is much more a test of the company's commitment to the customer than just being cheerful when answering the phone and taking orders. After the sale, if there is a problem, that is when you have the proof of a company's commitment to customers."

The key, Ron said, is the Cabela's call centers. "We're very lucky in a lot of ways," he said. "We've kept the Cabela's culture that started in Sidney. It's really just small-town America, rural America. It's something other companies can't match. They can copy our process, but they can't match our attitude."

"We always looked at everything from the consumer's point of view first. That came from Jim, Dick and Dennis. They would always ask, 'What is our customer going to think about this?' about everything we would do."

– Jeff Johnson, Merchandising Director of Footwear

2006 Sable in Zimbabwe.

"Four or five times a day guys would call just to say Cabela's was the greatest." – Gregg Severinson

Gregg Severinson, Director of Cabela's Outdoor Adventures.

Gregg Severinson, who is now Director of Cabela's Outdoor Adventures, began working in customer service in 1984. "Back then it seemed like there were so many guys building a fishing rod or planning to go duck hunting for the first time. They were not only asking, 'What do I need?' but also, 'How do I pick from all these different products?'"

Gregg believes most people think customer service is a complaint desk. "This was completely opposite at Cabela's," Gregg says. "Four or five times a day guys would call just to say Cabela's was the greatest."

And even dealing with complaints at Cabela's was easy, according to Gregg. "All you had to do was ask the customer, 'What do you want? Do you want to send it back? Do you want a refund? Do you want to replace it?'" Part of the ease of dealing with customers was Cabela's simple process for returning or exchanging merchandise. And, no phone calls or special authorizations were needed. Cabela's Legendary Guarantee exemplifies their desire to take care of their customers.

Cabela's catalogs have always been reference works and not merely listings of products. Care is put into every catalog to make it a means of communicating real information about the products, how they work and how they can benefit the buyer. Part of the Cabela's satisfaction philosophy is that they take responsibility for the products they sell, even if the products are not Cabela's own brand. The more typical policy for brand-name merchandise sold by other companies is: "Don't call us, contact the manufacturer. It's not our problem." Cabela's is different.

Even today, according to Jeff Johnson, Jim Cabela reads individual customer comment cards, and each department reviews them as well. "Letters from customers are passed on to us employees," Jeff said, "and we don't hesitate one second to pick up the phone and call our customers and let them know the people who work here care about their business, care about the quality of the product and are genuinely interested in hearing what they have to say. We bend over backward to take care of the customer and fix the problem."

Cabela's purchased original artwork from talented artists to illustrate its catalog covers, providing a unique look and feel to the catalogs. By doing so, Cabela's provided support for many wildlife artists and facilitated exhibition of their art to millions of outdoor enthusiasts throughout the world. Here are two examples. The 1982 cover is from a Rosemary Millette painting; the 1986 cover from a John Eberhardt original.

Cabela's Gets Into Camouflage

A wide variety of products are available in Cabela's camouflage patterns.

Camouflage fabric was first widely used in U.S. military applications during World War II. And it didn't take long for soldiers to realize the value of camouflage when they returned to their hunting grounds back home.

But the hunting world changed forever in 1980, when Jim Crumley invented Trebark, the first modern camouflage pattern.

This more realistic approach to camouflage led to the development of an industry dedicated to designing patterns tailored for hunting a variety of species in a wide variety of terrains.

For instance, a dark pattern, with black, brown and green colors, might be perfect for a deer hunt in New England, but it wouldn't be a great choice for a pronghorn hunt in a wide-open Western landscape. And the types of vegetation hunters hide in near a winter duck marsh in the North, are completely different than they'll encounter during a spring turkey hunt in the swamps of the Southeast.

As the number of available camouflage patterns grew, Cabela's product managers were able to add items to the lineup that appealed to hunters across North America, and around the world. When they couldn't find exactly what they were looking for, they called on their experience in the outdoors to design patterns that would be manufactured under the Cabela's brand.

According to Ev Tarrell, Merchandising Director for Hunting Apparel, Cabela's approach to developing its own camouflage products is pretty simple: "The easiest way to explain: It was to fill voids in the marketplace. For example, one of our challenges was to make rain gear that was quiet. It turned into a seven-year quest, and we introduced our Quiet Rainwear."

Cabela's involvement in camouflage pattern development started in 1988. Its first entry in the marketplace was Western camouflage in 1989. "It was a woodland-type pattern with grays, greens and tans to match the western high country," Ev said. "After that came Horizon, and BranchBark was introduced in 1991."

Ev said entering into the camouflage business was not viewed as a risky business proposition at the time because Cabela's had done its homework and had open lines of communication with Realtree and Mossy Oak, two vendors who dominate the category and sell huge volumes of camouflage products through Cabela's catalogs, retail stores and website. "We have great partnerships with both Realtree and Mossy Oak and have been very supportive of what they have been doing over the years. It's been a symbiotic relationship. Cabela's was just filling a void."

The Seclusion family of camouflage has received a lot of attention since its introduction. "The Seclusion pattern really is one of Cabela's major camouflage developments," said Ev. The original Seclusion pattern was launched in 2001; followed by Seclusion 3D® Open Country,

Ev Tarrell, Merchandising Director for Hunting Apparel.

Cabela's Seclusion 3D® pattern

Cabela's Outfitter Camo™ pattern

Seclusion 3D® Backwater and Seclusion 3D® Konifer. Once again, each pattern was the result of Cabela's filling a void in the camouflage market.

Retracing his footsteps from the time he started dedicating more time to camouflage, Ev remembers how ideas on paper eventually blossomed into retail product and how the process has evolved. "We were small enough back then that we were always interacting with each other. It was, 'Look at this; what do you think?' Cabela's is a breeding ground for developing ideas."

Ev is as excited about prospects for the future as he is about Cabela's past successes in the camouflage category. "Camouflage patterns typically have a three- to five-year life cycle," he said.

"It's no different than anything else. You constantly want to build a better product. New technology is there. All-purpose camouflage has yet to be maximized. Look what's going on with the military. They're making patterns more universal. When you consider light reflectants, studies of game-animal vision and looking at smaller geographic areas in terms of matching patterns you see there is room for growth." Cabela's and Tarrell's mission is clear. "We want to keep raising the bar. Cabela's brands have been built by filling voids and doing it the right way, making products practical and standing behind the products," he said.

"We work with a company and tell them what makes sense for us. The vendor then realizes he is going to have to raise the bar if he wants to do business with us." – Fred Neal

Testing Through Use

From the time Dick and Mary first welcomed vendor salesmen bringing their wares to Chappell for demonstration, Cabela's has always believed in self-testing products that go into their catalogs. By the 1980s, with thousands upon thousands of new and different products being offered to them, the system needed to be formalized.

Mike Wieser says, "We ask: would we use it, does it have a place in the market, or is it just a gadget or a gimmick? Next we evaluate quality, a critical element in product selection."

Cabela's receives thousands of products for consideration. "They are kept in a sample room where anyone on the merchandising staff is welcome to take a sample out, use it and provide feedback. This is a valuable means of ensuring the highest quality merchandise for our customers."

"I once went on a grizzly hunt in Alaska, outfitted with boots, clothing, everything from the sample room. Used the stuff for nine days and 900 miles on a snowmachine, and filed a report on the products when I got back," he said.

Over time, the testing procedure led to the development and improvement of products. "At times we would suggest the vendor make appropriate changes," he said. "Some listened, some didn't. If they didn't, that was our opportunity to make the product the way we wanted. That led to many of our later private-label products and product improvements."

Fred Neal, who came on board in 1984 and today is Cabela's Merchandising Director for Firearms/Shooting said even the new-product selection process is more formal than it was in the early years.

"What we do now, let's say with a new duck call, is look at our duck-call assortment and see we really don't need any more," Fred said. "So is there something about this new one that is meaningful enough to add to the assortment and get rid of an older one? It used to be we just kept adding them. We don't do that any more. We try to avoid duplication of products if there is no purpose. I mean, how many 10x42 binoculars do we need?"

Fred points out it has always been Cabela's unwritten law that if something was added, "we had to believe in it." But now, he says, there also has to be a reason beyond mere quality. "It has to fill a void. We ask, 'Is it something our customer needs or wants? We work it backward, starting from the customer's point of view."

The selection process has actually raised the bar for manufacturers who wish to be included in Cabela's catalogs. According to Fred, "We work with a company and tell them what makes sense for us. The vendor then realizes he is going to have to raise the bar if he wants to do business with us." The result is that Cabela's drives technology, product advancement and product quality to the benefit of their customers. No other catalog company has achieved such a successful formula or made such an impact on product development, and it's all because of Dick and Jim Cabela's original decision never to sell anything if they hadn't proved it worked and that customers needed it.

"We were all encouraged to think out of the box before there was a box," he said.

Fred underlines the importance of personal experience. "If you're in a goose pit, you are absolutely unforgiving of boots that don't keep your feet warm and dry. That has nothing to do with the price. They either keep your feet warm and dry or they don't. There are a lot of people putting together outdoor catalogs who have never been in a goose pit."

Fred Neal, Merchandising Director for Firearms/Shooting, with a roosterfish in Costa Rica, 2004.

The Cabela's/Leatherman Story

Tim Leatherman was out of options. It was 1983, and attempts to sell his idea of a multitool combining pliers, a knife and other tools weren't going anywhere. The U.S. government, large corporations — no one showed interest.

He and partner Steve Berliner decided to try one more avenue — mail-order catalogs. They sent letters to established mail-order companies describing the tool and offering to send a prototype. In Cabela's merchandising department, Dennis Highby read the letter and said yes, so Tim, who has a mechanical engineering degree, sent one of his few precious handmade prototypes and a letter explaining the development process — how in 1975 he conceived the original idea of combining pliers with a pocketknife during a low-budget trip to Europe with his wife.

"We had the good fortune, or made the mistake, of buying a used Fiat for $300 in Amsterdam thinking that would be the least expensive way to travel around Europe," Tim said. However, the Fiat required frequent repair. "I had a pocketknife, but that wouldn't handle everything I needed to do," he said.

Plus, being on a tight budget, they often stayed in inexpensive hotels with less than reliable plumbing and heating that often needed tweaking, such as trying to turn up a radiator with what was left of a twisted-off stem. Essentially, his pocketknife needed pliers and screwdrivers.

When Tim returned from Europe, he started working on a compact, versatile tool that would have made his recent travels easier. He contemplated designs and built prototypes — "I started with scrap metal," he said. "I picked up a hacksaw and file and tried to build what was in my mind." After three years, he had a prototype he liked.

Tim Leatherman, Chairman.

Efforts to sell his patent rights went nowhere. Together with Steve Berliner, a friend from college days, they decided they would have to start a company and manufacture the tool themselves.

"We were naïve in terms of business," he said. "We were hoping to make and sell 4,000 in the first year, which even we knew wouldn't pay us a penny for our time but hopefully would pay back the cash investment we figured we'd need to buy machines, materials and hire people. But before starting, we needed an order large enough to justify going into production."

Cabela's was the first to recognize the potential of Leatherman tools. Tim still has the original Cabela's purchase order, dated May 26, 1983, for 500 Leatherman Pocket Survival Tools, the first order his company received.

"You wouldn't believe how happy I was that day," Leatherman said. "After eight years of working in a garage developing the tool and trying to find a customer, we finally made a sale. Once I floated down to the floor, I realized it was only 500 tools, but we decided we would accept the order and go into production."

The seven-month lead time before Cabela's order was due was enough to buy machinery, hire people, arrange subcontracting and get started in production.

After the Cabela's order, another catalog company followed with a smaller order. When catalogs from Cabela's and the other company came out featuring Leatherman tools, more catalog companies took notice and started placing orders, too. In the meantime, Cabela's ordered more Leatherman tools to meet demand. "We were hoping to make and sell 4,000 tools that first year, and we ended up making and selling 30,000, and the year after that we sold 70,000, and it went on from there," Tim said. "Demand was off the charts. We were an overnight success, after eight years."

Leatherman said if he hadn't received the Cabela's order, if the attempt to sell Leatherman tools through mail-order companies hadn't worked, "none of this would have happened. I would have dropped the project and gone back to my day job – selling welding supplies.

"I am, and will always remain, grateful to Cabela's for giving me that first order," he said. "And I applaud Cabela's for having the foresight to see something in a product no one else did and, in doing so, launch my business."

An early catalog presentation of Tim Leatherman's new multitool, with the original purchase order that helped launch the business.

The Loomis Story

Gary Loomis at work on a stream; with Dennis Highby in the early '80s; and in the G. Loomis workshop.

The way Gary Loomis tells the story, "a handshake with Cabela's" made his dream of starting a successful fishing-rod company a reality.

In the early 1980s, after selling everything he owned to buy and redesign rod-manufacturing equipment, Loomis ended up with $32 to his name and unfinished business. He still needed to put the final touches on one piece of equipment before he could start producing rods.

Following a frank discussion with his wife, Loomis decided to go back to work as a machinist until he could save enough money to the get the business up and running. Then Cabela's called.

Dennis Highby, a merchandising manager at the time, told Loomis the company wanted him to produce 280 blanks a day for the next eight months. As much as he wanted to accept the order, Loomis instead had to explain to Highby his predicament. He needed capital. And to Loomis' surprise, Highby asked, "How much?"

Loomis figured he needed $50,000 to finish the equipment, purchase materials and staff the production.

"That much money back in the '80s was a tremendous amount," he said. "I figured they'd never give me that kind of money."

When Loomis told him the bottom line, Highby asked if the $50,000 would make it possible for him to fill the order. Loomis said yes, and Highby asked him for his bank account number.

Three days later, Loomis had the money in his account and G.Loomis, manufacturer of high-performance fishing rods, became a reality.

"I never signed anything," he said. "It was all on a handshake. I paid back the first half of the money that year and the second half the next."

Loomis continued making blanks for Cabela's even when he sold the company in the late 1990s. Today, not only rods, but also reels, accessories and clothing bear the G.Loomis name.

The Cabela's Dodge Concept Vehicle

Cabela's sizes up special Dodge

By JACKIE FLOHR
Regional Correspondent

JIM BEARDSLEY, (left) catalogue manager for Cabela's, Inc. in Sidney
the Dodge dealer in Sidney, discuss the prototype Ramcharger being eval
for Dodge.

SIDNEY — A special outdoors edition of a 1989 Dodge Ramcharger recently developed by Dodge Truck will be given a thorough workout by officials and employees of Cabela's Inc. of Sidney.

The special "Cabela's Edition" sport utility vehicle was introduced at a news conference held here Thursday.

The Ramcharger was presented to Richard Cabela, president of Cabela's, a leader in the outdoors catalog industry, by Michael G. Kelley, national advertising manager for Dodge Truck. A second Ramcharger will also be given to selected outdoor writers for evaluation.

The special "Cabela's Edition" sport utility prototype was modified with the sportsman in mind. After-market features such as a color-matching brush guard, running boards, fender flares and spare tire carrier were added to the exterior. A roof rack that can store game, and blacked-out rear windows for privacy was also added.

Dodge further installed an overhead outside temperature-compass gauge. A lockable gun storage drawer with removable carpeting on top, fishing rod carriers and movable dressing lights are also featured.

Dodge excited by vehicle

John Elwell, the Dodge dealer in Sidney, said Dodge is very excited about the new concept vehicle.

"From what I understand this concept vehicle is a beginning of quite an involvement with special sport utility vehicles," Elwell said. "Dodge is totally excited about it as are we. We just think that (Cabela's) input on the sport utility vehicle is going to be a wonderful thing for Dodge."

Jim Beardsley, catalog manager for Cabela's Inc., said the prototype would be given a thorough workout in testing the concepts for Dodge.

"We're looking at some of its features to see how feasible they are," Beardsley said. "We already have recommendations without even taking it out in the field.

"I can assure you that Jim Cabela has already driven it across some highways and some roads and he's found some things already. We're going to give it a tough workout and give Dodge exactly our evaluation as to what works and what doesn't. Hopefully we'll all come out with a better vehicle that Dodge can sell in the near future."

Road trip planned

Beardsley said Dodge sent the vehicle to "Cars and Concepts," an after-market specialty builder in Detroit, Mich. They did the after-market additions and customized it to Dodge's specifications, he said.

Beardsley said Dodge used Cabela's input as well as that of several other outdoor gear companies to get information of what was wanted in an outdoor vehicle.

Beardsley
mostly Cab
take the ve
this weeker
nament.

"We're g
midnight bo
Beardsley s
try out the
bulbs and s
dock. We w
can see v
without lau
well as the

Beardsle
would also
moose hunt
vehicle on a

Cabela's employees worked with Dodge to develop and test a specially-designed 1989 Dodge Ramcharger, the first Cabela's-edition vehicle to hit the streets and backroads.

The two-door sports utility vehicle featured, among other things, a lockable firearm/valuables storage drawer, brush guard, fishing rod carriers, roof rack and rear-facing halogen lights for such tasks as launching a boat at night. Dodge delivered the "concept vehicle" to Cabela's and Cabela's employees tested it on hunting, fishing and other excursions throughout the Midwest. Feedback on the design was provided to Dodge. The vehicle was a common sight in Sidney for years.

According to this Sidney Telegraph article, Dodge made a second similarly equipped Ramcharger available to outdoor writers for their evaluation. Other features included running boards, fender flare, spare tire carrier and Cabela's famous logo on the front quarter-panels.

The second Cabela's-edition vehicles, 2010 Ford F-250 and F-350 pickups, were introduced in late 2009 and were available to the buying public through Ford dealerships throughout the country. The specially designed pickups, with diesel engines, included such features as a hidden under-the-seat firearms locker as well as customized embroidery on the seats and floor mats.

A.C. Cabela and Marian posed with the Cabela's Concept Vehicle, a 1989 Ramcharger with features designed for outdoor enthusiasts.

Cabela's
Cabela's
FEDERAL
HI-POWER
SHOT SHELLS
410
25

Creating the Cabela's Brand

From extensively testing products in the field and consulting with manufacturers about improvements and features, it was only a short step to Cabela's commissioning manufacturers to develop exclusive products for Cabela's, then to having its own Cabela's product brand. In the beginning, this grew from field testers encountering a product that was basically good but could benefit from a few improvements or additions, such as boots with great features that needed a different type of lacing.

Fred Neal points out that the process can run in either direction along the quality/price scale. "One great example," he says, "was a boot manufacturer who brought us a really good product that was overbuilt for 80 percent of the people who wanted it, so it was overpriced for our customers." The Cabela's merchandising team suggested trimming and modifying some of its features to create a less expensive model that could better satisfy the larger part of the market. According to Fred, "They had more than half of it right, and all they had to do was make a couple adjustments to have the perfect boots. They became an exclusive model offered only through Cabela's. Over time, Cabela's catalogs contained brand-name products, products produced exclusively for Cabela's and eventually Cabela's own brand of products."

Hunting clothing and footwear were products where Cabela's rigorous field testing first began to impact manufacturers on a large scale. Pat Snyder notes, "Years ago, when I used to go waterfowl hunting with my dad, part of hunting was just sitting and shivering. You were cold; you were wet; that was just part of it. You didn't have the insulation; you didn't have the GORE-TEX; you didn't have the technology that's available today.

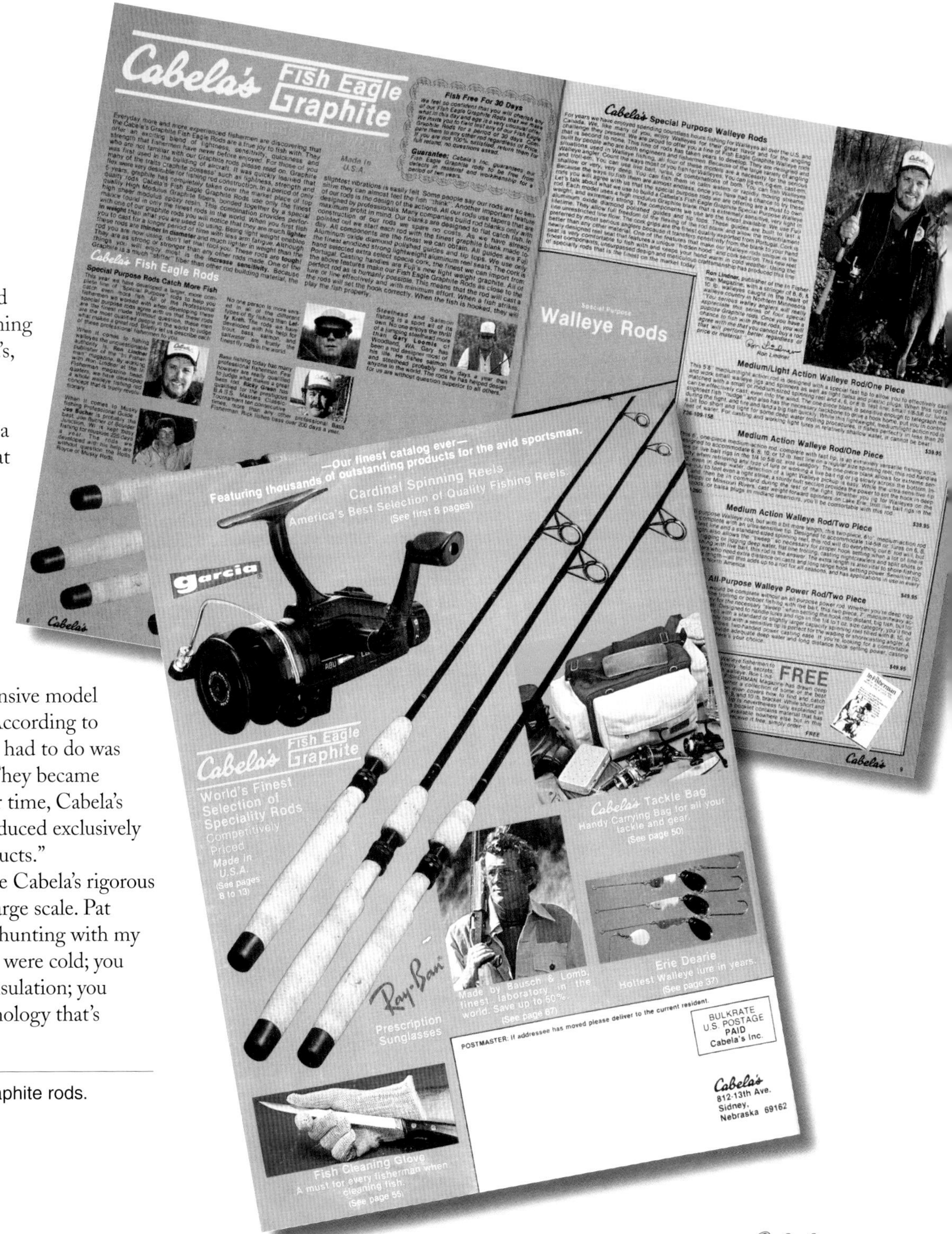

Significant product introductions by Cabela's included graphite rods.

Cabela's Innovations

- Mr. Mean Lure
- MagTouch Rod
- Hydro Troll
- Vortex Spinning Decoy Device
- RealImage Decoy Skin
- Cot-Side Nightstand

Cabela's product innovations have created popular items that have not only been huge successes, but also helped partner companies grow and succeed. One of the first was the Mr. Mean fishing lure, developed by Dennis Highby and eventually produced exclusively for Cabela's by Mister Twister. To develop this weedless, hidden-hook, soft-rubber lure that "ripples like a leech and swims like a minnow," Dennis melted plastic worms and made a plaster of Paris mold with a cutout outline in the plastic lid of a coffee can he took from the Cabela's break room. He then went next door to the auto parts place and bought Bondo, then ended up making a hob to make a lure. Cabela's sold over a million of them.

The Mr. Mean lure was never patented, but many other Cabela's innovations were. One of the earliest was the MagTouch Rod, which Dennis patented in the 1970s. Even back then, Cabela's could see the trend in fishing rods was to reduce weight and improve sensitivity. Dennis developed a process for drilling out fishing rod handles and wrapping them with cork instead of rubber so the rod blanks could be inserted from the bottom. A cutout in the handle allowed the fisherman's hand to touch the rod blank so that he could feel the slightest contact

Cabela's employees' in-the-field experience led to many new and improved products for outdoorsmen and women — and an impressive array of U.S. patents.

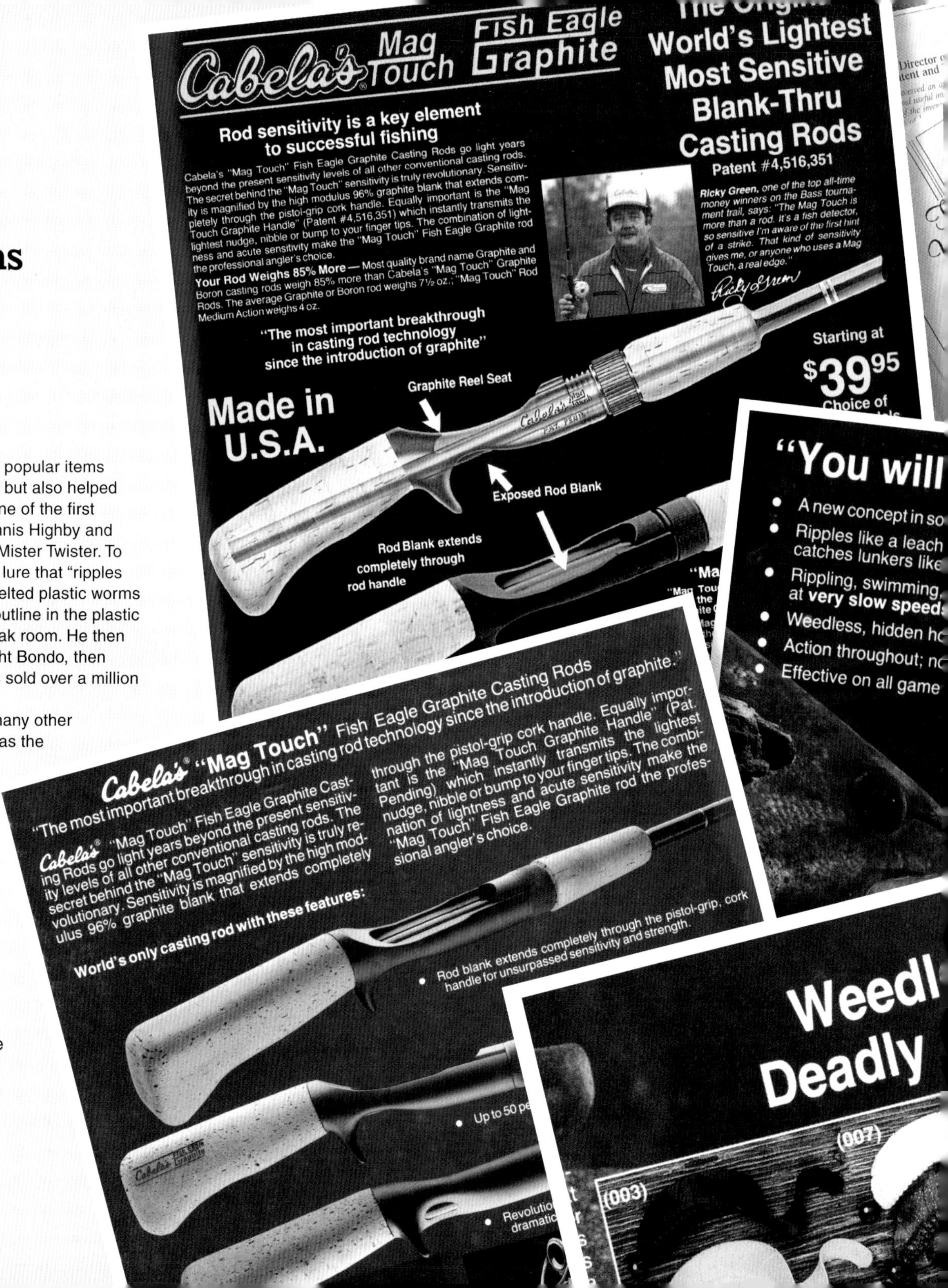

United States Patent
Canadian Patent
The United States of America
The Director of the United States Patent and Trademark Office
Has received an application for a new, original, and ornamental design for an article of manufacture. The title and description of the design are enclosed. The requirements of law have been complied with, and it has been determined that a patent on the design shall be granted under the law.
Therefore, this
United States Patent
Grants to the person(s) having title to this patent the right to exclude others from making, using, offering for sale, or selling the design throughout the United States of America, or importing the design into the United States of America for the term of fourteen years from the date of grant of this patent.
The Commissioner of Patents and Trademarks
Therefore, this
United States Patent
U.S. Patent
Oct. 13, 1998
Sheet 1 of 4
Des. 399,338
FIG. 1
Nov. 21, 2000
6,148,459
FIG. 3
United States Design Patent
Johnson et al.
BOOT UPPER PATTERN
Patent No.:
Date of Patent:
CLAIM
DESCRIPTION
US 7,195,025 B2
it's alive"
Cabela's
Mr. Mean
by Mister Twister
innow;
ever used!
(164)

of a fish with the bait. That design, combined with graphite rod blanks that came on the market during the 1970s, resulted in rods weighing about a third of other rods. MagTouch became a large part of Cabela's fishing business.

Other Cabela's patented products that have become popular, and set industry standards, include:

Hydro Troll (Patent #5,127,353 issued 7/7/1992).
A hydrofoil improves boat performance and fuel efficiency by allowing the boat to get on plane faster and stay on plane at slower speeds. A trolling plate makes it possible to achieve slow trolling speeds while using the main motor, eliminating the need for a kicker motor.

"We sold a lot of trolling plates, and we sold a lot of hydrofoils," said Ron Nelson, Cabela's Quality Assurance Manager (who at the time headed up the company's R&D department) who, based on Mike Wieser's idea, designed and built the Hydro Troll. "The idea was to create a single product that did the same thing as two other products," he said.

Ron said the Hydro Troll took more than one year to design and produce.

"We started selling them in 1991, and they were successful from the beginning," he said. "We're still selling them today. Most of the best stuff we developed over the years came from a lack of something, or as a way to make something work better."

Vortex Rotating Spinning-Wing System
(Patent #7,131,221 issued 11/21/2006).
The Vortex is another example of taking a successful product and making improvements.

"When we designed the Vortex, spinning-wing decoys were the craze," Ron said. "The thought was that if one decoy sitting on a stake worked, two circling in the air, looking like they were getting ready to land, should work even better. And it did."

The Vortex, the idea of Dennis Highby and Gregg Severinson, used a 12-volt motor to spin two spinning-wing decoys in a 10-foot diameter circle.

"We tested it right after the season closed (with ducks that were really educated) and ducks swarmed it," Ron said. "It just mesmerizes ducks."

Two Cabela's innovations: Hydro Troll and Vortex Rotating Spinning-Wing System.

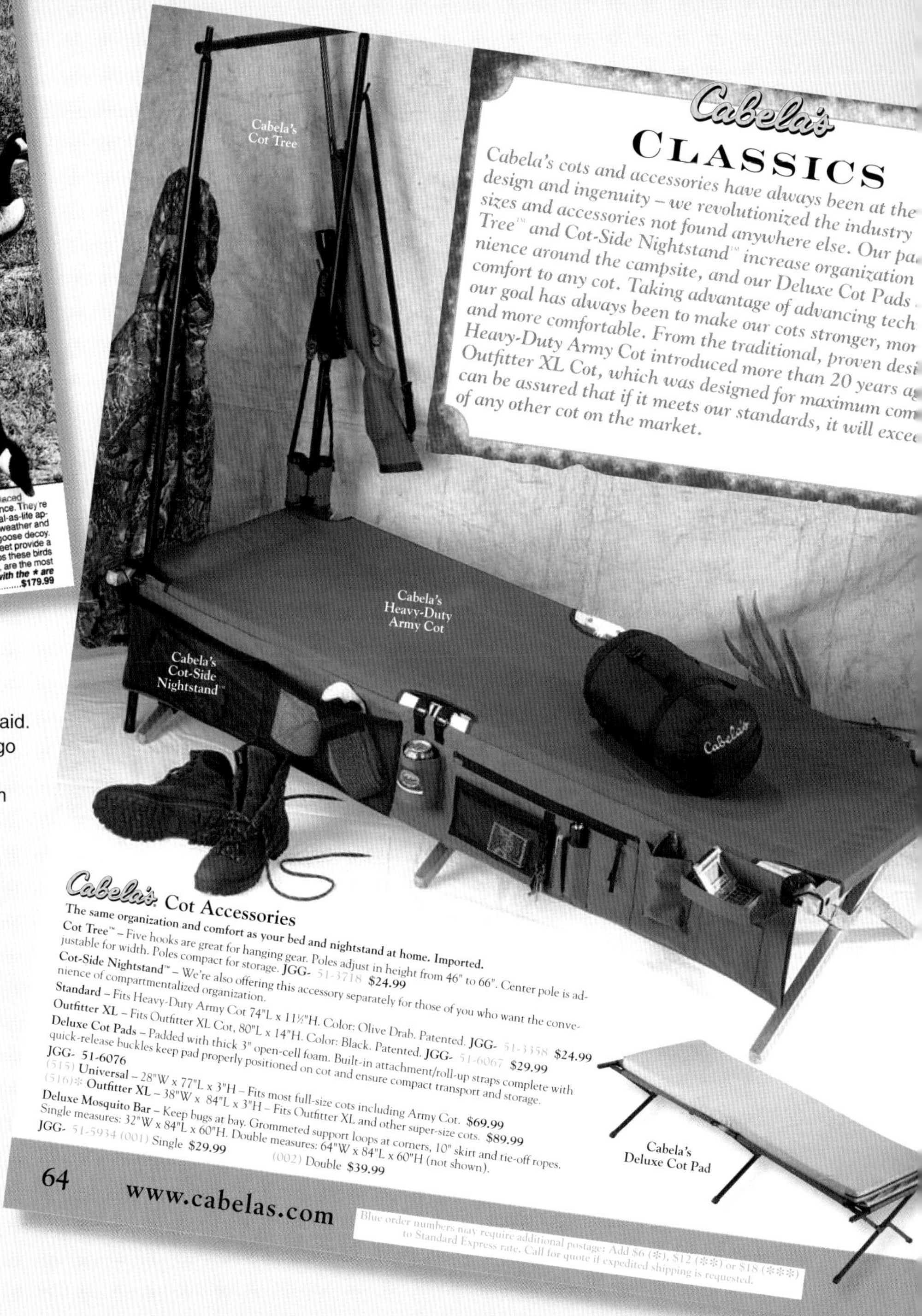

RealImage Decoys (Patent #5,983,552 issued 11/16/1999).
"At the time there were a lot of silhouette decoys with realistic images," Ron said. "I came up with the idea to print a realistic goose image on fabric that would go over a three-dimensional decoy."

The process started in the photo studio, where Ron's team took more than 60 photographs of a mounted Canada goose for a 360 – degree view of the bird. They used computer programs to put all the pictures together and then prepared the final image for transfer to the polyester "skin."

The RealImage Decoy skins were sold with Cabela's snow goose decoys, giving customers another two-for-one innovation.

Cabela's Cot-Side Nightstand
(Patent #6,148,459 issued 11/21/2000).
"This one was the idea of Roger Verhulst, who was the camping buyer at the time," Ron said. "It was the result of a lot of tent time."

The Cot-Side Nightstand keeps essentials close at hand. It has a shelf for an alarm clock, a beverage holder and multiple storage compartments. It also has a sleeve that will hold a shotgun or rifle.

"It's pretty simple, but there was nothing like it at the time," Ron said.

Real Canada geese mingled with Cabela's RealImage Goose Decoys during this catalog product shoot, illustrating how realistic and lifelike the decoys are. The Cot-Side Nightstand filled a need discovered through camping experience.

The GORE-TEX® Story

The GORE-TEX® brand is recognized around the world by hunters and anglers who rely on waterproof, breathable clothing and footwear to keep them dry and comfortable through a wide range of outdoor pursuits.

Cabela's was one of the first companies to recognize the potential for using GORE-TEX® technology in fishing and hunting products in the early 1980s.

The heart of all GORE-TEX® fabrics is the GORE-TEX® membrane. It contains more than 9 billion microscopic pores per square inch. These pores are 20,000 times smaller than a water droplet, but 700 times larger than a water vapor molecule, which makes the GORE-TEX® membrane completely waterproof from the outside, while allowing perspiration to escape from the inside.

GORE-TEX® fabric is actually a laminate in which the GORE-TEX® membrane is bonded between high-performance fabrics that are extremely breathable. All GORE-TEX® fabrics are waterproof, windproof and breathable.

Designed for the backpacking market, GORE-TEX® was sold commercially for the first time in 1976, but it was destined to make its way into the hunting and fishing worlds.

Steve Shuster started working for W.L. Gore & Associates in 1982 as a chemist in the research and development department. He had a passion for fly fishing and hunting, however, and quickly realized he didn't want to spend all his time in the lab, so he moved into a sales role in 1983 and was one of the first Gore employees to work with Cabela's.

At the time, Gore was just getting into the hunting and fishing product categories. And it didn't take long for Cabela's and Gore to develop a business relationship that would become mutually beneficial to both companies.

"Cabela's played a significant role in Gore's early success," said Steve, Gore's brand leader focused on enterprise. "They were passionate champions who were users of the products they were selling. Some of the other companies we worked with in the hunting field weren't users and that created challenges when we'd show them concepts and products.

"Cabela's and Gore shared a passion for innovation and uniqueness, and that helped successfully launch Gore in the hunting and fishing markets."

Soon after joining the Gore sales team, Steve traveled with Cabela's buyers Dennis Highby, Pat Snyder and Jeff Johnson to Alaska to hunt caribou and moose. As is typical in the Last Frontier, constant wind and rain pounded the hunters throughout their 10-day trip. But the possibility of encountering inclement weather was one of the reasons the group chose the destination.

"Because the weather was so bad, it was a great opportunity to collaborate and test new product," Steve said. "At the time, a lot of people in Alaska were using bread bags (worn between their socks and boots) to keep their feet dry. On this trip, Jeff Johnson came up with the idea of creating GORE-TEX® socks for the hunting and fishing market.

"We had a lot of discussions at night in the tent about what we could improve on. That really differentiated Cabela's from the rest. These kinds of experiences, when we used the products, really living through and feeling and seeing and experiencing everything from successes to failures, were very valuable."

Capitalizing on the successes, Cabela's merchandisers began designing and developing Cabela's-branded products that incorporated the GORE-TEX® waterproof and breathable technology.

Steve cited Cabela's MT050 hunting clothing, created by Ev Tarrell, who wanted to combine quiet fabric with waterproof protection; and a series of lightweight, waterproof hunting boots, designed by Jeff Johnson, as two early examples of beneficial collaboration between Cabela's and Gore.

"One of the things that has helped the two companies is we both wanted to make the best product possible for the targeted end-users," Shuster said. "That core value, the outfitter mentality, was to develop the best product for the specific activity."

And that was a philosophy that started at the top at Cabela's and Gore.

"The leadership in both companies really wanted to make sure they set a good example," Steve said. "Bob Gore was not a hunter like Jim Cabela was, but they both pushed their people not to compromise on quality, integrity and innovation. Ultimately that drove developing and pioneering great products the market needed."

The GORE-TEX® brand is a trademark of W.L. Gore & Associates

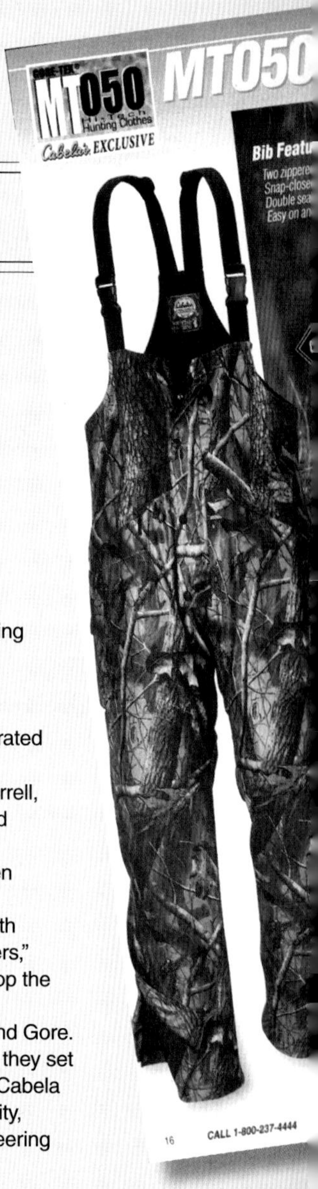

The finest big-game clothing you can buy. GUARANTEED.

ail Extreme

MT050 Hi-Tech Hunting Clothes

Cabela's EXCLUSIVE

Available with Scent-Lok

Mossy Oak New Break-Up Parka

Realtree AP HD Parka

NEW CAMO

GORE-TEX

Pant Features

- 150-gram Thinsulate Insulation
- Two front pockets and back pockets
- Double seat and knees for superior durability
- Easy on and off knee-length leg zippers

Jacket Features

- Three-piece adjustable drawcord hood
- Two handwarmer pockets and a zippered vertical chest pocket
- Two large lower cargo pockets
- Adjustable cuffs
- Dual storm flaps
- Drawcord at hem

DEMAND THE BEST...

MT050® – Think of every favorable attribute you could want in camo clothing and combine them all into one fabric. ***We did – it's called MT050.*** Nothing else compares with the innovative low-nap outer layer that is as soft as fleece with unmatched durability. Compresses extremely small, keeps a supple feel in temperatures well below zero, resists clingy vegetation. Plus, it's also pill- and fade-resistant, guaranteeing camo patterns look like new for the life of the garment.

GORE-TEX® – Unquestionably the finest waterproof, breathable fabric ever engineered. It delivers complete 100% water- and windproof protection, yet breathes so perspiration escapes, pre-

Cabela's **GORE-TEX® MT050® Whitetail Extreme™ Insulated Clothing** Scent-Lok® and Standard styles available

- ***Quiet as fleece, yet has unmatched durability***
- ***Ultrawarm Thinsulate™ Supreme Insulation***
- ***GORE-TEX® membrane is 100% waterproof and breathable***
- ***Engineered for exceptional fit and freedom of movement***

With our revolutionary Whitetail Extreme™ System you get durability, quietness, complete protection from the elements, total scent control, exceptional

Chest sizes: M-3XL.

Whitetail Extreme Bibs – The ultimate protection for your legs and Equipped with adjustable suspenders, leg zippers, a cargo pocket right side, an elastic waist, adjustable cuffs, a front zipper and a

Men's Styles

Thinsulate

at www.cabe

Cabela's **Gore-Tex Thinsulate Pac Boots**

Your feet will stay drier, warmer, and more comfortable than with any other boot of this type. From the flexible gum rubber bottoms to the top of the heavily oiled 5 1/2-6 oz. velva leather uppers, you stay absolutely dry, because of a built-in liner that has a 100% waterproof membrane of breathable Gore-Tex. In addition, the quilted liner utilizes Cambrelle, a durable material that absorbs perspiration then quickly dries. Further, the boot is designed so that the attached liner can be brought outside the boot overnight to be air freshened. As for warmth, these boots are insulated with 200 gram thickness Thinsulate, but we didn't stop there. We added a 3/8'' wool felt midsole that stops cold from coming up through the bottom. A special brush guard where the rubber meets the leather keeps brush and debris from working up into the seams. All seams are permanently treated with a heavy-duty waterproof sealant, to help prevent water from entering. Split back stay adds to the already-impressive durability of these boots. An extra-wide, three-piece gusset makes them easy to get on and off. As a result of these boots being designed to fit the contours of your feet better than some sloppily fitting pacs, you will enjoy improved walking comfort and support. The Frelonic innersole helps too. If you are a half-size or wear extra-heavy socks, we recommend that you go to the next size larger with this boot. Combination eyelets and speed lacing. Traction sole.

Sizes: Whole sizes only,6-13. Please specify.

76-95143 .... **$74.95**

Cabela's **15'' Thinsulate Hunting Pacs**

With Removable Thinsulate Liners

Extra tall boots for outdoorsmen who want to be ready for tougher-than-normal weather conditions; or, who prefer the looks and protection taller boots provide throughout the season. Featured, are removable Velcro-attached liners with Thinsulate thermal insulation. By purchasing an extra pair of liners, you virtually can have a fresh pair of boots every day. Liners use Cambrelle, a soft, durable, fast-absorbing material. Uppers are breathable, full-grain, water repellent oil-tanned leather. Padded collar. Sizes: Medium width, 7-13. Whole sizes only. Please specify.

76-95776 .... $72.95

76-90020 — **Extra liners, per pair. Sizes 7-13.** ... $16.95

Gore-Tex®/Thinsulate Pac Boots

With Removable Liners

A truly all-season boot, with versatility never before available. The removable Gore-Tex® Thinsulate inner liner provides a warm waterproof boot. Remove the liner, and you have a warm-weather boot. Further, you can buy one or more pair of extra liners and you, in effect, have a dry, fresh pair of boots in an instant. Uppers are triple-stitched to rubber bottoms. Speed lacing at top three eyelets. Cushioned felt insert under the insole for extra warmth and comfort. Choose from all-leather upper or camo Cordura, reinforced with leather.

Sizes: Medium and wide widths, 6-13. Whole sizes only. Specify **size** and **width.**

76-96771 — Leather **$69.95**

76-96781 — Camo Cordura **$69.95**

Extra Liners. Whole sizes only. Specify **size** and **width.**

76-90010 — Medium width 7-13 .... **$19.95**

76-96766 — Wide width 6-13 .... **$19.95**

Cabela's **Upland Thinsulate Hunting Pac**

With Removable Thinsulate Liners

This boot has Thinsulate thermal insulation in the form of removable liners. In the past, if you have had trouble drying your boots out for the next day's use, your troubles are over. With these boots, you simply remove the liners by way of Velcro attachments at the top, for fast easy drying. Purchase an extra pair of liners, so you have a dry pair on hand at any time. Lining of cambrelle for extra comfort and wicking away moisture. Lug-type rubber soles provide good traction. Choose from leather reinforced upper of Cordura nylon in Woodland Camo or uppers of full-grain, oil-tanned cowhide. Made in U.S.A.

Whole Sizes. Med. or wide width. 6-13. Specify.

10''Thinsulate Hunting Pac

76-96806 — Woodland Camo **$61.95**

76-96801 — Full Leather **$61.95**

Liners available in Med. & Wide width. Specify **size** and **width.**

76-96786 — Per Pair. Sizes 6-13 .... **$13.95**

46 Cabela's 1986 Fall

Seeing the benefit waterproof, breathable laminate GORE-TEX® could bring to hunting and fishing outerwear, Cabela's employees worked with Gore to improve design and implementation. At left, Pat Snyder, Jeff Johnson and Dennis Highby accompanied Gore employees on a hunt in Alaska to test GORE-TEX® products in adverse conditions.

"We built the waders and put them on the back cover of every catalog, and within two years the whole wader industry transitioned to Cordura waders."

– Pat Snyder

I think one of the real keys to Cabela's success is that early on, we recognized sportsmen would pay for appropriate technology. They weren't afraid to invest in high-quality products that performed and functioned for them. That is really the premise of everything we built, how we can put more quality into these products and still offer them at a fair value to our customers."

Pat drives home the point when remembering early in his career he and Dennis Highby were looking at waders. All waders at that time were made with thin fabrics, and wore out too fast or snagged and tore easily. Then a nylon fabric called Cordura was introduced into the luggage market. "We kept looking at this Cordura stuff," says Pat, "this heavy-duty fabric, and we wondered if we could make it into waders." They went to several manufacturers asking them to build Cordura waders and were turned down. Finally, they persuaded Endicott Johnson in New York to pilot a Cordura wader program.

"We built the waders and put them on the back cover of every catalog, and within two years the whole wader industry transitioned to Cordura waders. That's how much impact our catalog had on hunters and fishermen and the industry itself."

Pat points to GORE-TEX as another example in which Cabela's was instrumental to product development. "When the first GORE-TEX hunting coats came on the market in the 1980s, customers would send them back because they leaked. We tested them and discovered that the manufacturers weren't sealing the seams. So we went in and helped the Gore company establish standards for waterproofing garments made from its fabric. We did the same thing with leak problems in early GORE-TEX boots. Our customers recognized the improvements and responded with increasing sales. We are probably the largest retailer of GORE-TEX products in the world."

Jeff Johnson points out one key to making such new products successful was the informational nature of Cabela's catalogs. "We were able to take the mechanics of the product, the concept of the product, and convey the whole story to consumers. The consumers would get it and understand what this product is and what it will do for them. We took a lot of time in the catalog presentation and explanation of the product."

On a personal level, Jeff relates, "It was fun to sit down with a copywriter and pitch the product. If I could sell it to him, then I was successful and the copywriter could explain it convincingly to the customer."

Incorporating the then-new Cordura nylon fabric into the design and manufacturing process produced heavy-duty waders that could stand up to the wear and tear of hunting, filling a need for sportsmen and starting an industry-wide trend toward Cordura waders.

WORLD'S TOUGHEST WADERS

Cabela's® Cordura Nylon Brush Buster Waders

"1000 Denier Nylon Wears Like Iron"

Made in the U.S.A. These are the waders for the waterfowler who would crawl through the muck and the mire to put the sneak on a big greenhead, and for the angler who would cross a wall of barbed wire or make his way through a jungle of briars and brambles to get to the pool that is home for that big lunker. These waders are for anyone who wants the toughest, most durable wader on the market today. You would expect waders of this quality only from Cabela's. Only the best materials have been used. You know the name, Cordura. It became synonymous with long wear, abrasion resistance and durability in the use of backpacks. Since then, it has been used in a whole new generation of hunting boots and other apparel. Now, another name that has earned your trust, Cabela's®, offers you the "wears-like-iron" brush busting quality of Cordura in waders. And the quality doesn't stop with the Cordura outer. These waders feature cotton liners that add to the overall strength and keep condensation to a minimum. Soles are natural gum rubber, patterened to give a sure grip. You bet! They have steel shanks and cushioned insoles. Insulated models feature in-liner insulation, with heavy-duty, ½" thick wool felt at the midsoles. The chest waders feature a reinforced top with drawstring, inside storage pouch and belt loops. Hip waders have inside leg harnesses to provide a snug fit below the knees. Both chest and hip waders come in whole sizes only. If you are a half size, we recommend the next largest size.

Insulated Chest Waders — Brown Camouflage
793-954 — Regular sizes: 6-13, Specify **$129.95**
793-955 — Long sizes: 9-13, Specify **$129.95**
793-953 — Short sizes: 6-9, Specify **$129.95**

Non-Insulated Chest Waders — Green Camouflage
793-960 — Regular sizes: 6-13, Specify **$119.95**
793-961 — Long sizes: 9-13, Specify **$119.95**
793-959 — Short sizes: 6-9, Specify **$119.95**

Insulated Chest Waders — Dark Brown
793-957 — Regular sizes: 6-13, Specify **$129.95**
793-958 — Long sizes: 9-13, Specify **$129.95**
793-956 — Short sizes: 6-9, Specify **$129.95**

Non-Insulated Chest Waders — Dark Brown
793-963 — Regular sizes: 6-13, Specify **$119.95**
793-964 — Long sizes: 9-13, Specify **$119.95**
793-962 — Short sizes: 6-9, Specify **$119.95**

Hip Waders, Insulated — Whole Sizes: 6-13
793-965 — Brown Camouflage **$79.95**
793-966 — Dark Brown **$79.95**

Hip Waders, Non-Insulated — Whole sizes 6-13
793-967 — Green Camouflage **$69.95**
793-968 — Dark Brown **$69.95**

POSTMASTER - If addressee has moved please deliver to the current resident

Cabela's
812 - 13th Ave
Sidney
Nebraska 69160

ORDER TOLL FREE
800-237-4444

BULKRATE
U.S. POSTAGE PAID
Cabela's, Inc.

For fastest service, PEEL OFF THIS LABEL and affix in space provided on the Order Form. If the address or spelling is incorrect, please correct.

Cabela's Fish Eagle Graphite
Special Purpose Walleye Rods
For years we have enjoyed spending countless hours fishing for Walleyes all over the U.S. and Canada. We, like many of you enjoy Walleyes for their great flavor and for the angling challenge they present. We are proud to offer you a line of Fish Eagle Graphite Walleye rods that is second to none.
This line of rods has taken years to develop. They are designed and built by people who are both engineers and fishermen. Because of the large variety of angling situations used in Walleye fishing, all four of these models are a necessity for the serious Walleye angler.
Fish Free For 30 Days
We invite you to field test any of our Fish Eagle Graphite Rods for a period of 30 days. Compare them to any other rod regardless of Price. If you are not 100% satisfied, return them for full refund, no questions asked.
Handle Closeup
In most parts of the country walleyes bite best early in the spring when the ice has just gone out. The revolutionary cork handle used on our Fish Eagle Graphite Walleye Rods lets your hand touch mostly warm cork. This feature keeps your hand comfortable and ready to detect even the lightest strike.
Single Foot Guide — All four models of our Fish Eagle Graphite Walleye Rod Series feature light weight single foot Fuji Aluminum Oxide double braced guides on the first and largest guide for added strength. All thread wraps are finished with two coats of flexible polymer. The finest finish used on any guide wraps.
Ferrule System — All two piece rods feature a graphite-to-graphite ferrule that allows the same progressive tip to butt action normally found only in a one-piece rod. Because the ferrule is a tip-over-butt style, and an integral part of the tip section, the ferrule is unusually strong, efficient and streamlined.
FREE! We invite each of you Walleye fishermen to order this free booklet of closely held secrets, tricks and tips on how to catch walleye. Rod Lindner, publisher of the famed 'IN-FISHERMAN' Magazine has drawn deep into his resources and put together a collection of some of the best ways to catch walleye. A section even covers how to find and catch lunkers, those elusive fish in the 8, 9, and 10 lb. bracket. While short and to the point, each secret, trick or tip is nevertheless fully explained in terms of when, where and how. This booklet contains material that has never been in print before and is available nowhere else but in this special gift offer from Cabela's. To receive it free, simply order:
506-108-000 .... FREE
806-109-270 — 7' Med/Heavy, 8-12 lb.line, ¼-1 oz. lures $49.95
Garcia Cardinal Spinning Reels
Browning Mitchell 300 and 440 Series Reels
Shakespeare Sigma Pro Spinning Reels
$7.00 Factory Rebate on all 2300 series reels, Good thru June
Cabela's
WORLD'S FINEST QUALITY SPORTSMAN'S PRODUCTS
1982 SUMMER

Cabela's Found, Nurtured Local Talent

Always one to share outdoor adventures with friends, Jim Pohl, center, killed this elk with a bow during a 1993 hunt in New Mexico. With Jim were Jeff Johnson, left, and Fred Neal. Jim's career at Cabela's started on the dock, unloading trucks during summer breaks from college. But his artistic talent, shown in these drawings, led to his providing catalog illustrations and ultimately a position as Manager of Creative Services.

Walk the halls of Cabela's World Headquarters in Sidney, Nebraska, and you'll likely cross paths with workers from most any state and a few distant countries. But that doesn't mean the World's Foremost Outfitter always has to look far to find employees to support its global business. In fact, many of its biggest success stories are natives to the modest Western town Cabela's calls home. One such story involves a homegrown artist named Jim Pohl.

Jim's notable 25-year-career at Cabela's began in 1984 in one of the most inauspicious locales – the company's hot, dusty loading dock. At that time, Jim was sweating his way through school at the Colorado Institute of Art by unloading trucks during summer break.

One evening while spending some time with Jim, Cabela's fishing buyer Tom Rosdail (now the company's Vice President of Brand Marketing and Licensing) happened across some artwork he had created. Impressed by the dockworker's talent, Tom asked his boss, Cabela's future CEO Dennis Highby, for permission to pay Jim to produce a few illustrations for the company's famous mail-order catalog.

"It was obvious he had talent," Tom said. "He came in and did some line art and it was good, so I contracted him to do a few more things, and they were good. So, in 1985 we hired him full-time to help with our catalogs."

In the 1980s, Cabela's lacked a formal catalog-production team like it enjoys now. Back then, a small, versatile staff took on an "everyone-pitches-in" philosophy, and the homegrown artist's work ethic made him an ideal member of the team and the company's first true catalog employee.

"There wasn't anything he wouldn't do for you," Tom said. "We counted on him for anything that had to do with art, whether it was illustrating catalogs or making sure colors in photos were correct. He'd step in anywhere, anytime to help."

Jim's eye for art and commitment to Cabela's took him on a professional journey that eventually led him to become Cabela's Manager of Creative Services.

Like many Cabela's employees have over the years, Jim often volunteered his time and energy, especially to conservation and habitat organizations that offered opportunities for kids. Jim, along with many coworkers, were active supporters of Pheasant's Forever Chapter's Youth/Mentor Hunt – an event Jim contributed to right up to his untimely death in 2009.

That same year, Sidney's High Plains Chapter of Pheasant Forever made up largely of Cabela's employees, established a fund in Jim's name, the proceeds of which support the chapter's Youth/Mentor Hunt and other youth activities. In addition, each year, the Sidney Shooting Park conducts a Jim Pohl Memorial Shoot to benefit the local youth trap team.

Today, Cabela's Sidney, Nebraska, World Headquarters draws employees from around the world. Most have left some sort of mark on the company's 50-year history. But all you have to do is walk the company's hallways, hunt some of the area's pheasants or enjoy the smile on a young shooters face as he enjoys a round of clays to see the legacy of at least one local who stayed home to support the company and the town he loved.

Cabela's employees taking orders on the third floor of the downtown Sidney headquarters, 1983.

The busy Shipping Department on the second floor of the downtown facility, 1982.

Many, but not all, of Cabela's product ideas and innovations have been protected by patents. Fred Neal remembers a morning in 1984 when he and Jeff Johnson were sitting in a goose blind. "It was probably 15 to 20 below wind chill, and Jeff's Labrador retriever was shivering. Jeff had just started building neoprene waders. We came up with the idea for a vest to protect dogs from heat loss. We used scraps of neoprene from the waders to make a prototype." It took them a year measuring dogs and plenty of trial and error to come up with the vest. "We put it on the market but didn't patent the idea," he said. "Whether or not we could have gotten a patent, you never know, but we probably should have tried. Now many other companies sell them."

"Today," Pat Snyder says, "if we introduce a product in a catalog, six months later it's out in the market. We used to enjoy several years' exclusivity, but not any more. But we still have a tremendous advantage. If you look at our assortments today, we are probably twice as large as our closest competitor in terms of pure SKU count. Our customers come to us for unique specialty items. That is what we are known for, and they continue to shop and purchase products from Cabela's for that reason."

Approaching Maturity

At the end of the 1980s, Cabela's was positioned to truly become the World's Foremost Outfitter. A core management team of committed outdoorsmen were on their way to establishing the Cabela's brand as the premier source of quality products. The Cabela's system of hands-on product testing had set the standard for the outdoor manufacturing industry. And company growth was continuing, reaching $188.6 million in sales by the end of the decade — more than 10 times what it had been just 10 years earlier.

The company had acquired additional warehouse facilities at the former Sioux Army Depot. Cabela's had also launched Outdoor Adventures booking agency, established a stand-alone telecommunication center in Kearney, and opened its first separate-location retail store — all of which would play increasingly significant roles in the company's future in the coming years.

Successful businesses reach a critical point when future growth depends on adjusting business plans and recruiting appropriate talent without sacrificing values that led to their success. During the 1980s, the Cabela brothers made that transition.

Cabela's celebrated its 25th anniversary in 1986.

...fles

...ring an Ozark rifle un... ...merican tiger striped ...nsure that each Hat... ...fles are derived from ...was something you ...Horn; Front – Brass ...r. Weight: .36 cali-ber, 7¾ lbs. 45 and .50 caliber, 7¼ lbs. Brass trigger guard and butt plate. Hand sanded and carved stock, hand-rubbed and polished with homemade polish and wax formula. Barrel is browned with homemade formula.
Calibers: (036) .36 Cal., **(045)** .45 Cal. or **(050)** .50 Cal. Specify.
76-20228 — Percussion **$399.95**
76-20227 — Flintlock **$399.95**

Ⓑ **Frontier Muzzleloading Rifle and Rifle Kit** — Experience the thrill of a well-placed shot, as did the independent mountain man of the past. These rifles feature deep-grooved barrels precisely rifled for excellent round ball accuracy. Double set triggers. Select hardwood. Octagonal barrel, 15/16'' across the flats; 28'' long. Hooked breech. 44'' overall length. Screw adjustable sights, windage and elevation. Beaded blade front, partridge-style open rear sight. Solid brass trim. Weight, 6 lbs. 7 ozs. .50 caliber.
76-25053-000 — Rifle . . . . **$114.95** **76-25054-000** — Kit **$84.95**

Ⓒ **CVA Muzzleloader Black Powder Shotgun and Kit** — The trigger comes back, the barrel swings, there's a metallic "clunk" followed by a white cloud of smoke, which clears just in time to reveal the big honker coming down. This is hunting with a muzzleloader, a type of hunting that offers more challenge and excitement to the hunter's ever more limited time in the field. Cylinder bore. 12 gauge. 28'' barrel. Length overall 44''. Weight 6 lbs. 10 ozs. Engraved lock-plate and trigger guard. Brass bead front sight.
76-23411-000 — Shotgun . . . . . **$199.95** **76-23400-000** — Kit **$149.95**

Jennings Devastator Crossbow

...evastator features a Trackless, Quick Take-Down design for minimum ...wear, long power stroke and higher performance. Extra strong Muscle ...ave continuous fiber design for best possible stress distribution. Keyhole ...sign is lightweight; won't torque. Automatic safety when cocking. Bull ...k design for good balance. Pistol-style grip. Roller sear trigger mecha-...t stirrup cocking. Rear peep sight with multiple front pins. 125 lb. draw ...iecast magnesium riser. Extruded aluminum barrel. Glass filled nylon ...or: Camouflage.
...000 . . . . **$199.95**
...amouflage, anodized aluminum. Do not include points.
...00 — Per 6 . . . . **$21.95**
...or use with Jennings Devastator and other crossbows. Holds four ...
. . . . . **$12.95**
76-45033-000 . . . . **$19.95**
76-45034-000 — Extra String — 26'', 24 strand **$3.49**

1986
SPRING

Cabela's Professional Hunter Knife

Featuring a retractable gut hook that acts as a point protector so entrails are not accidently cut open. It's a very versatile knife for all uses that call for a superior knife. Also a handy 1½'' serrated edge for cutting through wire, rope, bone etc. Black hard rubber handle for secure grip. 2½'' fixed blade, 4½'' handle. Comes with a camouflage Cordura holster.
76-55017-000 . . . . **$37.95**

Browning Folding Saw/Knife

Browning builds quality into their knives just like they do in a fine gun. This beauty has a saw blade for cutting bone, cartilage and tree limbs when hunting from a tree, plus a 'field-dressing blade' with a blunt end that separates the hide from the meat without cutting the entrails or meat. A trailing point blade is ready for general dressing and skinning. A tough handle of Stamina Wood decorates this knife which also comes encased in a handsome, handmade, top grain leather sheath.
76-29582-000—Folding Pocket Knife - 3¼'' blades **$37.95**

Cabela's Super Sharpener

Super Sharpener puts a razor edge on a knife faster than any other device. It is compact for convenient carrying and storage. You don't have to know a thing about sharpening knives, scissors, hatchets and other tools in order to put a razor edge on these tools—simply stroke Super Sharpener across the edge and its carbide blades will do the rest. Also sharpens small garden tools and scythes; excellent for deburring. Handy in the kitchen, tool box, car, tackle box or packsack.
76-89871-000 . . . . **$6.95** **76-89766-000—Ex blade** **$3.49**
Super Sharpener for Larger Tools—This model is designed for larger tools and implements such as lawn mower blades, chisels, hoes, clipper blades, rototillers and all single-edge tools.
76-89801-000 . . . . **$6.95** **76-89696-000—Ex blade** **$1.79**

Lansky Knife Sharpener Set

Now, get a truly professional edge everytime—at the exact angle you select, the marked guide eliminates any error for the wrong angle on your blade. With the three different color coded grit stones, fine, medium and coarse you can sharpen any knife to a perfect razor edge. Just lock the back of the blade into the clamp and attach one of the stones in the desired angled slot and in just a few short minutes you can have any sized blade back to that factory edge. Set comes in a handy plastic carrying case with instructions and special honing oil.
76-50217-000 . . . . **$21.95**

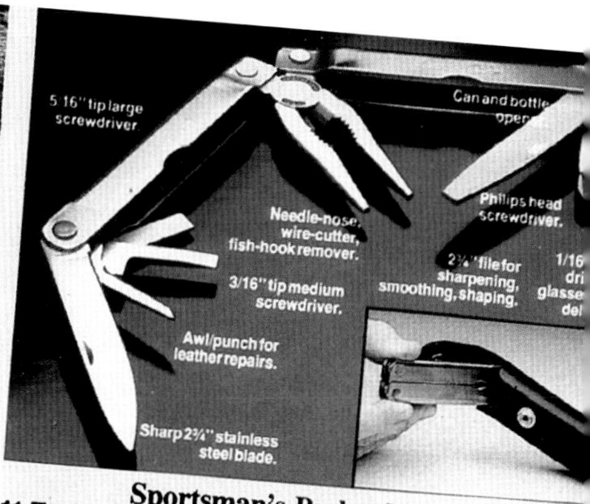

Sportsman's Pocket Multi-Tool

11 Tools in One—Here's a tool - or should we say eleven of them no less than an engineering marvel. The marvel is not only that 11 tools put in a 1''x4'' package, but also that the tools are arranged so that th... handy and practical to use. The swivel base on each tool is cammed s... when a particular tool is folded out for use, it snaps into place and stays the... til it is folded back into the self-contained case. The tools include: needle... pliers, cutters, knife, three sizes common screwdrivers, bottle opener, ruler, awl/punch, file, and Phillips head screwdriver. Originally made as ... vival tool, this tool is all stainless steel made to tough U.S. Military specifica... Each tool is warranted for life to the original purchaser. Comes with leathe... sheath.
76-83921-000 . . . . **$2...**

Gerber LST Folding Lockback Knife

LST stands for light, smooth and tough. And this knife is all of that and more. T... larger camouflage knife with 2⅝'' blade, weighs only 1.3 ozs; and the smal... black ultralight 2'' blade knife weighs a mere .6 oz. The knives open and clo... smoothly thanks to "lubricated for life" bushings. And they are tough as a result... their Zytel handle and Gerber's high carbon surgical quality stainless steel blade...
Ⓐ Knife only
76-55018-000 — 2¾'' closed; 4¾'' open; 2'' blade . . . . **$12.9...**
Ⓑ Knife only
76-50000-000 — 3½'' closed; 6⅛'' open; 2⅝'' blade . . . . **$18.9...**
Ⓑ Knife and Cordura Sheath
76-50013-000 — 3½'' closed; 6⅛'' open; 2⅝'' blade . . . . **$21.9...**

Cabela's Pac-Saws

Finally, a product that will place all your cutting needs at your fingertips. The Pac-Saw comes with heat treated carbon steel saw blade, coarse teeth on one side for wood, fine teeth on the other for meat. The saw fits neatly in a heavy top grain cowhide sheath, that easily stores at your side or in your pack.
Pac-Saw with Leather Belt Case and Folding Knife Case
Ⓐ **76-22883-000** **$24.95**
Pac-Saw with Camouflage Cordura covered leather Belt Case
Ⓑ **76-20069-000** **$25.95**
Pac-Saw with Leather Belt Case and 2-Level Shell Carrier
Ⓒ **76-20070-000** **$27.95**
Ⓓ **76-55912-000** — Sport Saw **$14.95**

Cabela's catalogs and catalog covers have evolved over the years, but from the beginning, customers waited anxiously for the catalogs to arrive in the mail.

Representation of Cabela's covers over the years.

Representation of Cabela's covers over the years.

Representation of Cabela's covers over the years.

Representation of Cabela's covers over the years.

Representation of Cabela's covers over the years.

Chapter 4

Bridges to the Future

Second-floor merchandise shelves and filling line at Cabela's in downtown Sidney, Nebraska – 1983.

Key elements helping spur Cabela's growth in the 1980s included implementation of an improved telephone system; construction of Cabela's first stand-alone store; and creation of Cabela's Outdoor Adventures booking agency. This growth helped Cabela's earn the title of World's Foremost Outfitter.

Revolution in Telemarketing

In the mid-1970s, Cabela's published its local Nebraska telephone number in its catalogs and started taking orders and customer service calls. Dick Cabela's first awareness of the phone-order revolution had come at a Direct Marketing Association conference where other mail-order companies were complaining about the growing number of customers who wanted to talk to a live representative. Initially, Dick says, "We considered these calls an inconvenience, but quickly saw it as an extension of customer service." But by 1981 the volume of calls required setting up a separate telemarketing department and installing an automatic distribution system to replace the original manual telephone switchboard.

Soon after, the phone company suggested the Cabela brothers install a then-new 800-number system so customers could call toll-free. Initially, Dick was not warm to the idea, thinking not only would Cabela's need separate phone and mail-order staff, "We would havc to pay for the calls, too." Then he realized his order takers on the phone could offer a personal customer service touch.

"All of a sudden, this 800-number thing began to make sense," says Dick. The toll-free system was installed in April 1983. Before long, telephone orders were half the business, mail-order the rest.

Second-floor packing line in Sidney, Nebraska – 1983.

Cabela's sales increased 12-fold from 1979 to 1989. With a continuing need to hire more telemarketing staff, it had outgrown the downtown Sidney headquarters and the employee resources of the Sidney area. It was clear the company was going to have to branch out. Again, good fortune intervened. In Kearney, Nebraska, about 200 miles to the east, an empty Rockwell International plant was available, Cabela's purchased it in 1985. Kearney, a college town of 28,000, offered a larger workforce. By November 1986, the new facility was operating with 300 employees answering phones 24 hours a day.

Cabela's Would Never Be the Same

Cris Hoehn, who joined Cabela's in 1982, serves as manager of four call centers. Call-center representatives take orders, handle customer service calls and product inquiries, and also handle Cabela's Web site live chat and e-mail response. "Cabela's legendary customer service will always be honored by the people manning Cabela's phones," says Cris.

Cris says the Cabela brothers have constantly rejected the automated "press one to continue" types of phone systems, insisting Cabela's phones always be answered by a person. "We try to make things easy for customers by having well-trained staff," Hoehn said. "It's hard enough if customers have a problem, but if they then have to wait or repeat the problem to several different layers of people, it is frustrating, and we try to avoid that."

"Our associates demonstrate great work ethics, which is critical to providing world-class customer service," she said. Cabela's has rejected solicitations to outsource their telemarketing services. "Superior customer service is a core value at Cabela's and is best provided by ourselves," Cris said.

As Cabela's continues to expand internationally, the need for multilingual staff grows. Cabela's call centers are staffed with

"Our associates demonstrate great work ethics, which is critical to providing world-class customer service." – Cris Hoehn

French- and Spanish-speaking representatives. In addition, Cabela's utilizes a service to translate other languages to provide world-wide customer service.

Newly hired associates receive extensive training, including how to get on the Web site, how to process an order, how to perform a 'where's my order?' search. Then after about eight hours of mentoring on the phone, they are on the phone helping customers.

The call centers also have a system for customer feedback comments. "We wanted to capture customer comments about product, service, anything the customer wanted to share with us," Cris said. "We would complete a form and send it to Jim in Sidney. Jim would read these comments every day and forward them to the appropriate department, asking that the customers concerns be addressed. Recently, we introduced a more efficient communication mode to provide better service to our customers."

Customer service representatives busy answering holiday-season calls at the call center in Kearney, Nebraska. December, 1992.

Focusing on Customer Experience

Ron Spath became the Director of Customer Service in 1995, replacing Dot Kruse who was one of Dick Cabela's first hires in Sidney when he convinced her to leave the Green Stamp Store to work for Cabela's. In the mid-1990s, the Customer Service and Telemarketing departments were separate units. In 1999, Ron combined the two, forming a division capable of not only taking inbound calls from consumers wanting to place orders, but also resolving customer service issues.

More than 10 years later, there are five Cabela's call centers across Nebraska. But that's not all that has changed. Ron's title was recently updated to Vice President of Customer Experience.

"It's not just a change in wording," Ron said. "It's a re-purposing of the company's customer service staff members and their critical role as they serve Cabela's growing family of outdoor enthusiasts. It's our company's mission to cherish and please every customer, every day. That's a bold statement."

But Cabela's customer service representatives are extensively trained to live up to the company mission. New associates go through over a week of training before handling calls on their own. As they receive additional training and demonstrate improved competency, they are given access to additional files and information to help them learn how to better serve Cabela's customers.

With the maximum amount of training followed by stringent testing, customer service representatives have the opportunity to become product specialists who handle the most challenging customer calls. Less than 10 percent of the company's 1,000-plus customer service associates reach this level. According to Ron, the specialists are rarely stumped by customer service inquiries.

"But when they are, they're on the phone instantly contacting company vendors or other experts in the field to find the correct answer," he said. "Specialists are very proud to have the opportunity to share their knowledge of the outdoors and our product selection directly with our loyal customers."

And each day, calls bring new stories from customers. Most often they want to thank Cabela's for handling their orders and questions in a swift and professional manner. But a few of their stories are sad (a family member passing away before they were able to use a new fishing reel), funny (an honest angler ordering one lure and receiving a box of 144) and just plain odd (a customer requesting a shirt, but receiving a pair of boots). Regardless of the situation, Cabela's representatives are charged with handling each call quickly and fairly while treating the caller like family.

Ron Spath, Vice President of Customer Experience.

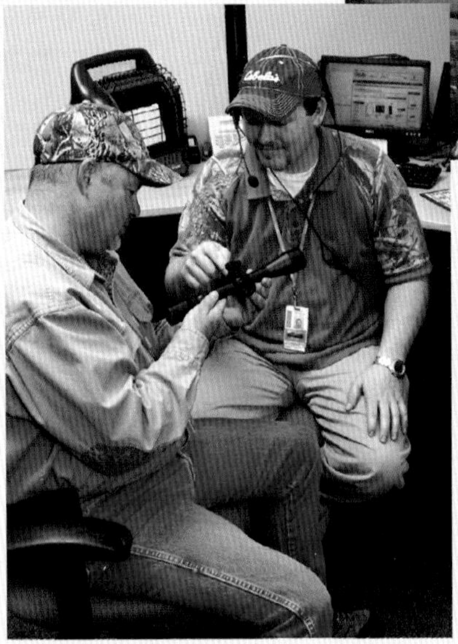

Cabela's product specialists receive frequent training along with stringent testing on product knowledge.

By the mid-2000s, company executives began holding monthly "voice of the customer" meetings, during which they listen to customer service calls. These listening sessions keep the executive team up to speed on everyday consumer concerns, including those relating to customer service, product quality and issue management. But to be sure Cabela's has "nailed every detail" of the customer experience.

"The company continually surveys retail, telephone and Internet consumers," Ron said.

"All company employees, from our customer service representatives to the members of our executive team, make decisions every day with our customers in mind," he said. "Our ultimate goal is for every customer to have an outstanding experience each time they interact with Cabela's – and, if not, we'll do whatever we can to make it that way."

Cabela's Outdoor Adventures

Cabela's most unique service to sportsmen is its Outdoor Adventures travel and booking agency, which offers turnkey services for travelers wishing to pursue their passion anywhere in the world.

Gregg Severinson joined Cabela's in 1984 and was tapped to develop the travel service the following year. Outdoor Adventures was started as a service to customers who wanted to hunt, fish and travel, but needed assistance in selecting the right destination and proper outfitters and guides who could provide them with the best experience.

The first Outdoors Adventures ad was in Cabela's December 1985 catalog, and the first trips were sold in 1986. "Initially, we just booked the destination, matching customers with outfitters," Gregg said. "Then we added full travel packages in 1991, providing door-to-door service to far-out-of-the-way places."

Gregg started Outdoor Adventures by studying outfitting and guide services. Once he determined likely prospects, he booked a trip so he could evaluate first-hand the outfitter and the operation. The process was a natural extension of Cabela's product-testing philosophy. No service would be included in Cabela's Outdoor Adventures' catalog unless it was proven worthy.

Gregg Severinson,
Director of Cabela's Outdoor Adventures

Early Outdoor Adventures Hunting Catalog

Read what some of our 1989 customers have to say . . .

Steve Reichard with his 30'' plus Wyoming mule deer. ''This is my 5th hunt with Cabela's Outdoor Adventures. They keep getting better & better!''

Norman Deleeuw with his 6 x 6 New Mexico elk. ''The guides and outfitters were excellent, made me feel right at home. Great hunt, would like to go back.''

Robert Farmer with outstanding barren ground caribou. ''This hunt fulfilled a life time dream.''

Craig Tinkham with his 10' Alaskan brown bear. ''By far and away the finest outfitter and guides I have ever come across. Nothing more needs to be said.''

Jim Schneider, with his exceptional Wyoming whitetail. Jim is going back in 1990.

Dennis Highby of Nebraska gives this sheep hunt in Alaska the thumbs up. Dennis' full curl ram was 8½ years old and sported 16'' bases.

Rick Ryan with his exceptional New Mexico bull. ''I would highly recommend this elk hunt to anyone interested in hunting for quality trophies with quality people. The hunt was more than I expected and worth every penny.''

Darrell Mitchell, with his possible Boone & Crockett Alaskan moose.

Sal DaBiere, New York, with his impressive 21-point Texas whitetail.

Cover and back photos by Leonard Lee Rue

Gregg Severinson, manager of Cabela's Outdoor Adventures with his Dall Sheep taken in Alaska, Fall 1989. This ram is a 37'' full curl with 15½'' bases.

Bruce Warren, Cabela's Outdoor Adventures, with his Yukon bull taken Fall 1989.

Where we have been and outlook for 1990 and 1991

Cabela's Outdoor Adventures is not an arm chair booking agency. We invest a considerable amount of time and money investigating outfitters for our customers. We want you to have a good hunt and get game. We rely on our repeat business. Many of our customers have booked several hunts with us.

Cabela's has compiled some of the finest hunting destinations in North America and Africa. These hunts are available to our customers at no extra cost. It is important for you to book now for the best dates available for 1990 and 1991.

Our customers do not realize how close we are to the big game hunting in the West. Sidney, NE is only 10 miles from Colorado and 60 miles from Wyoming. This enables us to make many trips each year to our Western states during and after the hunting seasons.

British Columbia

We made four trips to B.C. last year and visited a host of outfitters. We feel we have the best this province has to offer for our customers. Stone's sheep hunting is getting better and better. The ram numbers and age class is up considerably, if you hunt the right areas. The largest Canadian moose are killed in B.C. 13 of the top 25 Boone and Crockett bulls, including #1 and #2, have come out of B.C. We have outfitters opening up areas that have never been hunted. The Fall of 1990 will undoubtedly put some of our hunters in the book. The black bear hunting is phenomenal on the coast. We have been there and worked out a special price for our hunters to enjoy this exciting spot and stalk hunt. Grizzly success was also up last fall. One of our outfitters put 3 bears in the all time record books just from last fall. Goat hunting in our areas was fantastic. 100% success on trophy billies.

Yukon

The Yukon territories are two thirds the size of Alaska with only 23,000 inhabitants. This territory is what big game dreams are made of. We are working with one outfitter in this territory because of his success on trophy game. The fall produced a 45'' stone sheep. 100% success on moose averaging 60'' with several heavy-horned 65'' plus monsters. This outfitter also has an incredible area for mountain caribou and grizzly. He has only hunted half of this huge guide area. Each year he is opening up new areas that have not been hunted for 26 years. This area is different from most popular trophy big game areas. It is common not to hear or see another plane your entire hunt. Seeing another hunter is out of the question.

Quebec

We have access to the finest caribou hunting in Northern Quebec. If you are looking for a big Quebec Labrador Caribou we know where they are. We have been there. One third of the book heads have come from the Koroc herd. We can tell you when and where to go for big bulls. We offer these hunts fully guided and unguided.

Alaska

Big game hunting in Alaska is still fantastic. The largest trophies are in smaller pockets than 10 years ago. You have to hunt the right areas. This past fall we had clients take exceptional moose, caribou, sheep and a brown bear almost 11' squared. These hunters book early and pay a premium fee. There are no ''deals'' in trophy hunting. If you want an opportunity at outstanding trophies and are willing to part with a few extra dollars, let us know. Cabela's works with the best outfitters in Alaska. We visit Alaska several times each year to find you the best areas for trophy hunting.

Cabela's visits many different hunting camps each year. Not all of our homework pays off. Some outfitters do not have what they claim. By visiting these camps, we are able to sort out the best areas with the most aggressive outfitters. We do this so you have the best opportunity at game. We want you to be successful. We are offering an opportunity at game. We are not selling animals. We do not offer exotic hunts or any type of high-fenced hunts. All of our hunts are fair chase with no guarantees. We believe hunting is the most exciting sporting event available. We never know how the hunt will go, what will happen or what animals will be taken. We can tell you how your hunt might go or how it should unfold, but not the outcome. This is why it is called hunting.

Outdoor Adventures Cabela's 1

Cabela's T.A.G.S.

Trophy Application and Guide Service (T.A.G.S.), a division of Cabela's Outdoor Adventures, started in 2004. T.A.G.S. provides consultation to big-game hunters to help select destinations, and assists with filling out and submitting application forms. They will even float tag fees.

The easiest, most reliable and complete service assisting hunters in drawing premium big-game tags, T.A.G.S. is the fastest-growing portion of the Outdoor Adventures division, in part because it is so cost-effective and worry-free for the hunter.

Dick and Mary – Two Hearts, One Passion

Tanzania, 1992

"Some of us are just meant to be hunters."
– Dick Cabela, from Dick and Mary's book *Two Hearts, One Passion*

Mexico, 2001

Mexico, 2001

Cameroon, 2001

Tanzania, 2002

Tanzania, 1995

South Africa, 2003

South Africa, 1999

President Reagan welcomed Dick and Mary Cabela to the White House

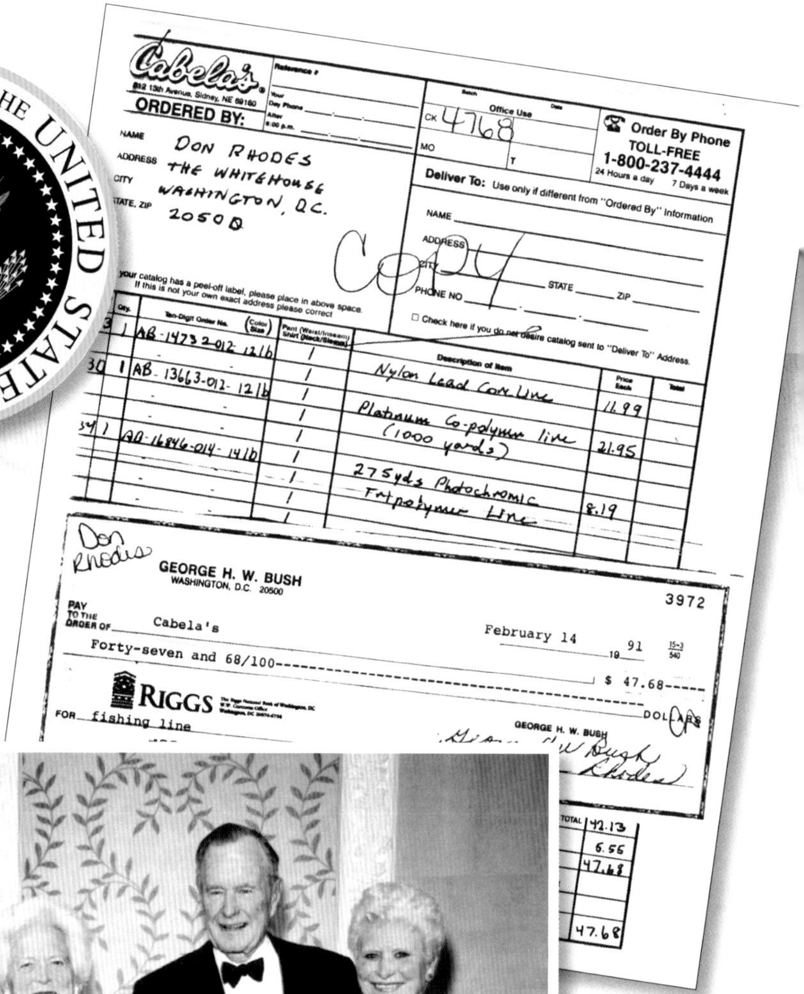
Cabela's
812 13th Avenue, Sidney, NE 69160
ORDERED BY:
NAME DON RHODES
ADDRESS THE WHITEHOUSE
CITY WASHINGTON, D.C.
STATE, ZIP 20500
Office Use
CK 4768
Order By Phone TOLL-FREE 1-800-237-4444 24 Hours a day 7 Days a week
Deliver To: Use only if different from "Ordered By" Information
NAME
ADDRESS
CITY STATE ZIP
PHONE NO
Check here if you do not desire catalog sent to "Deliver To" Address.
COPY
If your catalog has a peel-off label, please place in above space. If this is not your own exact address please correct

Qty.	Ten-Digit Order No.	(Color Size)	Description of Item	Price Each
1	AB-14732-012-12lb		Nylon Lead Core Line	11.99
1	AB-13663-012-12lb		Platinum Co-polymer line (1000 yards)	21.95
1	AB-16846-014-14lb		275yds Photochromic Tri-polymer Line	8.19

TOTAL 42.13
6.56
47.68
47.68

Don Rhodes
GEORGE H. W. BUSH
WASHINGTON, D.C. 20500
3972
PAY TO THE ORDER OF Cabela's
February 14 1991
Forty-seven and 68/100
$ 47.68
RIGGS
FOR fishing line
DOLLARS
GEORGE H. W. BUSH

President George H.W. Bush and First Lady Barbara Bush at an event with Dick and Mary Cabela in 2002.

General Norman Schwarzkopf (left) speaks with Dick Cabela at a 1995 function. The back of the photo is inscribed, "A meeting of two generals."

Mary and Dick and their daughter, Carolyn, and daughter-in-law, Cathy, exchange hunting stories with General Chuck Yeager.

Jim Cabela – Dedicated Outdoorsman

Grand Slam of North American Sheep

Desert Sheep
Mexico, 1998

Stone's Sheep
British Columbia, 1997

Dall's Sheep
Northwest Territories, 1997

Bighorn Sheep
Wyoming, 1999

"How much better can it get? You get to use the products you enjoy using and make some money on the side. It's a pretty good deal."
– Jim Cabela

Good News River, Alaska, 1986

Wyoming, 2002

Russia, 1996

Andros Island, Bahamas, 2008

Alaska, 1989

Wyoming, 2006

Jim and professional hunter, Rusty Labaschagne, Zimbabwe, 2003.

Dennis Highby – In The Field

Alaska, 1990

Zimbabwe, 2002

“It’s been the best job anyone ever had. There were a lot of good times. That’s what it was all about: working hard, playing hard and having fun doing it.”
– Dennis Highby

Kazakhstan, 1987

South Dakota, 2001

Boone and Crockett Whitetail
Typical, Measures 171⅞" net
Nebraska, 2003

Tanzania, 1998

10-foot Brown Bear, Alaska, 1994

From left, daughter Amy, Dennis, daughter Sarah, and wife Linda in Alaska.

Zimbabwe, 2001

Living the Cabela's Lifestyle

Jim and Dick Cabela, and then Dennis Highby, made sure employees got into the field to fish, hunt and camp as much as possible. Not only did some of the best and most productive business discussions occur in the field, the trips allowed employees to field-test products and, more importantly, get to know each other. This practice created a family atmosphere and led to a close-knit group of core employees, many of whom still lead the company.

On a successful goose hunt near Oshkosh, Nebraska, from left, are Pat Snyder, Jim Cabela, Matt Highby and his father, Dennis.

Cabela's monthly company newsletter "Hook, Line & Sinker" showcases employees in the field in four special Trophy Editions each year.

TROPHY EDITION OCTOBER 2010

Jon Dincau, Owatonna, Minn., asset protection manager; and his son Chandler, took these Merriam turkeys in the Black Hills of South Dakota on opening day 2010. Chandler was happy to learn that his bird was 1-lb. heavier and had a 1" longer beard than his dad's bird.

Phil Krohn, fishing/fly fishing/marine sales manager in Rogers, Minn., caught this huge 46½" northern pike in August 2010 on Red Lake in Ontario, Canada.

Aquarium Manager in Hoffman Estates Jim Galeno caught this 5-lb. smallmouth bass in Boulder Junction, Wis.

Nicole Pugliano, senior softlines manager in Billings, Mont., took these two feral billy goats on North Island New Zealand earlier this year using a Remington 700 rifle in .300 ultra short mag.

Wesley Sytsma, asset protection manager in Wheeling, W. Va., and his brother Colin (left) caught these walleye on Sturgeon Bay of Lake Michigan in August. Both fish were over 29" in length and weighed 10 and 7-lbs.

Brian Snowball from Cabela's Canada store harvested this whitetail buck in Interlake, Manitoba last November.

10

OCTOBER 2010 TROPHY EDITION

Robert Reznak, corporate RACM for marine accessories and electronics, caught this musky in Ontario, Canada with a Cabela's Pro-Guide combo and Cabela's Flat Tire Swimbait.

Post Falls Event Coordinator Pete Marion introduced Glendale Event Coordinator Pat Zeman to Lake Roosevelt in Kettle Falls, Wa., this summer where Pat caught her first walleye.

Chris Harris, nephew of Lisa Stewart, category administrator in the hunting/archery/optics department at Corporate, took this turkey with his 12-gauge in Chariton, Iowa.

Owatonna Retail Back End Manager Steve Meschke harvested these two pheasants on opening day 2009 at the Meschke family farm in Morristown, Minn.

Mike Campos, brother of Bryan Campos, onboarding specialist in the Sidney, Neb. corporate offices, shot this nice 4x5 mule deer in full velvet with his PSE X-Force Bow in Nevada in early fall 2009.

Evan Harpster, cousin of Jared Dirkschneider, research analyst at WFB, caught this giant walleye in May 2010. The fish measured 32" and weighed 10½-lbs.

11

Cabela's Executive Team

South Dakota, 2004

Tommy Millner, Chief Executive Officer

Austria, 2009

New Mexico, 2010

Labrador, Canada, 1995

Cabela's Executive Team

Pat Snyder,
Executive Vice President and Chief Marketing Officer

Ralph Castner, Executive Vice President
and Chief Financial Officer

Brian Linneman,
Executive Vice President and Chief Merchandising Officer

Cabela's Executive Team

Michael Copeland,
Executive Vice President and Chief Operations Officer

Charles Baldwin, Executive Vice President
and Chief Administration Officer, and son Cameron

Doug Means, Executive Vice President
and Chief Supply Chain Officer

Joe Friebe, Executive Vice President
Chief Executive Officer, World's Foremost Bank

BEAR
OF AN OUTDOORSMAN
CHARLES KROLL

Chapter 5

Retail Becomes Tourism

– The 1990s –

North American diorama at Cabela's in Kearney, Nebraska.

Although Cabela's was founded as a mail-order catalog company, there had been a retail-store element from the beginning. After all, those first fishing flies Dick bought in Chicago in 1961 were intended to be sold in the sporting-goods section of the family furniture store. Walk-in customer traffic began with Cabela's locations in Chappell and continued at the headquarters in Sidney, where the first-floor retail department became a stopping point for regional outdoor sportsmen.

"When we moved to the old John Deere building, there was not a formal retail presence," said Sharon Robison. "Local people would walk in the front door and say, 'My couch broke. Can you fix it?' They thought they were coming to Cabela's furniture store, which was well-known throughout the area." Eventually, an appropriate retail space was created to meet customer demand for outdoor gear, not furniture.

Tom Rosdail remembers walk-in customer traffic growing and growing and growing. Many would stop by Sidney to visit the store as they traveled through western Nebraska, particularly after the opening of Interstate 80. "Customers would stop to get things they had seen in our catalog," he said. "In a sense you could say Cabela's was already a 'tourist destination' long before today's huge stores were even dreamed of."

In 1985, Cabela's purchased the Rockwell building in Kearney to accommodate the growing telemarketing department. In 1987, a portion of the building was remodeled into retail space. The new store provided a unique outdoor-experience style of shopping with more than 250 wildlife mounts, including a diorama depicting a mountain lion attacking a mule deer. It was an immediate success, beyond expectations, and provided a blueprint for the next major step in Cabela's growth and evolution – a chain of retail stores across the United States and into Canada.

Retail sales had been a minor sideline, almost a distraction from the company's fundamental identity as a mail-order business. With the Kearney store's success and unexpected volume of customers – and sales, the Cabela brothers realized their customers were not only eager to order by mail and phone, but also anxious to visit a store where they could see, handle and purchase Cabela's products.

The new Kearney store did not divert much walk-in traffic from Sidney, even though it was closer to the population centers in the eastern part of the state. Ever-growing numbers of traveling Cabela's customers continued to drive into downtown Sidney, wanting to visit the "real" Cabela's. Looking ahead, Cabela's had already purchased 45 acres of property near Sidney's I-80 exit. In 1991 the brothers took another leap into uncharted territory and opened the first stand-alone Cabela's catalog showroom.

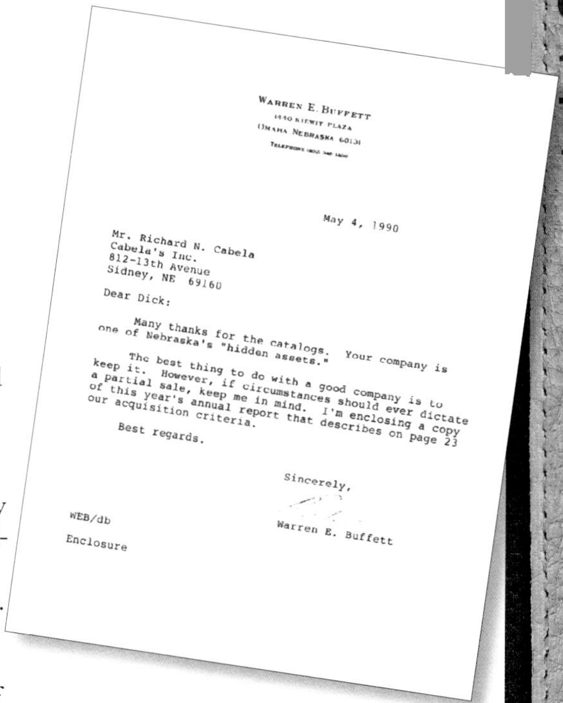

WARREN E. BUFFETT
1440 KIEWIT PLAZA
OMAHA, NEBRASKA 68131
Telephone [illegible]

May 4, 1990

Mr. Richard N. Cabela
Cabela's Inc.
812-13th Avenue
Sidney, NE 69160

Dear Dick:

Many thanks for the catalogs. Your company is one of Nebraska's "hidden assets."

The best thing to do with a good company is to keep it. However, if circumstances should ever dictate a partial sale, keep me in mind. I'm enclosing a copy of this year's annual report that describes on page 23 our acquisition criteria.

Best regards.

Sincerely,

Warren E. Buffett

WEB/db

Enclosure

Cabela's Time Line

1990s

1990

- Nick Wilson hired. Vice President of Distribution Centers
- Total revenue: $188,656,402.

1991

- Sidney catalog showroom opens in July.
- Gun Library introduced
- Total revenue: $208,251,174.

1992

- Cabela's acquired five additional buildings at the former Sioux Army Depot
- Total revenue: $234,488,141.

1993

- Total revenue: $283,341,786.

1994

- Dick and Jim Cabela inducted into Nebraska Business Hall of Fame.
- First specialty catalog: Tackle Shop
- Partnership contract signed by Cabela's and National Bank of Commerce to create Cabela's CLUB Visa.
- Total revenue: $346,557,490.

1995

- Ron Spath hired, now Vice President of Customer Experience.
- Total revenue: $420,736,663.

Artist's rendering of Sidney, Nebraska catalog showroom.

The Sidney showroom was 85,000 square feet (later to grow to 104,000 square feet with the addition of a boat shop), with a ceiling rising more than 50 feet. Designed to provide a unique outdoor atmosphere, it contains more than 500 trophy mounts and includes a 27-foot-tall mountain replica with 40 full-body North American big-game mounts. Outside is a 34-foot-wide bronze sculpture of two battling elk, titled Royal Challenge.

The Sidney store contained many of the items offered in Cabela's catalogs, plus special items only available in the store. The former bargain basement became the Bargain Cave, containing overstocked, discontinued, one-of-a-kind and returned goods at marked-down prices. The hunting department also featured the first Cabela's Gun Library, offering collectible, investment-grade and limited-edition firearms.

Cabela's did not advertise the first day the store would open, but word of mouth alone brought in 3,000 customers. The official grand opening, in September 1991, attracted more than three times that many. By the end of the decade, nearly 1 million customers per year would be pulling off I-80 or flying into the Sidney airport to visit the showroom. It had become a top tourist attraction.

The lessons were not lost on the Cabela's management team. For one thing, the success of the Sidney flagship showroom completely upended all marketing experts' long-held belief that the three most important elements of success for any kind of retail operation are location, location, location. Sidney is located nearly 200 miles from the nearest major population center of Denver. But given the passionate loyalty of Cabela's huge and ever-growing customer base, the Sidney catalog showroom instantly proved the concept

"If you build it, they will come." Its continued success meant the only question remaining was where to build the next store.

The Retail Boom Begins

By 1998 that question was answered with the opening of the next Cabela's catalog showroom in Owatonna, Minnesota, about 50 miles south of Minneapolis on Interstate 35. Minnesota is a popular hunting and fishing state for residents and thousands of sportsmen and women who travel there each year. Dick and Jim decided to make the new store even larger than Sidney's. The 150,000-square-foot store would feature a 35-foot Conservation Mountain with more than 100 full-body mounts and more than 600 other trophy mounts throughout. An eight-ton bronze whitetail sculpture outside the front entrance stands 27 feet tall.

Dick and Jim during construction of the Sidney, Nebraska catalog showroom.

The scale model of "Royal Challenge" the 34-ft. bronze statue at the Sidney, Nebraska store.

1996
- Marketing Department created
- Joe Friebe hired. Executive Vice President of Cabela's and President and CEO of World's Foremost Bank.
- Total revenue: $496,027,686.

1997
- Total revenue: $558,918,588

1998
- Headquarters moved into new 120,000-square-foot facility in Sidney, Nebraska adjacent to the retail store.
- Third store opened April in Owatonna, Minnesota (120,000 customers opening weekend).
- Distribution center completed in Prairie du Chien, Wisconsin; the attached store opened in September
- cabelas.com launched
- Total revenue: $666,120,538.

1999
- Brian Linneman hired for supply chain administration, now Executive Vice President and Chief Merchandising Officer
- Cabela's listed by Fortune magazine as one of 100 Best Companies to Work For.
- Fifth store opened September 29 in East Grand Forks, Minnesota
- Dick and Jim Cabela receive the Ernst & Young Entrepreneurs of the Year award in Retail/ Consumer Products category.
- Total revenue: $770,631,000.

Owatonna, Minnesota catalog showroom.

Owatonna, Minnesota Conservation Mountain.

Owatonna, Minnesota aquarium.

The Owatonna showroom opened on April 1, 1998, and welcomed 120,000 customers its first weekend. The official grand-opening week from May 30 to June 7 included celebrity guests such as Iditarod Trail Sled-Dog Race champion Jeff King, General Chuck Yeager and former Minnesota Vikings head coach Bud Grant. By July the customer count had exceeded 1 million, and in the first year of operation nearly 4 million shoppers had walked through the front doors.

Dick and Jim's confidence in Owatonna's success led to the decision to build a fourth catalog showroom connected to the new distribution center in Prairie du Chien, which opened only five months after Owatonna. The Prairie du Chien showroom is a "mere" 40,000 square feet, sized for a town of 5,500 people located in a popular outdoor destination area.

The store also has a unique capability to offset its smaller size. By being attached to Cabela's 720,000-square-foot distribution center, its in-house catalog-order department allows customers to select almost any item in any Cabela's catalog and have it brought directly to them from the warehouse. This is a grand-scale throwback to the early days in Chappell when walk-in customers had their pick of in-stock items direct from the shelves and, later, the days of dropping merchandise floor-to-floor in the Sidney store. Even with the huge Owatonna store nearby, nearly 200,000 customers visited the Prairie du Chien showroom in its first three months of operation, drawing traffic from regional population centers from Cedar Rapids, Iowa, to Madison, Wisconsin, to Chicago.

The final Cabela's catalog showroom to be built in the 1990s opened in East Grand Forks, Minnesota, in September 1999. In a sense it represented a return to the original concept of the Sidney showroom, being relatively modest in size (60,000 square feet) and located in a community of 8,000 adjacent to Interstate 29, just 80 miles south of the U.S./Canada border. Like the Sidney store, it draws traffic from traveling hunters and anglers, as well as Canadian residents. It is a full-fledged Cabela's showroom nonetheless, with features keyed to its regional location.

With a map of the United States tracking Cabela's rapid growth across the country as a backdrop, Dick and Jim pose with their father, A.C. in 1992.

Cabela's store in Prairie du Chien, Wisconsin.

Smoke from the opening shot hasn't settled before the dash for bargains begins at this 1990s sidewalk sale in Sidney, Nebraska.

The rapid pace of openings for Cabela's retail stores continued into the 2000s, with 31 stores in operation as of 2010, ranging from Scarborough, Maine, to Lacey, Washington, and from Buda, Texas, to Winnipeg, Manitoba. Their impact on both Cabela's customers and the economies of the towns and regions in which they are located has been remarkable. They have also changed the face of tourism for hundreds of thousands of outdoorsmen and their families, who now mark Cabela's stores as destinations on their vacation maps. Cabela's retail employees from coast to coast report thousands of customers who check off visits to stores one by one just as they keep track of their national park passport stamps. It is a mixture of shopping trip and vacation unique in American business history.

There is no better proof of this fact than the Sidney store's sidewalk sale, first instituted at the old brick headquarters building in the early '70s. According to Sharon Robison, sidewalk sales originated as a means of clearing returned items. "At that time, we didn't really categorize anything that came back. We just put it in piles downstairs. The sales were just a 'get rid of everything cheap' way of cleaning out the returned and discontinued merchandise."

By the end of the 1990s, the annual sidewalk sale was drawing more than 15,000 customers, more than twice Sidney's population. The earliest arrivals showed up as early as two weeks and camped out to hold their place in line. License plates on vehicles in the parking lot represented every state except Hawaii. It was a national "family reunion" for outdoorsmen, and many who had attended for years planned family vacations so they could meet with friends in the Cabela's parking lot before the opening gun announced the beginning of the sale.

How far can Cabela's spread its retail stores? Based on their experience so far, the Cabela's management team sees no limit. According to Pat Snyder, "I don't think it will stop. As of 2010, the retail portion is just more than 50 percent of Cabela's revenues. With a very successful and profitable retail model, we expect to grow much,

Cabela's Stores in High Demand

Cabela's receives a steady stream of requests from customers across the country clamoring for stores to be built in their hometowns. They insist the company has the potential to make a lot of money. "People love to hunt and fish here," they say. And there's no doubt that's true. But a lot of research goes into choosing a new Cabela's store location.

When considering a potential store site, the company's market research team analyzes everything from catalog and Internet sales histories to demographics, competition, traffic flow and market demand in the area.

"We examine every piece of meaningful information," said Michael Copeland, Cabela's Executive Vice President and Chief Operations Officer. "But it has to make sense. All of the data must support the choice, not just one or two pieces of the puzzle."

To Copeland, it comes as no surprise Cabela's stores are in such high demand.

"A Cabela's store brings hundreds of jobs to a city and our reputation as a growing, reliable company makes us a sought-after neighbor," he said.

Once a location has been selected, the company gets to work on specifics, like square footage, department layout and product selection. Most Cabela's stores are new, stand-alone buildings, but a few are attached to shopping malls, some of which have been re-purposed. The Grand Junction, Colorado, location, which opened in 2010, previously housed a department store.

The Grand Junction store is one of the company's smallest at around 80,000 square feet. But some stores, in Hamburg, Pennsylvania, Dundee, Michigan, and Fort Worth, Texas, cover more than 225,000 square feet. Copeland said that every square foot of space is accounted for and the product selection varies depending on location.

"Our merchandisers begin aligning product based on the needs of the customers in the area well before we break ground for the building," he said. "Before a single truckload of gear arrives at a new store it has been assigned a shelf number or allotted floor space."

Copeland added that there is little room for error in all the planning it takes to prepare a store for opening, not only in terms of product assortments, but also personnel.

"Many of our customers are experts when it comes to outdoor recreation," he said. "We can't afford to hire employees who are anything less than specialists in their area of expertise. We even invest in internal education programs to further hone our associates' knowledge.

"We're willing to do whatever it takes to exceed our customers' expectations and make sure Cabela's locations continue to be the most popular destinations for outdoor enthusiasts."

A sidewalk sale in Sidney, Nebraska.

much more. If a market is suitable, if profitability is there, we will continue to build stores."

Looking at how the retail channel fits into the overall Cabela's picture, Pat observes, "Not long ago, everybody said the Internet was the place for growth. Well, we now have the largest Internet site in the sports-and-fitness market, and it is growing, and our catalog is the same. Yes, we do give up a certain amount of catalog and Internet business in the area when we open a store. But within 12 to 18 months we are back to where we were with catalog. In fact, both of those increase because of the exposure created by the retail stores."

> **"In-Store Pick Up assures customers that the merchandise they want is available and is being held for them at a store. It makes our customers' shopping trips more productive."**
>
> – Pat Snyder

Pat believes all three approaches complement each other. "Some customers prefer to shop out of a catalog, so they call the 800 number. Some want the convenience of shopping via the Internet. Some customers want to touch and feel, look at the product, have someone demonstrate it and talk to someone about it face to face. They go to our stores. That face-to-face market is limited only by how many people have a store within driving distance. In that sense, retail expansion is virtually unlimited for us."

Pat also points to a new era of integration that will help shoppers. Under the In-Store Pick Up (ISP) program, a customer can select a product from a catalog, the cabelas.com website, or while at a store and have it shipped free of charge from a distribution center to any store where they can then pick it up. This program essentially makes accessible the entire range of in-stock Cabela's products by networking Cabela's catalog, website, retail and distribution operations.

"ISP assures customers that the merchandise they want is available and is being held for them at a store," Pat said. "It makes our customers' shopping trips more productive."

Gun Library – Boise, Idaho

Gun Library – Hamburg, Pennsylvania

Gun Library – Mitchell, South Dakota

Gun Library – Owatonna, Minnesota

Gun Library – Richfield, Wisconsin

Gun Library – Sidney, Nebraska

The Gun Libraries

Gun Libraries are a unique aspect of Cabela's stores. Before they had retail locations, Cabela's could not sell firearms, except for black-powder firearms, through catalogs because of federal law. But with retail locations, the Cabela brothers' life-long appreciation for fine guns finally had an outlet. According to Tom Rosdail, "We always had firearms in the store in downtown Sidney, but the Gun Library concept we have now wouldn't work if we didn't have the national network of stores to support it."

Cabela's Gun Libraries are not gun stores per se, though conventional production firearms are sold in all Cabela's stores. Gun Libraries feature some of the finest, most historically significant and collectible guns in the world.

Tom says the Gun Library "is like the World's Foremost Used Gun Store, on steroids." He adds, "Two full-time firearms experts scour the country looking for firearms. The best sources are leads from customers. For example, someone wants to sell their firearms collection. We make arrangements to appraise it. The seller is able to liquidate the collection and we put great firearms back on the market."

Cabela's Gun Libraries are like firearms museums, a museum where displayed items can be purchased. Prices can be as low as a few hundred dollars, though turning over some price tags can reveal a five- or six-figure price. And historical finds can turn up anytime, including a "1 of 1,000" Winchester Model 73 Cabela's purchased from a pioneer family in Montana. That's the "Winchester 73" title gun of the famous James Stewart movie. "We have found famous outlaws' guns with notches in the handles; guns with stories to tell if they could talk," Tom said. "One of our stores once had a World War II anti-aircraft gun that had been converted to shoot shotgun shells. That was certainly unique. I think it sold for $20,000."

Cabela's first specialty catalog targeted at a specific customer segment.

Diversifying the Catalogs

Even as the retail stores and later online sales grew to prominence in the Cabela's story, Cabela's catalogs remained its core business, growing and diversifying with each passing year. And from the beginning, the creation and production of catalogs have been an in-house operation. That's significant, considering Cabela's mails more than 130 million catalogs a year.

During the early 1990s, as other special-focus companies began to imitate some of Cabela's business practices, it became apparent to Cabela's that its traditional format of all-encompassing spring and fall catalogs needed to be refined and more targeted. That led to Cabela's first specialty catalog, the Tackle Shop catalog, which was published in 1994. Today, Cabela's annually publishes more than 90 titles, including the prized, limited-edition 1,300-plus-page hard-bound catalogs.

Doug Zingula, Vice President of Merchandising Support Services, remembers, "When I started in 1981, we had about $19 million in annual sales, and you wore a lot of hats like you would in any small company. We would meet with vendors and make product selections, then we had to produce the catalog. The catalog was the business." The process of designing catalogs was carefully thought out. "We also set up our pages," says Doug. "Which pages will have which products and which products will I place where on the page? We would draw on blank sheets of paper for the photographer to show how we wanted the products laid out and how much copy block to allow. There were no copywriters, so we wrote our own copy. We did everything, down to working with photographers to get the shots. It was really a cradle-to-grave process. Still is, just much, much bigger."

Another important aspect of the business was the mailing lists, Doug said. "We might have the best system for producing catalogs, but if we don't have somebody in our marketing department who understands our customers and is making an accurate analysis to ensure we are sending catalogs to the right people, it doesn't matter," Doug said.

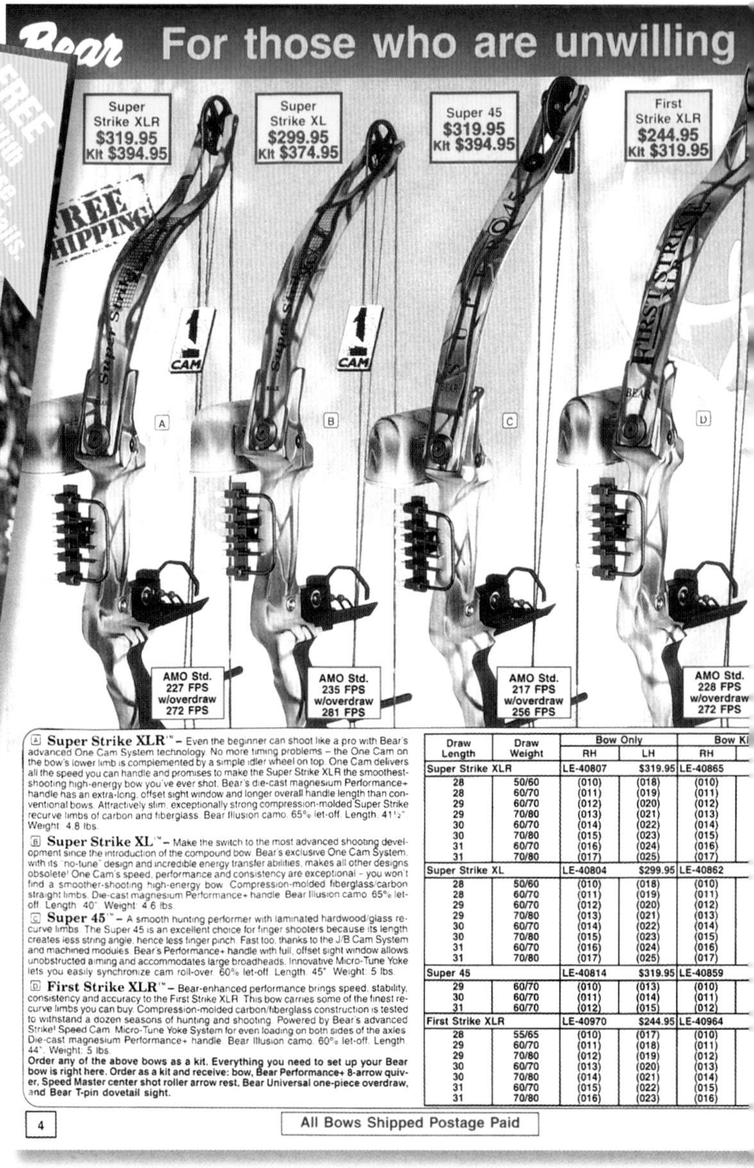

Bear For those who are unwilling

Super Strike XLR $319.95 Kit $394.95

Super Strike XL $299.95 Kit $374.95

Super 45 $319.95 Kit $394.95

First Strike XLR $244.95 Kit $319.95

FREE SHIPPING

A — AMO Std. 227 FPS w/overdraw 272 FPS

B — AMO Std. 235 FPS w/overdraw 281 FPS

C — AMO Std. 217 FPS w/overdraw 256 FPS

D — AMO Std. 228 FPS w/overdraw 272 FPS

A **Super Strike XLR™** – Even the beginner can shoot like a pro with Bear's advanced One Cam System technology. No more timing problems – the One Cam on the bow's lower limb is complemented by a simple idler wheel on top. One Cam delivers all the speed you can handle and promises to make the Super Strike XLR the smoothest-shooting high-energy bow you've ever shot. Bear's die-cast magnesium Performance+ handle has an extra-long, offset sight window and longer overall handle length than conventional bows. Attractively slim, exceptionally strong compression-molded Super Strike recurve limbs of carbon and fiberglass. Bear Illusion camo. 65% let-off. Length: 41½". Weight: 4.8 lbs.

B **Super Strike XL™** – Make the switch to the most advanced shooting development since the introduction of the compound bow. Bear's exclusive One Cam System, with its "no-tune" design and incredible energy transfer abilities, makes all other designs obsolete! One Cam's speed, performance and consistency are exceptional – you won't find a smoother-shooting high-energy bow. Compression-molded fiberglass/carbon straight limbs. Die-cast magnesium Performance+ handle. Bear Illusion camo. 65% let-off. Length: 40". Weight: 4.6 lbs.

C **Super 45™** – A smooth hunting performer with laminated hardwood/glass recurve limbs. The Super 45 is an excellent choice for finger shooters because its length creates less string angle, hence less finger pinch. Fast too, thanks to the J/B Cam System and machined modules. Bear's Performance+ handle with full, offset sight window allows unobstructed aiming and accommodates large broadheads. Innovative Micro-Tune Yoke lets you easily synchronize cam roll-over. 60% let-off. Length: 45". Weight: 5 lbs.

D **First Strike XLR™** – Bear-enhanced performance brings speed, stability, consistency and accuracy to the First Strike XLR. This bow carries some of the finest recurve limbs you can buy. Compression-molded carbon/fiberglass construction is tested to withstand a dozen seasons of hunting and shooting. Powered by Bear's advanced Strike! Speed Cam. Micro-Tune Yoke System for even loading on both sides of the axles. Die-cast magnesium Performance+ handle. Bear Illusion camo. 60% let-off. Length: 44". Weight: 5 lbs.

Order any of the above bows as a kit. Everything you need to set up your Bear bow is right here. Order as a kit and receive: bow, Bear Performance+ 8-arrow quiver, Speed Master center shot roller arrow rest, Bear Universal one-piece overdraw, and Bear T-pin dovetail sight.

Draw Length	Draw Weight	Bow Only		Bow Ki
		RH	LH	RH
Super Strike XLR		LE-40807	$319.95	LE-40865
28	50/60	(010)	(018)	(010)
28	60/70	(011)	(019)	(011)
29	60/70	(012)	(020)	(012)
29	70/80	(013)	(021)	(013)
30	60/70	(014)	(022)	(014)
30	70/80	(015)	(023)	(015)
31	60/70	(016)	(024)	(016)
31	70/80	(017)	(025)	(017)
Super Strike XL		LE-40804	$299.95	LE-40862
28	50/60	(010)	(018)	(010)
28	60/70	(011)	(019)	(011)
29	60/70	(012)	(020)	(012)
29	70/80	(013)	(021)	(013)
30	60/70	(014)	(022)	(014)
30	70/80	(015)	(023)	(015)
31	60/70	(016)	(024)	(016)
31	70/80	(017)	(025)	(017)
Super 45		LE-40814	$319.95	LE-40859
29	60/70	(010)	(013)	(010)
30	60/70	(011)	(014)	(011)
31	60/70	(012)	(015)	(012)
First Strike XLR		LE-40970	$244.95	LE-40964
28	55/65	(010)	(017)	(010)
29	60/70	(011)	(018)	(011)
29	70/80	(012)	(019)	(012)
30	60/70	(013)	(020)	(013)
30	70/80	(014)	(021)	(014)
31	60/70	(015)	(022)	(015)
31	70/80	(016)	(023)	(016)

4

All Bows Shipped Postage Paid

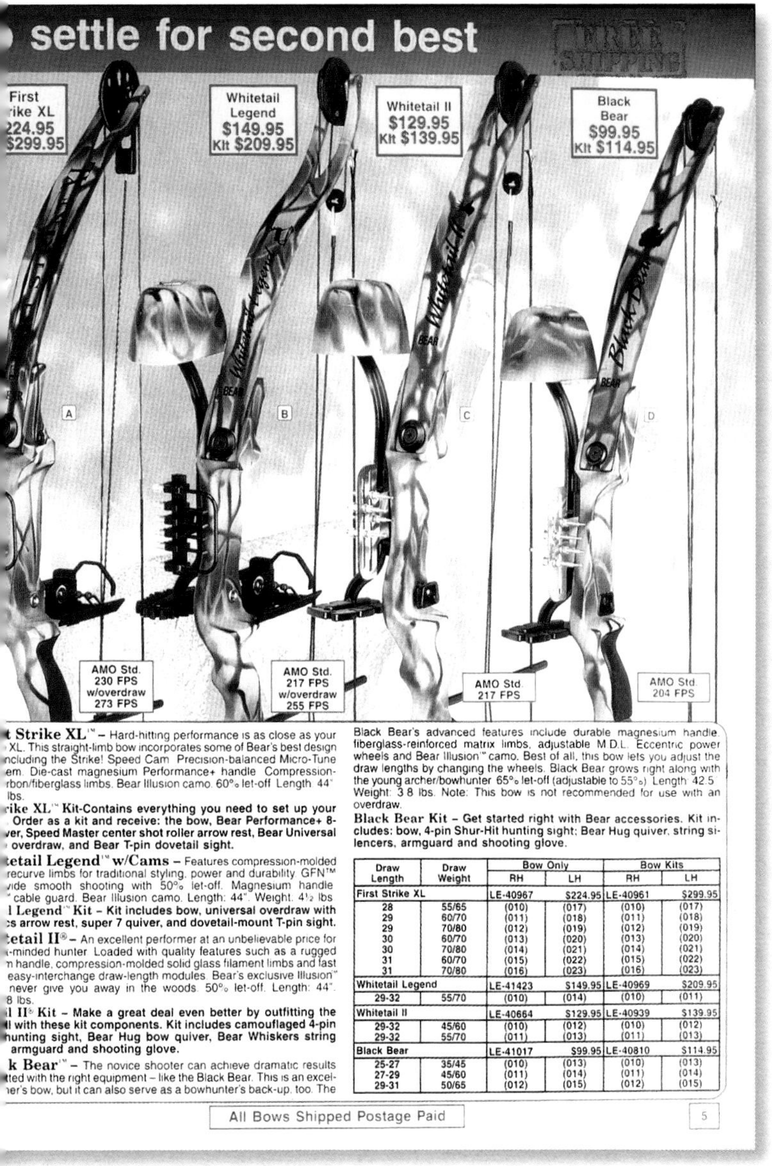

settle for second best

FREE SHIPPING

First
rike XL
224.95
$299.95

Whitetail
Legend
$149.95
Kit $209.95

Whitetail II
$129.95
Kit $139.95

Black
Bear
$99.95
Kit $114.95

A

B

C

D

AMO Std.
230 FPS
w/overdraw
273 FPS

AMO Std.
217 FPS
w/overdraw
255 FPS

AMO Std.
217 FPS

AMO Std.
204 FPS

t Strike XL™ – Hard-hitting performance is as close as your XL. This straight-limb bow incorporates some of Bear's best design ncluding the Strike! Speed Cam. Precision-balanced Micro-Tune em. Die-cast magnesium Performance+ handle. Compression-rbon/fiberglass limbs. Bear Illusion camo. 60% let-off. Length: 44" lbs.

rike XL™ Kit-Contains everything you need to set up your Order as a kit and receive: the bow, Bear Performance+ 8-ver, Speed Master center shot roller arrow rest, Bear Universal overdraw, and Bear T-pin dovetail sight.

tetail Legend™ w/Cams – Features compression-molded recurve limbs for traditional styling, power and durability. GFN™ vide smooth shooting with 50% let-off. Magnesium handle " cable guard. Bear Illusion camo. Length: 44". Weight: 4½ lbs.

l Legend™ Kit – Kit includes bow, universal overdraw with cs arrow rest, super 7 quiver, and dovetail-mount T-pin sight.

tetail II® – An excellent performer at an unbelievable price for -minded hunter. Loaded with quality features such as a rugged n handle, compression-molded solid glass filament limbs and fast easy-interchange draw-length modules. Bear's exclusive Illusion™ never give you away in the woods. 50% let-off. Length: 44". 8 lbs.

l II® Kit – Make a great deal even better by outfitting the ll with these kit components. Kit includes camouflaged 4-pin hunting sight, Bear Hug bow quiver, Bear Whiskers string armguard and shooting glove.

k Bear™ – The novice shooter can achieve dramatic results tted with the right equipment – like the Black Bear. This is an excel-ner's bow, but it can also serve as a bowhunter's back-up, too. The Black Bear's advanced features include durable magnesium handle, fiberglass-reinforced matrix limbs, adjustable M.D.L. Eccentric power wheels and Bear Illusion™ camo. Best of all, this bow lets you adjust the draw lengths by changing the wheels. Black Bear grows right along with the young archer/bowhunter. 65% let-off (adjustable to 55%). Length: 42.5". Weight: 3.8 lbs. Note: This bow is not recommended for use with an overdraw.

Black Bear Kit – Get started right with Bear accessories. Kit includes: bow, 4-pin Shur-Hit hunting sight; Bear Hug quiver, string silencers, armguard and shooting glove.

Draw Length	Draw Weight	Bow Only		Bow Kits	
		RH	LH	RH	LH
First Strike XL		LE-40967	$224.95	LE-40961	$299.95
28	55/65	(010)	(017)	(010)	(017)
29	60/70	(011)	(018)	(011)	(018)
29	70/80	(012)	(019)	(012)	(019)
30	60/70	(013)	(020)	(013)	(020)
30	70/80	(014)	(021)	(014)	(021)
31	60/70	(015)	(022)	(015)	(022)
31	70/80	(016)	(023)	(016)	(023)
Whitetail Legend		LE-41423	$149.95	LE-40969	$209.95
29-32	55/70	(010)	(014)	(010)	(011)
Whitetail II		LE-40664	$129.95	LE-40939	$139.95
29-32	45/60	(010)	(012)	(010)	(012)
29-32	55/70	(011)	(013)	(011)	(013)
Black Bear		LE-41017	$99.95	LE-40810	$114.95
25-27	35/45	(010)	(013)	(010)	(013)
27-29	45/60	(011)	(014)	(011)	(014)
29-31	50/65	(012)	(015)	(012)	(015)

All Bows Shipped Postage Paid

5

Cabela's Catalogs

Tim Joseph, Director of Brand Management and Creative Services

In 2010, Cabela's produced 93 catalog titles for a total of more than 13,000 individually designed pages.

That's no simple feat. The company deals with all aspects of catalog preproduction internally. That means Cabela's employees handle everything from photography (more than 10,000 new photos were taken in 2010 alone), graphic design, art direction and page layout to writing, editing, proofing and legal oversight of the catalogs. From start to finish, it's a four-month process on average.

"We do everything but print and deliver them to mailboxes," said Tim Joseph, Cabela's Director of Brand Management and Creative Services. "On an average day, we have more than 500 catalog pages in various stages of production."

And Cabela's is always expanding its catalog selection. The company not only adds new titles each year, but also regularly refines its catalog format. In 2010, Cabela's started producing microbooks, characterized by their 8-inch-square size and specific product selections.

"Despite their relatively small size, these books are like regular catalogs, but much more focused," Joseph said. "We take very specific product categories, like game management, predator hunting or sporting dogs to the next level by weaving informational pieces and tips into the catalogs. It's another way for us to share knowledge of the outdoors."

It's this kind of attention to detail, he said, that makes Cabela's catalogs such a key component in Cabela's multichannel business model. The catalogs grab customers' attention and help them make selections before visiting a store or placing an online or phone order.

"Of course we're also reaching out to our customers through other channels as well as via social, digital and mobile marketing," Joseph said. "But catalogs built the foundation of this company decades ago and they still serve as the heart of Cabela's today."

Catalog production is a major team effort, too. Each page is honed to perfection as it's reviewed multiple times by dozens of employees across several departments. In addition to the designers, art directors, photographers, copywriters and pre-press coordinators who provide and manage the content and layout, Cabela's merchandisers go to great lengths to ensure each product assortment is on target.

But one of the most painstaking parts of the process, according to Joseph, is finalizing the cover, because it must convey the theme of the entire catalog in a single page.

"We have to consider whether to use art or photography, mood or product shots, and whether to include headlines or redirect copy," he said. "All these pieces have to work in harmony to demonstrate, at a glance, what that particular catalog is all about."

"With the majority of the production process handled in-house, we have complete control over the connection our catalogs make with our customers – that's important because catalogs are a vital part of our brand and, to us, they are more than just catalogs. Each is an opportunity for us to reinforce the passion for the outdoors we share with our customers."

Red River $119.95

Cabela's Red River Rifle

Red River Rifle – Though considered the best "starter" blackpowder gun on the market, the Red River is all the gun you'll ever need for hunting or target shooting. We'd say "new and improved" but that just makes you think of gimmicks and there's nothing gimmicky about this solid Hawken-style rifle that delivers pure accuracy, shot after shot. What we've done is pare away the frills that have no serious function and included all the features that affect performance. That way, we keep it affordable without sacrificing the hallmark of Cabela's blackpowder rifles – accuracy. The octagonal barrel features optimum twist for dead-on shooting. At just over 7 lbs., it's easy to carry on the trail of a trophy rack. Features include adjustable rear buckhorn sight; solid brass, oversized, trigger guard, fore-end cap, ferrules and ramrod fittings; case-hardened heavy-duty quick reacting coil spring lock for solid cock and half-cock positioning and smooth trigger pull; fine-grained hardwood stock and subtle rubber recoil pad.

Cabela's Sporterized Hawken Hunter Rifle

We've taken the Percussion Hawken and added features that make it an even better choice for today's blackpowder hunter – like a rubber recoil pad, sling swivels and blued fittings to reduce glare. Still, the foundation is the unbeatably accurate barrel with a fully-adjustable rear sight you adjust to your personal zero and double set triggers that flawlessly transmit your shooting instinct. Other features include checkered walnut stock, leather sling and engraved case-hardened lock plate.

Carbine – With lighter weight and quick-handling features, these shorter-barreled carbines are favored by timber hunters and those who face long hikes or stalks. Nothing but weight is sacrificed. They have all the stylish and functional features of the Rifle, including bull's-eye accuracy.

Synthetic Stock Carbine – With Cabela's exclusive Carbelite™ synthetic stock, this Hawken Carbine is impervious to weather and humidity that can affect your zero. Same features as the wood-stock carbine, including the leather sling.

Sporterized Hawken $179.95

Style	Land & Grooves	Barrel Length	Overall Length	Rate of Twist	Order No.	Gun Only	Order No
Sporterized Hunter (RH) Sporterized Hunter (LH)	5/5	28" 28"	45½" 45½"	All cal. 1 in 48"	XS-25851 XS-21414	$179.95 $189.95	XS-21654 XS-21657
Hunter Carbine (RH) Hunter Carbine (LH)	5/5	21" 21"	38½" 38½"	45/58 cal. 1 in 48" 50/54 cal. 1 in 24"	XS-20542 XS-20543	$179.95 $189.95	XS-20536 XS-20537
Syn. Stock Hunter Rifle	5/5	28"	45½"	All cal. 1 in 48"	XS 20866	$179.95	NA
Syn. Stock Hunter Carbine	5/5	21"	38½"	50/54 cal. 1 in 24" 45/58 cal. 1 in 48"	XS-20867	$179.95	NA
Red River Rifle (RH) Red River Rifle (LH)	5/5	28" 28"	45" 45"	50 cal. 1 in 48" and 54	XS-20784 XS-21237	$119.95 $119.95	XS-2091 XS-2280

Calibers: (045, 45 cal), (050, 50 cal), (054, 54 cal), (058, 58 cal). Red River available in 50 & 54 cal. only.

Blue order numbers designate items shipped ground UPS. Allow extra time for delivery. For Cabela's Express Delivery on iter order numbers, see page 53 for details. **MI and NY residents: Please call Cabela's Customer Service Department 1-800-237-888 ordering information. NJ resident: We cannot ship guns to your state.**

26

Cabela's 1-800-237-4444

Specialty catalogs are produced to appeal to specific customer interests.

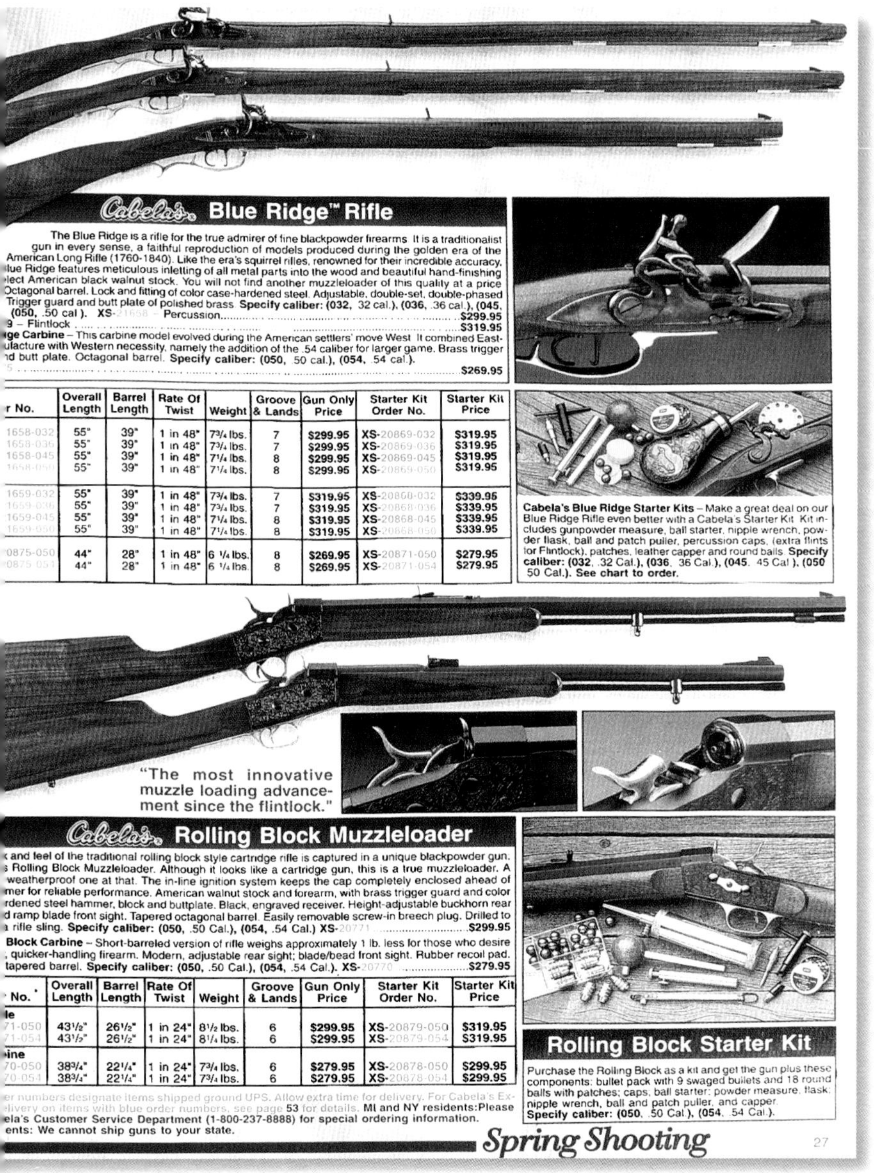

The targeted specialty catalogs proved effective, allowing Cabela's to provide a wider, more targeted range of products than could be contained within the pages of a single catalog. The annual spring and fall master catalogs continued, of course, but increasingly included only the most popular products in the most popular categories. Regular purchasers of particular product categories were identified and tracked, and they would then receive the more detailed specialty catalogs for their specific areas of interest. Another big advantage was it allowed Cabela's to respond more quickly and cost-effectively to product preference changes in particular categories, such as the rapid growth in deer hunters' use of trail cameras.

Another unforeseen benefit of the specialty catalog program was that it expanded the range of products Cabela's could successfully sell. Tom Rosdail remembers a group discussion some years ago in Dick Cabela's office concerning the high value their customers placed on the integrity of the Cabela's brand. Dick said, in jest, "Our brand is so strong, we could sell dresses." Tom said, "We all laughed, saying, 'Sure, like Cabela's is going to sell dresses.' Now the Women's Clothing catalog is one of our best specialty books." The key to its success, Tom thinks, is twofold. The first element is that every product in that catalog carries the same guarantee of satisfaction as every other product Cabela's sells. The second is that women are more likely to flip through it than they would to look for the same items buried in a master catalog.

This same strength of brand has also provided final vindication of Dick Cabela's failed "housewares flyer" notion from the early 1960s. The final key was tweaking the concept in a way that would relate it directly to the Cabela's outdoor lifestyle. Fred Neal recalls, "It was like a lot of things back in the old days. It was run and gun, try stuff, if it didn't work, you learned from it and moved on." Fred says that when he was new with the company, "Part of my category was the gift area, which was just six pages of one of the regular

Cabela's FT Series Fly Rods and Combos

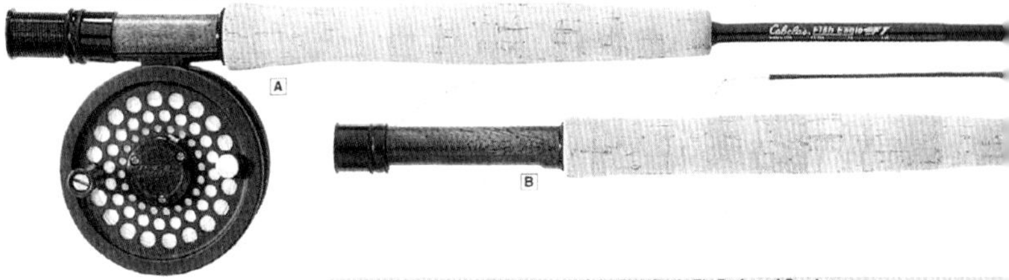

Cabela's Fish Eagle FT 2- to 4-Wt.

Fast-action rods designed for light lines with crisp actions. For tight casting situations like small, tree and brush-lined streams try the 6'6" model that really lets you feel the fight. The 8'6" model is designed for anglers who like a longer rod and want to deliver light presentations. The 8', 4-piece travel rod is designed for backpackers and travelers who never leave home without their fly rods.

					2-piece Fish Eagle Fly Rods and Combos			
					Trout	Panfish		
Model	Lgth	Line	Rod Wt.	Handle	TX-31-2115 Rod Only	TX-31-3396 Fin-Nor CR	TX-31-2116 HP	TX-31-1304 CD
FT662	6'6"	2	2.0	B	$200.00	$375.00	$335.00	$295.00
FT703	7'	3	2.1	A	$200.00	$375.00	$335.00	$295.00
FT764	7'6"	4	2.4	A	$205.00	$380.00	$340.00	$300.00
FT863	8'6"	3	2.4	A	$210.00	$385.00	$345.00	$305.00
FT904	9'	4	2.7	A	$215.00	$390.00	$350.00	$310.00
					4-piece Fish Eagle Fly Rods			
FT804-4	8'	4	3.0	A	$250.00	$425.00	$385.00	$345.00

Cabela's Fish Eagle FT 5-6 Wt.

The fast actions of this series of fly rods makes them the easy choice for casting anything from weighted nymphs and streamers to bushy, air-resistant dries and smaller dry flies and terrestrials. The 8' and 8'6" models are excellent choices for working smaller waters or when casting in challenging streams. The 9' and 10' rods are the choices when you are fishing bigger water. The 906 is our favorite when we fish bigger western waters where everything from stonefly to baetis hatches are found.

					2-piece Fish Eagle Fly Rods and Combos			
					Trout	Panfish		
Model	Lgth	Line	Rod Wt	Handle	TX-31-2115 Rod Only	TX-31-3396 Fin-Nor CR	TX-31-2116 HP	TX-31-1304 CD
FT805	8'	5	2.5	A	$210.00	$385.00	$345.00	$305.00
FT865	8'6"	5	2.6	A	$215.00	$400.00	$350.00	$310.00
FT866	8'6"	6	2.7	A	$215.00	$400.00	$360.00	$315.00
FT905	9'	5	2.8	A	$220.00	$405.00	$365.00	$320.00
FT906	9'	6	2.9	A	$220.00	$405.00	$365.00	$320.00
FT1006	10'	6	4.0	A	$240.00	$425.00	$385.00	$340.00
					4-piece Fish Eagle Fly Rods			
FT-865-4	8'6"	5	3	A	$255.00	$430.00	$390.00	$350.00
FT-905-4	9'	5	3.2	A	$260.00	$445.00	$405.00	$360.00
FT-906-4	9'	6	3.3	A	$260.00	$445.00	$405.00	$360.00

FT SERIES FLY RODS
1-800-237-4444

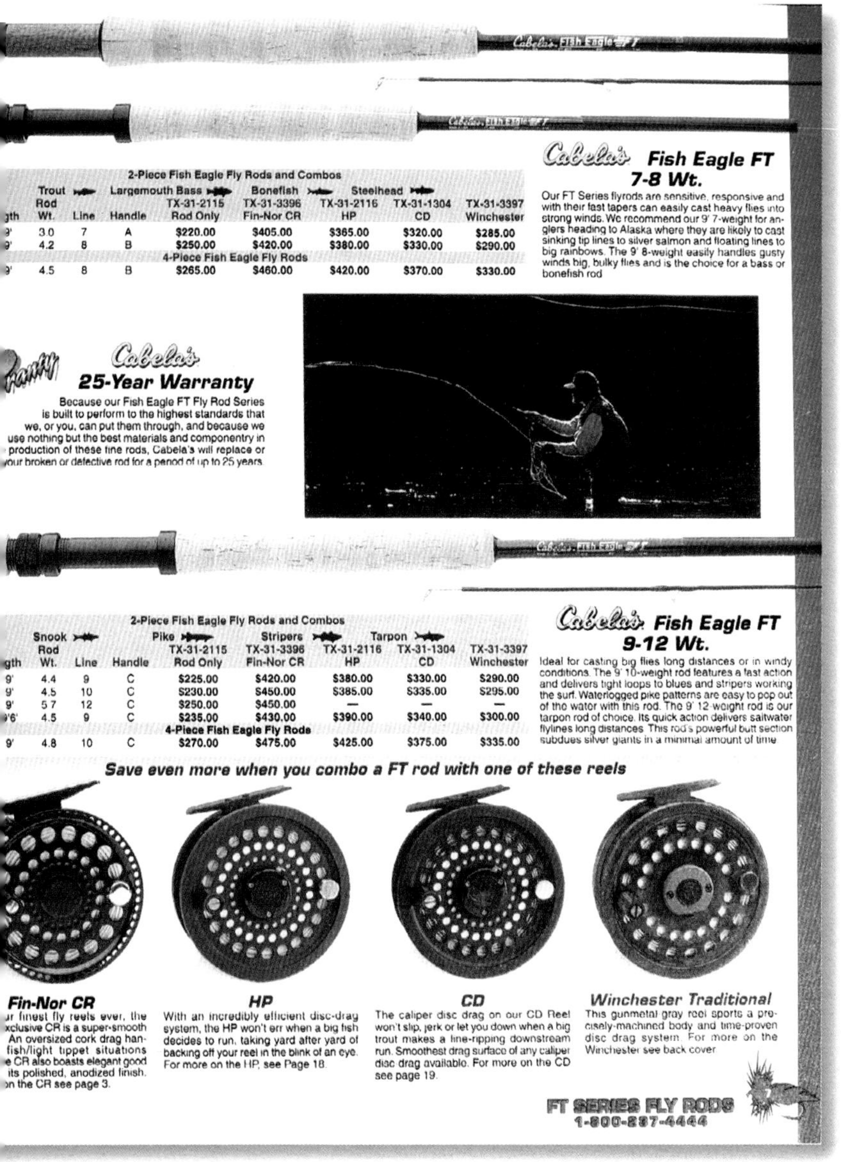

Cabela's Fish Eagle FT 7-8 Wt.

Our FT Series flyrods are sensitive, responsive and with their fast tapers can easily cast heavy flies into strong winds. We recommend our 9' 7-weight for anglers heading to Alaska where they are likely to cast sinking tip lines to silver salmon and floating lines to big rainbows. The 9' 8-weight easily handles gusty winds big, bulky flies and is the choice for a bass or bonefish rod

2-Piece Fish Eagle Fly Rods and Combos

Trout, Largemouth Bass, Bonefish, Steelhead

gth	Rod Wt.	Line	Handle	TX-31-2115 Rod Only	TX-31-3396 Fin-Nor CR	TX-31-2116 HP	TX-31-1304 CD	TX-31-3397 Winchester
9'	3.0	7	A	$220.00	$405.00	$365.00	$320.00	$285.00
9'	4.2	8	B	$250.00	$420.00	$380.00	$330.00	$290.00
4-Piece Fish Eagle Fly Rods								
9'	4.5	8	B	$265.00	$460.00	$420.00	$370.00	$330.00

Cabela's 25-Year Warranty

Because our Fish Eagle FT Fly Rod Series is built to perform to the highest standards that we, or you, can put them through, and because we use nothing but the best materials and componentry in production of these fine rods, Cabela's will replace or your broken or defective rod for a period of up to 25 years.

Cabela's Fish Eagle FT 9-12 Wt.

Ideal for casting big flies long distances or in windy conditions. The 9' 10-weight rod features a fast action and delivers tight loops to blues and stripers working the surf. Waterlogged pike patterns are easy to pop out of the water with this rod. The 9' 12-weight rod is our tarpon rod of choice. Its quick action delivers saltwater flylines long distances. This rod's powerful butt section subdues silver giants in a minimal amount of time

2-Piece Fish Eagle Fly Rods and Combos

Snook, Pike, Stripers, Tarpon

gth	Rod Wt.	Line	Handle	TX-31-2115 Rod Only	TX-31-3396 Fin-Nor CR	TX-31-2116 HP	TX-31-1304 CD	TX-31-3397 Winchester
9'	4.4	9	C	$225.00	$420.00	$380.00	$330.00	$290.00
9'	4.5	10	C	$230.00	$450.00	$385.00	$335.00	$295.00
9'	5.7	12	C	$250.00	$450.00	—	—	—
9'6'	4.5	9	C	$235.00	$430.00	$390.00	$340.00	$300.00
4-Piece Fish Eagle Fly Rods								
9'	4.8	10	C	$270.00	$475.00	$425.00	$375.00	$335.00

Save even more when you combo a FT rod with one of these reels

Fin-Nor CR
ur finest fly reels ever, the xclusive CR is a super-smooth An oversized cork drag han- fish/light tippet situations e CR also boasts elegant good its polished, anodized finish. on the CR see page 3.

HP
With an incredibly efficient disc-drag system, the HP won't err when a big fish decides to run, taking yard after yard of backing off your reel in the blink of an eye. For more on the HP, see Page 18.

CD
The caliper disc drag on our CD Reel won't slip, jerk or let you down when a big trout makes a line-ripping downstream run. Smoothest drag surface of any caliper disc drag available. For more on the CD see page 19.

Winchester Traditional
This gunmetal gray reel sports a precisely-machined body and time-proven disc drag system. For more on the Winchester see back cover

FT SERIES FLY RODS
1-800-237-4444

"Our basic customer is the consummate outdoorsman."
– Fred Neal

catalogs. My supervisor would introduce me as the 'junk buyer.' When I moved to fishing, we hired a product specialist for the gift section, and he just wouldn't quit. He'd go out on a limb with something, and if it caught on with customers, he'd go even further out. Slowly, he grew it to where we came out with a successful Home and Cabin catalog."

"It makes sense," Fred said, "our basic customer is the consummate outdoorsman. If he isn't out hunting and fishing, he's thinking about hunting and fishing. But the average guy gets to spend a limited time in the field, so he wants to surround himself with it in his home. It may be just one room or it might be the whole house. Now we're there to help him do that, to bring the outdoors indoors."

Cabela's employees moved into the 120,000-square-foot World Headquarters building in Sidney, Nebraska in early 1998. Between the headquarters building and green-roofed store in the background is Cabela's campground, which is popular with Cabela's shoppers and travelers on nearby Interstate 80. By 2002, the headquarters building had more than doubled in size.

Dick gave the welcoming speech and Jim cut the ribbon during the grand opening of the Cabela's World Headquarters in 1998.

Approaching the 21st Century

Cabela's overall sales growth during the 1990s was astronomical, increasing from $188.6 million in 1990 to $770.6 million in 1999. Since the only new Cabela's catalog showroom in operation until 1998 was in Sidney, the overwhelming portion of this growth was in the traditional Cabela's mail-order and phone-order channels. Still, as in the company's previous three decades, growth brought a never-ending search for space. In 1992 Cabela's acquired the final five buildings of the former Sioux Army Depot near Sidney, once and for all maxing out the area's existing warehouse infrastructure. It sufficed for a few years.

Not only was warehouse space an issue, personnel was running out of room in the old three-story building downtown, even after several key departments were transferred to the Sioux Depot location. Dick and Jim Cabela, therefore, followed their long-standing practice of turning revenue into growth and arranged for the construction of a new 120,000-square-foot Cabela's World Headquarters near the Cabela's store along Interstate 80. The move to the new quarters took place in early 1998, the same year as the opening of the new distribution center and store in Prairie du Chien and the Owatonna store.

It wasn't long before the new headquarters building was full. Employees were being added at an accelerated rate to keep up with demands of growth, particularly as Cabela's retail presence expanded across the country. Construction began on a 178,000-square-foot headquarters addition, nearly 150 percent larger than the original building, and in 2002 employees moved in. In addition to the headquarters building, retail showroom and adjacent campground, Cabela's employees are housed in three off-campus facilities in Sidney.

Nick Wilson, Vice President of Distribution

Even though the company had reached a size unforeseen by its founders or any early employee's wildest imaginations, its core philosophy and management style had changed little from its earliest days. Nick Wilson, who was hired in 1990 to oversee Cabela's distribution and fulfillment operations, remembers the story of how the Prairie du Chien distribution center came to be. "We were growing out of our clothes and just couldn't find any more people or places in western Nebraska. We were growing fast and needed another distribution center ASAP. I think about how simple it was. Jim told me to find a suitable location. There was no committee; there wasn't a group of people; it was just me."

Nick scouted in Iowa, southern Minnesota, the northwest corner of Illinois and southwest Wisconsin. Cabela's had a long-standing tradition of hiring people from those areas, and Nick, now Vice President of Distribution Centers, had come to Cabela's from Minnesota. "I found this location outside Prairie du Chien. Small town, six to eight thousand people, rural America, small farms around the area, a lot of small communities. I talked to local residents and asked a lot of people if they would be interested in working for us. I really got a good feeling about the area. That's how we ended up in Prairie du Chien, Wisconsin."

As the 20th century drew to a close, two developments would set the stage for continued success in the new millennium. The first was establishment of the Cabela's CLUB Visa credit card. The second was the launch of the cabelas.com website.

Cabela's 760,587 square-foot Sidney, Nebraska distribution center.

"I talked to local residents and asked a lot of people if they would be interested in working for us. I really got a good feeling about the area. That's how we ended up in Prairie du Chien, Wisconsin."

– Nick Wilson

Cabela's 1,071,000 square-foot Prairie du Chien, Wisconsin distribution center and store.

Cabela's 1,161,388 square-foot Wheeling, West Virginia distribution center.

Cabela's Partnerships

Cabela's contributions to outdoor causes and sportsmen and women have gone far beyond the long list of product innovations and comprehensive selection of items in their catalogs. Cabela's has always given back directly to the people and organizations who make the outdoor lifestyle possible. From contributions of support to local civic and outdoor organizations in the early days, to multi-million-dollar donations to hundreds of national and international outdoor sports organizations and advocacy groups, Cabela's has been a model of philanthropy for the outdoor industry.

Cabela's – with Dick, Mary and Jim leading the way – is dedicated to preserving the outdoor way of life not just because it is their business, but it is their way of life. Like Cabela's itself, the organizations it supports are dedicated to conserving the fish, game and wild places that are our heritage.

Plus, Cabela's employees are typically stalwart members of local conservation organizations, often taking leadership roles–including Dick and Mary Cabela. Dick is currently Chairman of the Board of the U.S. Sportsmen's Alliance, and Mary is chairwoman of USSA's Trailblazer Adventure Program. Another example is Cabela's President and Chief Executive Officer Tommy Millner, who serves on the Congressional Sportsman's Foundation Board of Directors and the Wildlife and Hunting Heritage Conservation Council.

Partial list of organizations with Cabela's Partnerships

4-H
Alaska Professional Hunters Association
Amateur Trapshooting Association
American Sportfishing Association
Archery Trade Association
Arizona Deer Association
Arizona Elk Society
Big Brothers & Big Sisters - Pass It On
Boone & Crockett Club
California Deer Association
California Waterfowl Association
Coastal Conservation Association
Congressional Sportsmen's Foundation
Conservation Force
Cornhusker Trapshoot
Dallas Safari Club
Deer Hunters of Idaho
Delta Waterfowl
Ducks Unlimited
Federation of Fly Fishers
FFA
Hunt of a Lifetime
International Hunter Education Association
Kids and Clays-Ronald McDonald House
Michigan Bear Hunters Association
Minnesota Deer Hunters Association
Mule Deer Foundation
Muskies Inc.
National Archery in Schools Program
National Muzzle Loading Rifle Association
National Retail Federation
National Rifle Association
National Shooting Sports Foundation
National Wild Turkey Federation
Nevada Bighorns Unlimited
North American Versatile Hunting Dog Association
Oregon Hunters Association
Outdoor Industry Association
Ovis Grand Slam
Paralyzed Veterans of America
Pheasants Forever
Pope & Young Club
Quality Deer Management Association
Rocky Mountain Elk Foundation
Ruffed Grouse Society
Safari Club International
Scholastic Clay Target Program
Sportsmen for Fish & Wildlife
Texas Parks & Wildlife
Texas Wildlife Association
Theodore Roosevelt Conservation Partnership
Tread Lightly
Treestand Manufacturer Association
Trout Unlimited
U.S. Sportsmen's Alliance
U.S.A. Shooting
Whitetails Unlimited
Wildlife Management Institute
Wild Sheep Foundation
Youth Shooting Sports Alliance

American Sportfishing Association

Boone and Crockett Club

California Deer Association

California Waterfowl

Coastal Conservation Association

Congressional Sportsmen's Foundation

DSC Dallas Safari Club

Delta Waterfowl

Ducks Unlimited

International Hunter Education Association IHEA Responsible Hunting

Minnesota Deer Hunters Association Hunting Habitat Education Legislation

The Mule Deer Foundation

NASP National Archery in the Schools Program

National Bowhunter Education Foundation Bowhunter Education

National Muzzle Loading Rifle Association Founded 1933

National Rifle Association of America Incorporated 1871

National Shooting Sports Foundation Promote • Protect • Preserve

NWTF

Pheasants Forever

Pope and Young Club

PVA Paralyzed Veterans of America

Quality Deer Management Association

Rocky Mountain Bighorn Society Founded in 1975

Rocky Mountain Elk Foundation

Ruffed Grouse Society

SCI First for Hunters

Sportsmen for Fish & Wildlife

Theodore Roosevelt Conservation Partnership Guaranteeing You a Place to Hunt and Fish

tread lightly! Leaving a good impression

Trout Unlimited

USA Shooting Team

U.S. Sportsmen's Alliance

Whitetails Unlimited

Wild Sheep Foundation

Cabela's
Mag Touch
GCII 603A Length 6' Line wt. 10-17 lbs. Lure wt. 1/4-3/4
Cabela's
A ROD THAT FE
Cabela's LSi
LSI 905-2
9'0" 5wt
Cabela's
HUNTING
Cabela's
Cabela's
Daiwa
Cabela's
2008 EDITION

Chapter 6

The World's Foremost Outfitter

– The 2000s –

In the year 2000, Cabela's was named one of the 100 Best Companies to Work for in America by Fortune magazine. Cabela's sixth and seventh retail stores opened in Mitchell, South Dakota, and Dundee, Michigan — encompassing 84,000 square-feet and 227,000 square-feet respectively. The first issue of the magazine, Cabela's Outfitter Journal, was published in July. Cabela's was experiencing growth unheard of in the outdoor industry, with total sales revenue topping $947 million. The following year, revenues would surpass $1 billion and would more than double in the next five years. By the end of 2009, Cabela's topped $2.6 billion, and there were more than 30 Cabela's retail stores in the U.S. and Canada.

Cabela's was transforming itself from a small-town mail-order company into a complex multichannel international powerhouse by incorporating cutting-edge developments in marketing and business techniques. Yet, unlike other companies in the high-tech world of the 21st century, it maintained its commitment to customer service.

The Internet Age

Nothing better exemplifies the Cabela brothers' ability to identify and adopt innovation than their early entry into online sales. According to Fred Neal, Cabela's Merchandising Director of Firearms/Shooting, "Back then, none of us knew what the Internet was, but Dick, Jim and Dennis had heard about it and they had foresight. Because Dick was so strong in direct marketing, and was the forward-thinking, big-picture guy, he figured out early that the Internet would be the catalog of the future, and he knew exactly when we should get into it."

Cabela's first website was a static informational site. In 1998, Cabela's launched a new website that allowed online ordering.

Cabela's website continues to evolve through the 2000s.

Cabela's Time Line

2000s

2000

- Cabela's named in Fortune magazine's 500 list of the 100 Best Companies to Work for in America.
- Sixth store opens in Mitchell, South Dakota.
- First issue of *Cabela's Outfitter Journal.* Joe Arterburn and Bill Bynum, founding editors.
- Seventh store opens in Dundee, Michigan
- Total revenue: $947,392,000.

2001

- World's Foremost Bank chartered for Cabela's CLUB Visa credit-card management.
- Sue Saathoff hired, now Vice President of World's Foremost Bank and Executive Vice President of Operations.
- Rated fifth most-popular catalog by Catalog Age magazine.
- Total revenue: $1,077,599,000.

"We didn't have any money budgeted for website development and had to do the whole thing on a shoestring." – Joe Friebe

Joe Friebe, Cabela's Executive Vice President and President and Chief Executive Officer of World's Foremost Bank, says, "Dick was not a technical expert on computers, but he understood that if a customer wants to place an order a certain way, you need to provide the service that allows him to do it. Did he really believe our customers needed it? I don't know. But he was smart enough to say, 'Let's let the customers tell us. Let's not presume we know what they want.' Jim agreed we should give it a shot. I wish I would have saved the letters and e-mails from people who said we were stupid to jump into it — that the Internet would never amount to anything."

Joe recalled, "When I first got to Cabela's in 1996, I was in marketing and we started talking about the Internet. Internally, we named the project 'SkunkWorks.' Dick Cabela was behind it. We built a team and their efforts resulted in a website we launched in 1996. It was a static site, not a sales site."

Joe heard about a small Internet company in Lincoln, Nebraska, that had helped develop an online store system. "We didn't have any money budgeted for website development and had to do the whole thing on a shoestring. I spent three or four days in Lincoln with tech guys from Cabela's, and we designed the system. Then some merchandising people were assigned to the project, and we pulled it together and launched the online order website in October 1998 and immediately got the first order. From that point on it snowballed."

The layout of the website was designed from a catalog perspective. "For the Internet, we coined the term 'POD,' for Product Offer Display," Joe said. "We likened it to a catalog copy block. We would visualize a catalog page with a hat, pants, coat, all the different pieces, and we could present the ensemble. We built the structure so we could show a bunch of products or a single product."

Joe is convinced the website was a major milestone for the company. "Timing was critical. Even a one-year delay would have been a problem and we would have fallen behind the competition. Today, when we talk about our direct sales, it is catalog and Internet combined that makes it work."

Cabela's decision-makers realized from the outset of the Internet era that it was not the be-all and end-all. According to Executive Vice President and Chief Merchandising Officer Brian Linneman, "Some of our customers would stop being customers if we discontinued catalogs. But there are customers to whom a catalog means nothing."

Brian believes the key to keeping Cabela's on top is to seamlessly integrate all electronic media. "Not just websites or e-mail, but the whole social marketing phenomenon, like Facebook, Twitter and YouTube. Many Cabela's customers utilize all three channels — catalog, Internet, retail — to make informed selections and then crisscross channels to buy," Brian says.

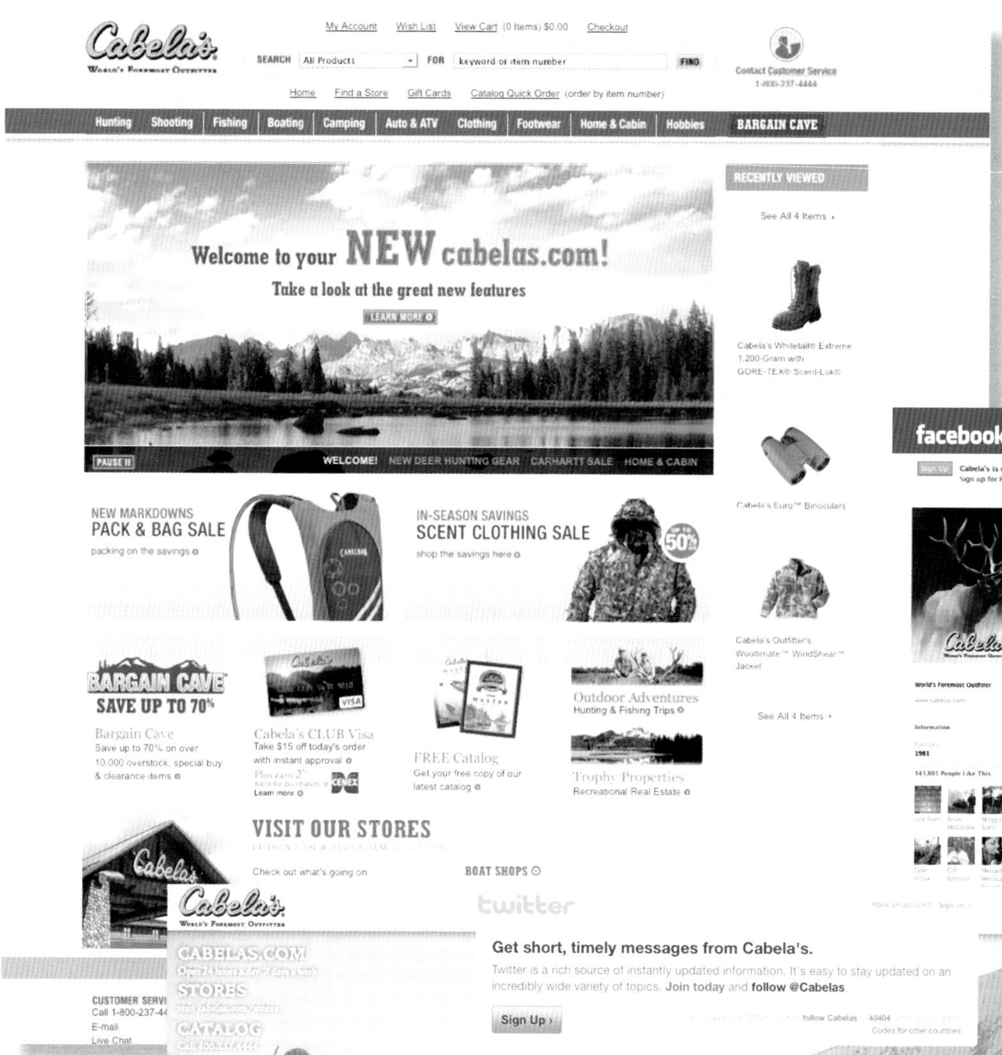

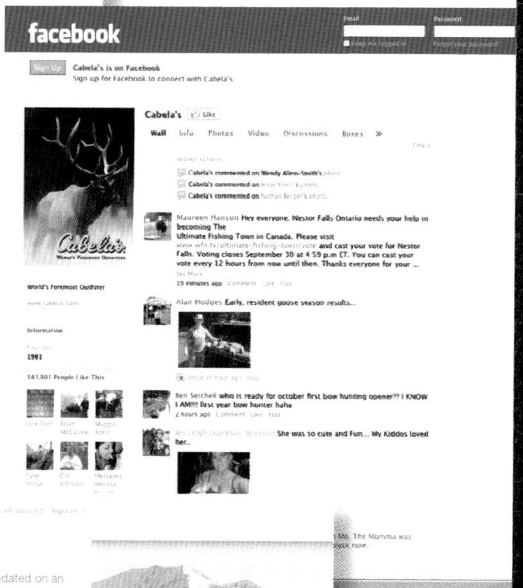

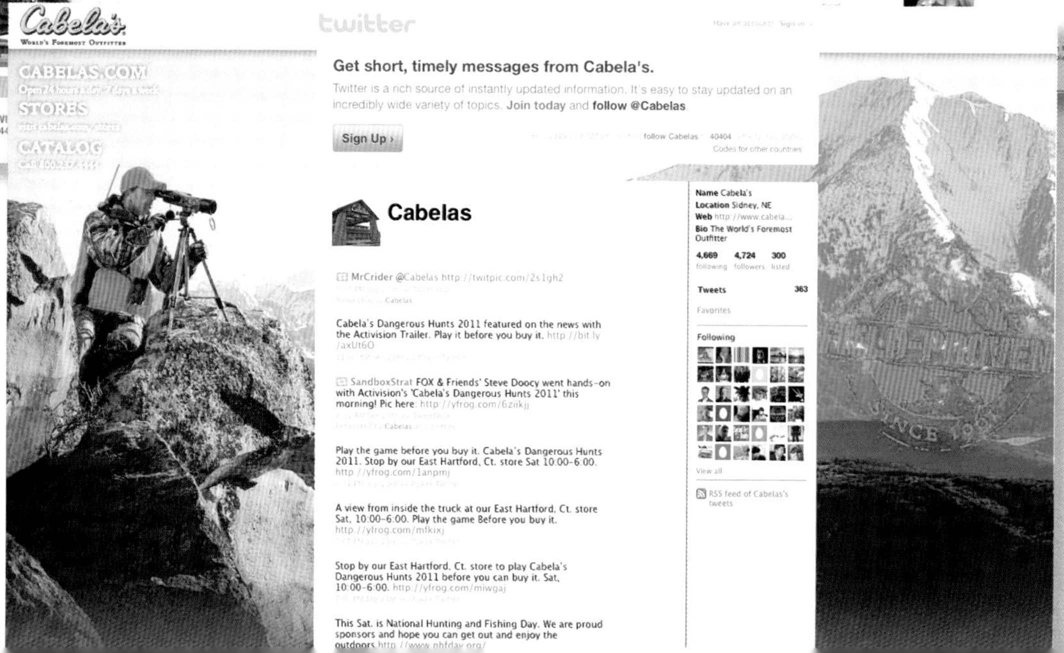

Internet-based media allows customers to easily communicate with Cabela's — and vice versa.

2002

- Eighth store opens in Kansas City, Kansas.
- Total revenue: $1,224,581,000.

2003

- Ninth store opens in Hamburg, Pennsylvania.
- Dennis Highby named President/CEO.
- Total revenue: $1,392,423,000.

2004

- Cabela's goes public on NYSE.
- 10th store opens in Wheeling, West Virginia.
- Total revenue: $1,555,974,000.

2005

- 11th store opens in Fort Worth, Texas.
- 12th store opens in Buda, Texas.
- 13th store opens in Lehi, Utah.
- 14th store opens in Rogers, Minnesota.
- Total revenue: $1,799,661,000.

> **"The reviews allow our customers to weigh in publicly on our products."**
>
> – Brian Linneman

Customer product reviews and ratings on the Cabela's website have become a popular shopping tool, and one of the major elements driving even dyed-in-the-wool print catalog shoppers online. Product reviews are often the first point of reference because shoppers can check what other people who have bought and used the products think about them.

"The reviews allow our customers to weigh in publicly on our products," Brian says. "What amazes me is how many people take time to write those reviews. It's great, the time and thought they put into it."

"The only way an online 'virtual catalog' will replace paper catalogs is when website pages finally become as easy to flip through as the paper ones," Brian says. "The technology is there. We have tried it, we have tested it. You press a button, go to the table of contents, and, say, the things you are interested in start on page 146. Click that line, and there are all the different items, just like in the catalog. Then you can flip forward or back through the pages, click on a product, and zoom in for more detail. Read the customer reviews if you want. Click on your selection; add to your cart, and place your order. It's what's coming."

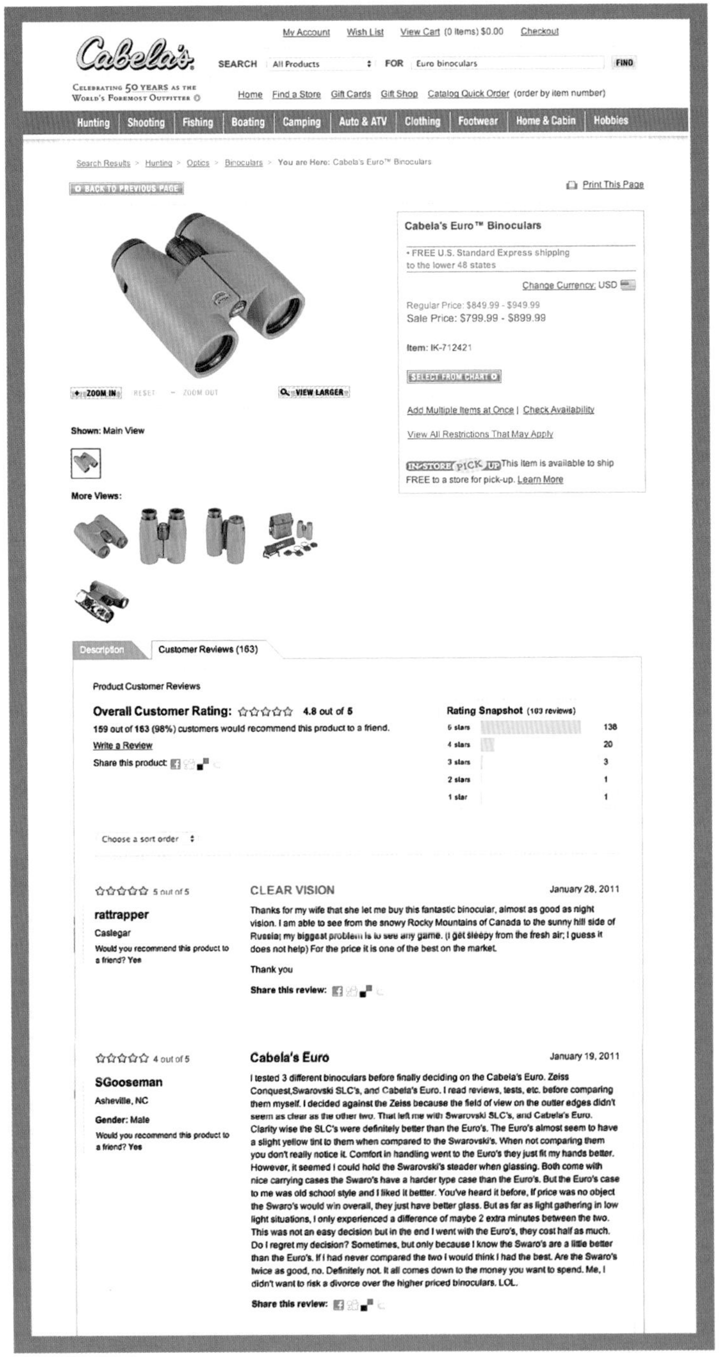

Cabela's products, service and culture available online

Mark Thompson,
Senior Director of E-Commerce.

Cabela's launched its e-commerce website in 1998, during the Internet boom. In the years since it has been recognized as a leading online source of outdoor gear and information. Most recently, industry publications have named cabelas.com one of the top five most-trusted e-commerce sites as well as the No. 1 outdoor retail site for holiday shopping.

"Part of the success is due to its vast selection," says Mark Thompson, Senior Director of E-Commerce. "Cabela's customers can find online every item featured in the company's catalogs, in addition to a wide variety of products available only on the Internet."

"Outdoor enthusiasts come to cabelas.com not only to find the best selection of gear, but also to stay informed about the company and outdoor recreation in general," Mark said. "Educational content, from product reviews to how-to articles, keep people coming back for more."

The Cabela's website also serves as a research tool for customers making in-store purchases. So it's essential that the more than 40 employees responsible for maintaining cabelas.com keep all aspects of the site polished and up to date.

In the fall of 2010, the company unveiled its most significant website redesign to date. The new site design boasted more customer-friendly navigation and the flexibility to keep pace with Cabela's ever-changing business needs.

"We're always striving to keep up with advancements in the industry and respond to what our customers want in their online experiences," Mark says. "Even before the new website was operational, we were looking at improvements to be made in the future."

But Cabela's goes to great lengths to uphold its dedication to customer service while pursuing its goal of staying on top of innovative electronic technology. Mark says the company does not take lightly its responsibility of protecting customer information.

"We're proud of our best-in-class online protection of personal information," he said. "And we back that up with diligent in-house watchdogs who work to further safeguard that data."

Whether online customers want to place an order, research products, find store locations, or manage their Cabela's and World's Foremost Bank accounts, the website offers them countless opportunities to interact with the company.

But most importantly, Mark says, "Cabelas.com makes our legendary service and gear available to outdoors people throughout the world – anytime, anyplace."

2006

- 15th store opens in Glendale, Arizona.
- 16th store opens in Boise, Idaho.
- 17th retail store opens in Richfield, Wisconsin.
- 18th retail store opens in La Vista, Nebraska.
- Total revenue: $2,063,524,000.

2007

- 19th store opens in Hazelwood, Missouri.
- Cabela's announces purchase of S.I.R. Sports Warehouse in Winnipeg.
- 20th store opens in Hoffman Estates, Illinois.
- 21st store opens in Gonzales, Louisiana.
- Cabela's CLUB Visa ranked 4th in customer satisfaction by Consumer Reports.
- 22nd store opens in East Hartford, Connecticut.
- 23rd store opens in Hammond, Indiana.
- 24th store opens in Post Falls, Idaho.
- 25th store opens in Reno, Nevada.
- 26th store opens in Lacey, Washington.

"When we open a new store, people take their kids out of school; skip work and come in wearing their Cabela's T-shirts and hats."

– Michael Copeland

Stores, Stores and More Stores

With the addition of the Mitchell and Dundee locations, the number of Cabela's stores reached seven. With the opening in 2002 of the eighth store in Kansas City, Kansas, and the ninth in Hamburg, Pennsylvania, a year later, it was time for the Cabela brothers and their management team to develop a strategic retail plan.

According to Brian Linneman, "Until 2003, store ventures were not seen as a growth strategy. Every new store increased our customer base, so the new stores were building our brand. We had our first annual strategic planning meeting in 2003. We established a vision of how we were going to grow the overall business strategically. That's when we settled on retail as a significant growth channel for Cabela's."

From then on, says Cabela's Executive Vice President and Chief Operations Officer Michael Copeland, "The decision on where to place new stores has been primarily based on where we have a substantial number of existing direct-channel customers making purchases from the catalog or online. You could say, we reward our established customers with a brick-and-mortar store in their neighborhood."

Hamburg, Pennsylvania, on opening day.

- Michael Copeland hired, now Executive Vice President and Chief Operations Officer.
- Total revenue: $2,349,599,000.

2008

- S.I.R. reopens as Cabela's 27th store.
- 28th store opens in Scarborough, Maine.
- 29th store opens in Rapid City, South Dakota.
- Total employees: 14,700
- Total revenue: $2,552,721,000.

2009

- Tommy Millner named Cabela's President/CEO.
- 30th store opens in Billings, Montana.
- Total revenue: $2,632,240,000.

2010

- 31st store opens in Grand Junction, Colorado.
- New stores announced for Allen, Texas, Springfield, Oregon, and Edmonton, Alberta, Canada.
- Total revenue:$2.7 billion.

2011

- New store announced for Wichita, Kansas.

Cabela's culture attracts employees

Employees in Rogers, Minnesota, store.

Charles Baldwin, Executive Vice President and Chief Administrative Officer.

According to Charles Baldwin, Cabela's Executive Vice President and Chief Administrative Officer, it is not uncommon for the company to receive an average of 10 applications for every open position in a new retail store. For instance, in early 2010, hiring managers sifted through more than 2,500 applications in an effort to fill about 250 jobs.

Cabela's employs more than 14,000 people among its retail stores, call centers, distribution facilities and corporate headquarters. But the company receives more than 100,000 applications for employment throughout the year, putting Cabela's in the enviable position of having access to a great depth of applicants when making hiring decisions.

"One might assume we have difficulty recruiting, as many of our locations are in smaller communities across the United States," Baldwin says. "However, most of our employees are also our customers, and they're outdoor enthusiasts."

He added that the camaraderie among Cabela's employees as well as the company's values-based policies and principles are a major draw for job seekers. For many, the network of Cabela's employees is an extension of their family. "They become part of a culture club of passionate outdoors people," Charles says.

"And it doesn't hurt that we are a growing company which sells fun."

But working at Cabela's is more than just a job; for many employees it turns into a career. Whenever possible, Cabela's strives to promote within the company. Almost two-thirds of promotions go to existing employees, Charles says.

As the company grows, so do external hires. But one commonality among employees remains: passion for the great outdoors. And that culture keeps people with the company for many years.

"Our formula is working," Charles says. "We have high tenure and low turnover.

"Cabela's employees share a common family-oriented, conservation-minded heartbeat, and we work hard to attract the best employees to serve our loyal customers."

Dundee, Michigan

From 2003 to 2010, an additional 23 stores were built and opened, in sizes appropriate for their locations. By 2007, total retail sales had nearly matched Cabela's overall direct-channel sales, and the next year would slightly surpass them. The impact was profound, adding an additional $1 billion to Cabela's revenues.

Michael had been a longtime Cabela's catalog customer and visited his first store two years before he joined the company in 2007. "When I saw the Fort Worth store for the first time, my reaction was, Wow! When you walk into that store, the size and atmosphere are overwhelming. It vastly exceeded my expectations."

"Cabela's is not like other retail brands," Michael emphasizes. "Cabela's customers are fiercely loyal. When we open a new store, people take their kids out of school; skip work and come in wearing their Cabela's T-shirts and hats. Thousands line up to be the first ones in the store. When we open the doors, they don't close for more than 20 minutes because of the crowd pouring in."

The tourist-center aspect associated with the stores has not been

Sidney, Nebraska, Gun Library.

diminished by their growing number. "When we opened our Billings, Montana, store in 2009," Michael says. "I took a photo of a man, his wife and a half-dozen buddies who had driven three hours to get to the store so they could celebrate his 42nd birthday there. His friends and family had given him Cabela's gift cards and he was so happy his birthday was on the same day we opened our store. That's an example of what I mean when I say it's much more than just a store. It's an event in customers' lives."

Bus loads of students visit Cabela's stores to see the animal displays and learn about wildlife and natural resources. Cabela's is also a popular destination for tour buses.

As for how many Cabela's stores there will eventually be, Michael says, "We aren't even close to a saturation point. We have people climbing all over us to get a Cabela's store in their community. Letters come every day, 'Please build a store here.' With only 30-plus stores, we are not anywhere close to capacity. We have a long way to go. We could more than double in size, and still not hit the saturation point."

Keeping pace with Cabela's growth

Angelo Sakis, Vice President of International Business Development and Operations.

To keep pace with company growth, Cabela's implemented state-of-the-art inventory-control systems.

In the 15 years Angelo Sakis spent managing Cabela's inventory-control operations, sales increased 500 percent – and so did inventory.

"Things got tricky," he says. "When a catalog-based company builds dozens of stores and launches a dot-com channel along the way, demand skyrockets. The move was great for business, but made for interesting times in the inventory department."

Angelo, Vice President of International Business Development and Operations since 2009, said the inventory control process was largely manual when he joined Cabela's in the mid-1990s. Today, computer programs have made these operations much more efficient.

"People don't use 10-key calculators much anymore," he says. "Our state-of-the-art inventory-control programs do much more than report numbers; they help us figure out when and how much inventory to plan, allocate, forecast and replenish."

These technological advancements make it possible for Cabela's employees to do more work, and do it faster. But thanks to the company's growing product selection, the inventory control staff grew from a handful of people in 1994 to more than 100 in 2009, when Angelo was Vice President of Inventory.

Like many longtime Cabela's employees, Angelo has had a hand in a variety of projects across all aspects of the company's business. In his time at Cabela's, he's also been involved in getting the company's first television program, "Under Wild Skies," up and running, as well as assisting in the initial launch of cabelas.com.

"When I came to Cabela's, if something needed to be done, we all jumped in," Angelo says. "That's the way things are today, too. Employees have more defined roles now, but we're still willing to pitch in anytime, anywhere the company needs us."

Cabela's Loyalty Programs

In 1987, Cabela's joined with National Bank of Commerce, a privately held bank in Lincoln, Nebraska, to introduce a Cabela's Visa affinity credit card. This card carried Cabela's name, and featured either a hunting or fishing scene, but offered no benefits.

Dave Roehr, then Vice President of Marketing, envisioned a credit-card program to reward customer loyalty, merging a bank's financial operations with Cabela's millions of devoted customers into a mutually profitable venture. He submitted proposal requests to a dozen banks and ultimately selected National Bank of Commerce, with whom Cabela's had the existing affinity card relationship. In 1995, Cabela's and NBC mailed the first pre-approved offers for Cabela's CLUB Visa.

The 5,000 customers who held the original affinity cards formed the CLUB Visa customer base. That group and newly signed-on cardholders, received a Cabela's Visa card with a mountain scene, the same image found on CLUB Visa Classic cards today.

Sue Saathoff, Vice President of Cabela's and Executive Vice President of Operations at World's Foremost Bank, was involved in the initial promotion of Cabela's CLUB Visa card, now held by millions of customers worldwide.

"The people we worked with at Visa were always impressed by Cabela's CLUB Visa growth and stability," she says. "But what really caught their attention was the simplicity of our loyalty program. It was all very easy for our customers. It's just one more way Cabela's puts customers first."

CLUB Visa members earn two percent in CLUB points for Cabela's purchases and one percent in CLUB points for other purchases using the card. They also receive exclusive promotions and offers throughout the year, including zero-percent interest offers, multiplied points on purchases, specific merchandise for value-priced offers, Internet specials and retail events for members. CLUB Visa membership levels – Classic, Signature and Signature Black – are based on annual spend.

Sue Saathoff, Cabela's Vice President and World's Foremost Bank Executive Vice President of Operations.

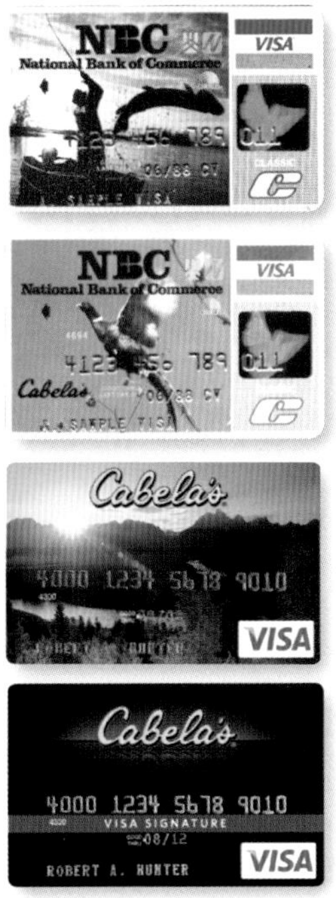

CLUB points are used to purchase merchandise from Cabela's and redemption is easy. Members can redeem points when they place orders from a catalog or on cabelas.com, or make a purchase at Cabela's U.S. retail locations. Points don't expire and are available whenever the customer chooses.

Over the years, customer acquisition efforts grew from pre-approved mailings to advertising in Cabela's catalogs and taking applications when customers placed phone orders. In addition, cabelas.com carried advertising and CLUB booths were set up in U.S. retail locations.

Cabela's stores have proven excellent settings for CLUB events. For example, at the first CLUB Visa members-only promotion in Owatonna, Minnesota, cardholders were invited to attend and receive $50 in CLUB points. The response was overwhelming. The nearby interstate exit was backed up with bumper-to-bumper traffic and the store was filled beyond capacity. This successful promotion was repeated for several years at many Cabela's stores.

World's Foremost Bank headquarters building in Lincoln, Nebraska.

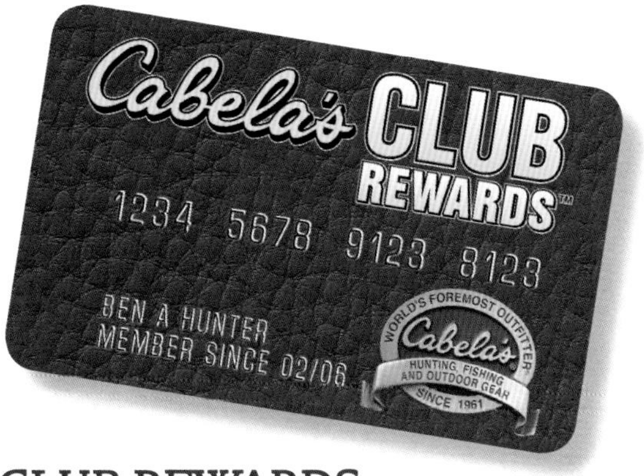

World's Foremost Bank

Wells Fargo purchased National Bank of Commerce in 2000. This paved the way for Cabela's to act on a contract clause allowing Cabela's to buy the CLUB Visa portfolio in the event of an ownership change. Dave Roehr and Tom Boatman, then Vice President of National Bank of Commerce, put the wheels in motion to start Cabela's own bank. World's Foremost Bank was chartered in 2001.

Joe Friebe, Cabela's Executive Vice President and President and Chief Executive Officer of World's Foremost Bank, says the decision to own and operate a bank had profound implications for the company.

"No one expected Cabela's CLUB Visa to be as big as it has become," he says. "We owe its success, as well as the company's success, in part, to World's Foremost Bank. We wouldn't be the same company without the bank. Cabela's CLUB is the glue that holds the business together." Cabela's ownership of the bank ensures that when CLUB Visa cardholders call for customer service assistance they speak with a Cabela's employee based in Nebraska, Joe says. "No overseas call centers for us," he says. "Cabela's has combined its relatively new financial business with its own unique, customer-oriented approach. Our loyalty program is as customer friendly as every other aspect of our business. An outside bank could never match that level of service."

Cabela's CLUB REWARDS

Sharon Robison, currently Manager of Cabela's CLUB REWARDS loyalty program, was on the original CLUB Visa team. Sharon says, "When offering the CLUB Visa card to retail shoppers, some said they didn't want another credit card. These customers were pushing carts filled with merchandise, so shouldn't they also be part of a Cabela's loyalty group?"

An examination of Cabela's customer database revealed a large pool of customers who were high-volume buyers but were not CLUB Visa cardholders. So Cabela's created Cabela's CLUB REWARDS, a non-credit card program that was tested in 2006, evaluated in 2007 with positive results, and officially launched later that year.

The CLUB REWARDS program is very basic. Members receive two percent back on purchases from cabelas.com, phone orders and at U.S. retail locations regardless of how they pay for their order, and can redeem CLUB points for Cabela's merchandise whenever they wish. There is no membership fee, no limit on the number of points earned and no expiration of points on accounts in good standing.

Cabela's commitment to customers has never been more obvious than through these two loyalty programs – Cabela's CLUB Visa and CLUB REWARDS – which benefit several million customers.

Going Public

On June 25, 2004, Jim Cabela rang the opening bell at the New York Stock Exchange and Cabela's went public. For more than 40 years the company had been privately owned, but in the early 2000s it faced two issues. Cabela's needed an influx of cash to fund the company's planned retail expansion, and to provide liquidity to its major shareholders, including the founders.

After much deliberation, Cabela's decided to make an initial public offering of Cabela's stock. The historical move marked a major business transformation. Cabela's Executive Vice President and Chief Financial Officer Ralph Castner recalled a contentious, months-long process.

"It was important to provide some level of control to the Cabela family," Ralph says. "It required a six-month effort involving investment bankers, accountants and attorneys to properly communicate the Cabela's story through a 130-page prospectus."

In one instance, he says, two weeks of passionate and lively discussion resulted in completion of one page of the prospectus. But a significant amount of time was also devoted to drafting the necessary communication to Cabela's employees and crafting the "road show" presentation to potential investors across the United States and Europe. In addition to Ralph, key players in the IPO preparation included Dennis Highby, Pat Snyder, Brian Linneman and Mike Callahan. Dennis, Ralph and Mike were the road show crew.

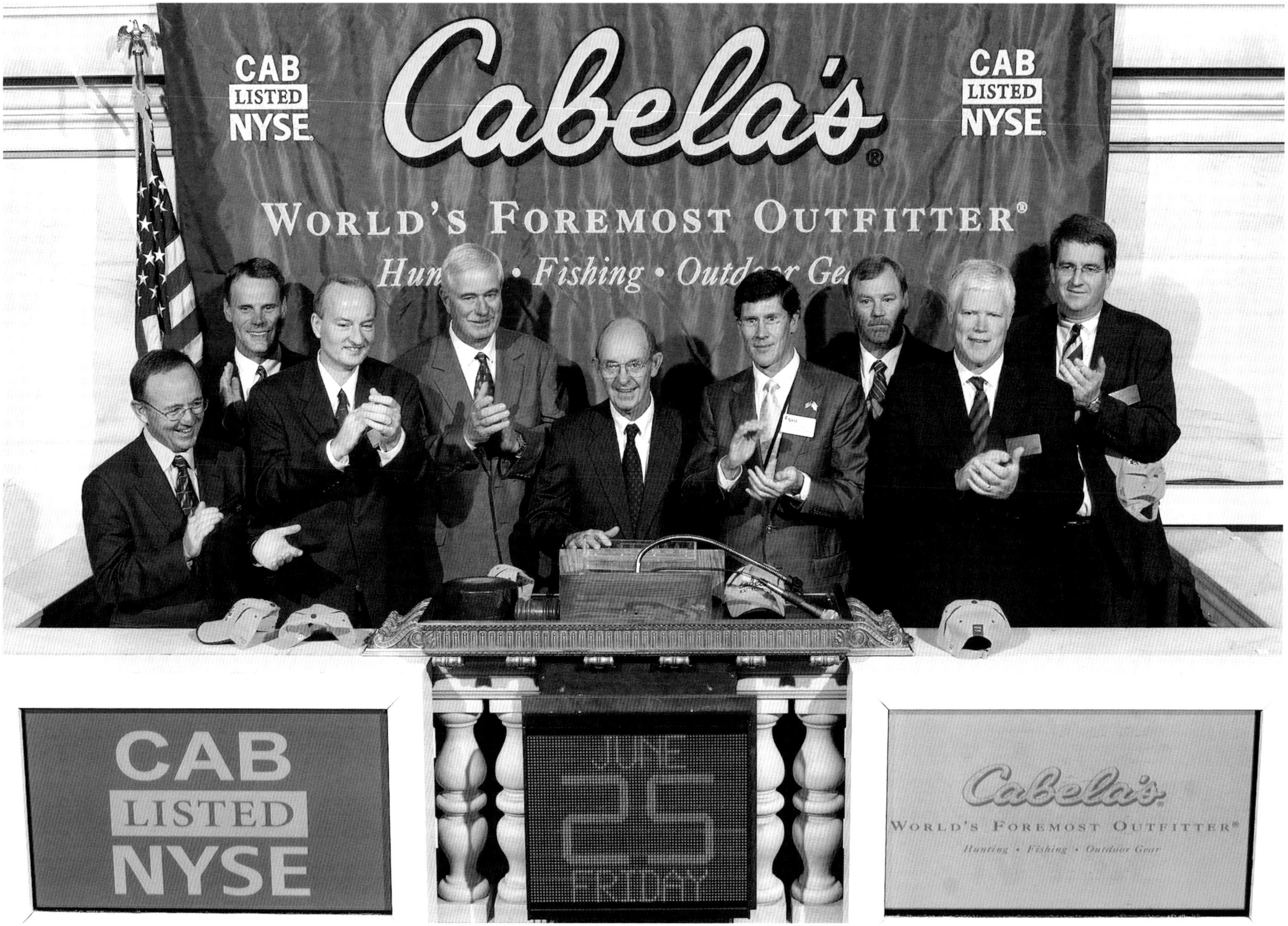

On the day of Cabela's initial public offering, June 25, 2004, Jim Cabela rang the opening bell of the New York Stock Exchange. Pictured, from left, are Cabela's Board of Directors Member Michael McCarthy, Brian Linneman, Dave Roehr, Dennis Highby, Jim Cabela, NYSE CEO John A. Thain, Pat Snyder, Mike Callahan and Ralph Castner.
Left: Cabela's employees in Sidney celebrate the company's successful initial public offering.

With a giant Cabela's banner draped over the front of the New York Stock Exchange building, Cabela's employees, spouses and members of Cabela's Board of Directors throw their caps in the air in celebration of the company's initial public offering.

"It was an easy sell," Ralph says. "Cabela's is the category leader in the outdoor industry. With our multichannel model, historic profitability, strong customer service, high-quality products and consistent growth and profits, the Cabela's brand wasn't a high-risk bet."

And in the summer of 2004, investors made it clear they agreed. Cabela's stock, at an IPO price of $20 per share, jumped 40% in the first few minutes of trading on the New York Stock Exchange and closed at $26, raising $156,300,000. But with this success came a new challenge: quarterly earnings calls.

"We spent 80 hours preparing for our first call in July of 2004," Ralph said.

While it was difficult to let go of the family's lifetime endeavor when the company went public, Dick Cabela said and continues to maintain, "Cabela's will stay Cabela's."

A sample of Cabela's stock certificate.

Cabela's Canada

Winnipeg, Manitoba

In 2007, Cabela's purchased S.I.R. Warehouse Sports Store in Winnipeg, Manitoba, and announced it would be headquarters for further expansion into Canada.

S.I.R. was founded in 1924 by Sydney Isaac Robinson and grew into one of Canada's leading outdoor outfitters through its mail-order operation and a 44,000-square-foot store in the heart of Winnipeg's shopping district.

Sharon Robison recalls how Cabela's Canadian venture began.

"Now Cabela's has a world-class electronic data warehouse where a simple computer query will extract amazing information," she says. "But before that, we relied on individual interpretation of what was happening within our customer structure."

"In the early '70s, I noticed a developing trend — orders from Canada were on the rise. About that time, my husband and I were on a fishing trip at a resort on the Campbell River near the Strait of Georgia. I asked, and none of the guides — a couple dozen or so — knew about Cabela's. At the time, I was in charge of mailing catalogs, so when I got home I asked Dick if I could allot some catalogs to Canada, that I thought we might be missing an opportunity there. Dick said, 'Sure, how many do you need?' and I said 'Oh, 10,000,' and he said, 'OK. Do it.'"

"Over the next five years, the Canada market grew substantially and that growth trend has continued."

The S.I.R. purchase, and the physical move into Canada, was a natural extension of Cabela's growing retail vision, according to Dennis Highby. "We had a loyal customer base in Canada, and our brand is very well recognized there, and that convinced us to expand our platform," he says. "We already did significant business in Canada through mail-order and cross-border shopping, so we felt it was important to have a Canadian footprint. The S.I.R. acquisition allowed us to accelerate the retail, catalog and Internet expansion."

The S.I.R. retail facility was remodeled to Cabela's style and became such a success that in 2010 Cabela's acquired a 345,000-square-foot facility in Winnipeg to serve as Canadian corporate headquarters, call center and distribution center for the catalog, Internet and retail operations. Also in 2010, Cabela's announced construction of a second Canadian catalog showroom, with 70,000 square-feet, to be opened in Edmonton, Alberta, in 2011.

Cabela's refined catalogs to address customer needs for specific regions and activities.

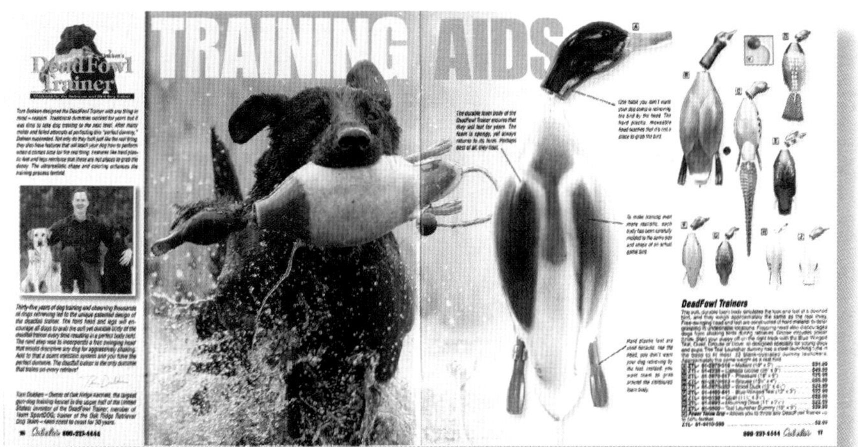

Visions of the Future

As Cabela's first half-century mark approached, the nature of the company had greatly changed from what it had been even just 10 years before. The integration of the developing multichannel elements of the business had added new departments and new management requirements. The move from private to public ownership required a more organized and mapped-out approach to future planning and expectations. A new group of senior executives had been brought on board since the mid-1990s to complement the continuing "old-timers" with decades of experience at Cabela's.

Looking toward the future, all of Cabela's leaders share a central concern: How can Cabela's continue to grow and prosper in a changing world, as a publicly regulated concern, under a new generation of leadership, without losing the essential character, the core values, that earned Cabela's its success in the first place?

Whether a 20-year Cabela's veteran or a person who joined recently, all Cabela's core managers agree it can continue and are committed to ensuring it does.

The Cabela's story is far from complete, but the best way to wrap up this 50th anniversary tale is to hear from Jim, Dick, Dennis and Cabela's Chief Executive Officer Tommy Millner. Tommy was named CEO in 2009, the first from outside the company; replacing Dennis, who transitioned from CEO to the Cabela's Board of Directors as a Vice Chairman.

Cabela's micro catalogs were the next step in the evolution of specialized product offerings.

"This love for the company, the depth of passion our employees have, is greater than in any company I have ever been associated with or even heard about, and it's not going away." – Tommy Millner

Chief Executive Officer Tommy Millner fishing in the Bahamas, 2010.

After 30 years as an executive in the outdoor industry (most recently at Remington Arms Company) and a longtime Cabela's customer, Tommy offers a unique inside view with an outsider's objective perspective.

"Because of the way Dick, Jim and Dennis treated people through 50 years of building Cabela's, there is among our employees a deep trust for the company and everything it stands for," Tommy says.

The Cabelas have always been quick to attribute their success to loyal employees. "Cabela's isn't Jim, Mary and Dick Cabela," Dick says. "Cabela's is our family of employees who work passionately every day to make us the best. Cabela's succeeded beyond our wildest dreams because it became the dream of so many dedicated employees."

"This love for the company, the depth of passion our employees have, is greater than in any company I have ever been associated with or even heard about," Tommy says. "And it's not going away.

"'Respect for Individuals' is one of our five Core Values and for Dick, Jim and Dennis it started with employees. Employees and customers. The employees know it; they feel the respect and they understand they are to pass on that respect to co-workers and customers. It's instilled that if we – each and every employee – don't please our customers every time we interact, we won't have a company. The focus of the entire company is laser-beamed at pleasing our customers every day. That says a lot for how ingrained those founding principles are."

To Jim Cabela, it's a simple matter of fact. "You can get all kinds of answers about how your business is doing but if you listen to your customers, they'll tell you what you need to know," he says.

Simple or not, it is taken to heart at Cabela's.

"Every month we hold a one-hour meeting with all our directors and vice presidents and we listen to customer-service calls," Tommy says. "That meeting will never come off the schedule because it brings to light and reinforces what's important to our customers. That's how deep our culture is, how ingrained our Core Values are in our fiber."

Cabela's Core Purpose and Core Values are displayed throughout the company.

Cabela's culture, Tommy says, "has migrated all over the United States and into Canada right along with our retail stores; and throughout the world via our catalogs and website."

Loyal Cabela's customers live what has become known as the Cabela's lifestyle – an active outdoor-recreation-oriented lifestyle, across the age spectrum, with an appreciation of the natural world and the health and well-being benefits it provides. The advent of the Internet and rapid, widespread sharing of information has accelerated the growth, as thousands and thousands of outdoor recreation enthusiasts bond over shared values and beliefs in a company grounded in tradition and heritage.

Cabela's has acquired a legendary cult-like status, a positive, family-like cult status, in which loyal customers express pride in their relationship with the company. And, Cabela's has entered the mainstream lexicon. During the 2000 and 2004 presidential elections, the national press played up the "Cabela's bloc of voters," a sought-after political force composed of grounded, informed outdoor enthusiasts.

And, the representation of a whole demographic continues in mainstream-media discussions of outdoor recreation, conservation, wildlife and environmental issues with mention of the "Cabela's crowd," referring to the hundreds of thousands of hunters, anglers, campers, hikers, wildlife watchers and others with a strong appreciation of outdoor tradition, heritage and our role in the natural world.

With so many sharing that appreciation, Tommy envisions no end to Cabela's growth or its role as an anchor, a manifestation, a gathering point for outdoor enthusiasts across diverse age, income, geographic, interest and educational demographic definitions, all sharing a common belief in values, ethics, tradition, heritage and culture.

"Cabela's is a phenomenon," he says. "It's a rolling snowball, growing in size and momentum as employees, customers and shareholders get on board realizing this culture created 50 years ago by Jim and Dick Cabela represents something special, something they want to be part of."

It's amazing, Dick says, what can happen by simply following what he and Jim learned from their father: "Customers come first; provide a good value for their hard-earned dollars and treat everyone with respect. Be honest, work hard and give everyone a fair shake."

Dennis knows these are not hollow words. All these years he has carried in his wallet Dick's business card, on the back of which is printed this Dale Wimbrow poem:

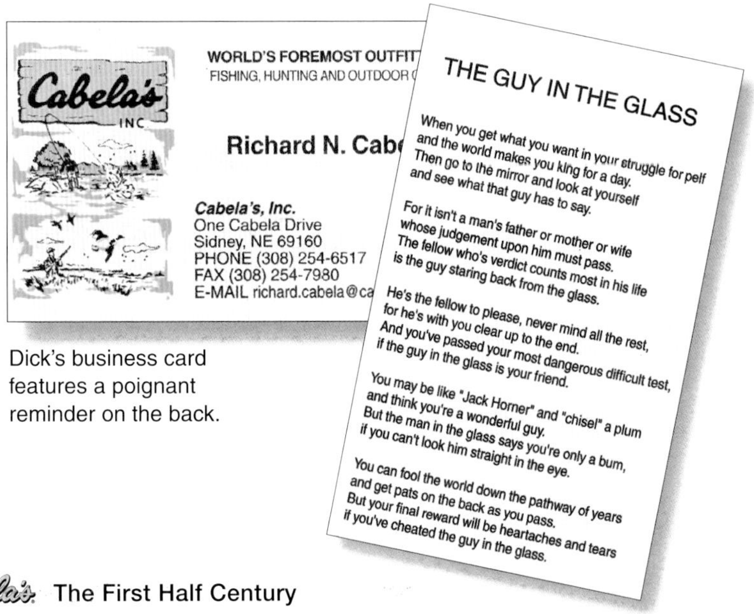

Dick's business card features a poignant reminder on the back.

The Guy in the Glass

When you get what you want in your struggle for pelf,
And the world makes you King for a day,
Then go to the mirror and look at yourself,
And see what that guy has to say.

For it isn't your Father, or Mother, or Wife,
Whose judgement upon you must pass.
The feller whose verdict counts most in your life
Is the guy staring back from the glass.

He's the feller to please, never mind all the rest,
For he's with you clear up to the end,
And you've passed your most dangerous, difficult test
If the guy in the glass is your friend.

You may be like Jack Horner and "chisel" a plum,
And think you're a wonderful guy,
But the man in the glass says you're only a bum
If you can't look him straight in the eye.

You can fool the whole world down the pathway of years,
And get pats on the back as you pass,
But your final reward will be heartaches and tears
If you've cheated the guy in the glass.

Copyright 1934

"Imagine working for someone who has that on his card," Dennis said. "That says a lot about Dick and about how Cabela's was built and what it stands for. It's about knowing who you are and what Cabela's is; about being able to look in the mirror every day. If you can live up to that standard, you're doing your job.

"I'm proud to have worked for a guy who has that on his business card."

Dick with a trophy Lord Derby eland in Cameroon, 2001.

The handmade sign on Jim Cabela's desk.

On Jim's desk is a desktop sign he made stating: Be brief, Be blunt, Be gone.

The sign, in place when Dennis arrived in 1976, intimidated salesmen and vendors, especially those intent on over-hyping products, but it also served as an important reminder to employees, Dennis says.

"It's effective in reminding you there is a time for visiting and then it's time to get to work," he says. "You can't just sit and hypothesize all the time; you have to get the work done."

Dennis reflects on changes and accomplishments during his tenure at Cabela's:

"When I started I was the 40th employee; and toward the end of my term as CEO, there were 14,000 employees.

"When I got here we were doing $5 million a year. For it to grow from $5 million to $2.6 billion in 2009, our growth averaged 20 percent each year.

"We were housed in one building and even then the third floor was locked up and the basement was empty. Now we have 31 retail stores; three huge distribution centers, call centers, our bank and other facilities.

"And back then we produced two catalogs a year, one in the spring and one in the fall. During my time, that had grown to more than 100 catalogs each year."

But the growth didn't come without hard work and sacrifice.

"I'm most proud of having raised four good kids. And I have 12 grandkids and a very understanding wife who put up with a lot of long hours we put in," he said. "As we were growing so fast, the core team put in a lot of long hours. We often worked every night until 10 or 11 o'clock, so we missed a lot our kids were involved in. Plus, we worked Saturdays and would come back in after church on Sundays."

Nevertheless, he says he wouldn't trade it for anything.

"It's been the best job anyone ever had," he says. "There were a lot of good times. That's what it was all about: working hard, playing hard and having fun doing it."

The most valuable aspect, Dennis says, was the close relationships that formed. "The most important thing to me has been to work for two fellows who were also my friends," Dennis says. "Jim and Dick were very enjoyable to work for. They have to be the best bosses in the world. They never once raised their voices. Imagine that."

"How much better can it get?" asks Jim, reflecting on 50 extraordinary years of combining work with his passion for the outdoors. "You get to use the products you enjoy using and make some money on the side. It's a pretty good deal."

Dennis closes with this advice to Cabela's employees for the next half century: "For the next 50 years, it will still be very important to always listen to our customers and continue to dominate the competition," he says. "And pay attention to the guy in the glass."

"For the next 50 years, it will still be very important to always listen to our customers and continue to dominate the competition."

– Dennis Highby

Dennis and Jim shooting clay targets, 2005.

Cabela's

Chapter 7

Cabela's Destination Stores

It is impossible to convey the Cabela's retail experience in a handful of photographs. Each store has its own features, each has its unique wildlife displays and special features, yet there is a common feeling connecting them all. It's a feeling of belonging, a feeling of being among friends who share common bonds and beliefs; who share appreciation for outdoor traditions and heritage.

Were they filled with only Cabela's great products, that would be enough. But Cabela's showrooms feature museum-quality wildlife displays and nostalgic outdoor memorabilia, all steeped in 50 years of rich Cabela's outdoor history. The stores are educational, entertaining and mesmerizing to anyone with an interest in our natural heritage, our natural surroundings, our national traditions.

Cabela's stores have been the backdrop for engagements and weddings, birthday shopping sprees and family gatherings. School buses and travel coaches offload their passengers for educational, enjoyable field trips. Families plan vacations to include Cabela's stores; hunters and anglers stop when en route to (and from) their destinations. Some track their visits, checking off each store from a well-traveled list.

Cabela's store openings are major events, drawing thousands who line up early to be some of the first inside. The excitement is palpable, and returned by the courteous, knowledgeable employees who share the same excitement. Cabela's employees are known for living the Cabela's lifestyle, an active outdoor-oriented lifestyle. Many loyal Cabela's customers live the Cabela's lifestyle too and that is the underlying feeling, the shared beliefs, the common experience, connecting them.

What follows is a photographic representation of all Cabela's retail locations. No matter how clear, how well-framed the photograph, none carry the feeling of stepping inside a Cabela's store. Come see for yourself. Welcome to the Cabela's shopping experience.

Customers flock to Cabela's grand openings.

EDMONTON
LACEY
WINNIPEG
EAST GRAND FORKS
POST FALLS
SPRINGFIELD
BOISE
BILLINGS
SCARBOROUGH
ROGERS
RAPID CITY
OWATONNA
RICHFIELD
EAST HARTFORD
MITCHELL
PRAIRIE DU CHIEN
DUNDEE
LEHI
SIDNEY
LA VISTA
HAMBURG
HOFFMAN ESTATES
HAMMOND
RENO
KEARNEY
GRAND JUNCTION
WHEELING
KANSAS CITY
HAZELWOOD
WICHITA
GLENDALE
ALLEN
FORT WORTH
BUDA
GONZALES

gain Cave

Sidney, Nebraska

- **Year opened:** original store, 1969; flagship store, 1991
- **Square feet:** flagship, 104,000
- **City population:** 6,000
- **GPS coordinates:** N 41° 06.885'   W 102° 57.355'
- **Fact:** original downtown building remained Cabela's corporate headquarters until new corporate office building was built in the late '90s

SIDNEY, NEBRASKA

Kearney, Nebraska

- **Year opened:** October 1987
- **Square feet:** 57,000
- **Miles from Sidney:** 220
- **City population:** 24,400
- **GPS coordinates:** N 40° 42.421'   W 99° 01.984'
- **Fact:** Kearney campus also home to large Cabela's call center

Owatonna, Minnesota

- **Year opened:** April 1998
- **Square feet:** 163,000
- **Miles from Sidney:** 720
- **City population:** 22,300
- **GPS coordinates:** N 44° 08.103'   W 93° 14.965'
- **Fact:** the first Cabela's showroom to include a furniture and art gallery

Prairie du Chien, Wisconsin

- **Year opened:** September 1998
- **Square feet:** 53,000
- **Miles from Sidney:** 740
- **City population:** 5,700
- **GPS coordinates:** N 43° 04.324'   W 91° 08.222'
- **Fact:** adjacent to a 600,000-square-foot Cabela's distribution center

KANSAS CITY, KANSAS

Kansas City, Kansas

- **Year opened:** August 2002
- **Square feet:** 192,000
- **Miles from Sidney:** 540
- **City population:** 147,000
- **GPS coordinates:** N 39° 7.230' W 94° 48.933'
- **Fact:** first Cabela's store to feature a trophy deer museum; building adjacent to the Kansas Speedway

Cabela's

Dundee, Michigan

- **Year opened:** August 2000
- **Square feet:** 227,000
- **Miles from Sidney:** 1,120
- **City population:** 2,700
- **GPS coordinates:**
  N 41° 57.850'   W 83° 40.500'
- **Fact:** first Cabela's store located in Eastern time zone; only two larger Cabela's stores have been built since

DUNDEE, MICHIGAN

Hamburg, Pennsylvania

- **Year opened:** September 2003
- **Square feet:** 246,000
- **Miles from Sidney:** 1,560
- **City population:** 4,100
- **GPS coordinates:** N 40° 33.46' W 76° 00.19'
- **Fact:** Cabela's largest store, located just a couple miles from the Appalachian Trail

HAMBURG, PENNSYLVANIA

East Grand Forks, Minnesota

- **Year opened:** September 1999
- **Square feet:** 60,000
- **Miles from Sidney:** 895
- **City population:** 8,700
- **GPS coordinates:**
  N 47° 55.715' W 97° 01.599'
- **Fact:** Cabela's second Minnesota location and the company's northernmost U.S. store; traditional stop for travelers heading to and from Manitoba, Canada

Mitchell, South Dakota

- **Year opened:** March 2000
- **Square feet:** 84,000
- **Miles from Sidney:** 440
- **City population:** 1,400
- **GPS coordinates:**
  N 43° 41.441' W 98° 01.035'
- **Fact:** grounds feature a larger-than-life-size bronze sculpture of a fox flushing pheasants among cornstalks

Wheeling, West Virginia

- **Year opened:** August 2004
- **Square Feet:** 175,000
- **Miles from Sidney:** 1,320
- **City Population:** 31,400
- **GPS coordinates:**
  N 40° 03.978' W 080° 35.774'
- **Fact:** Wheeling campus also home to a 1,000,000-square-foot-plus distribution center

Buda, Texas

- **Year opened:** June 2005
- **Square feet:** 192,000
- **Miles from Sidney:** 1,070
- **City population:** 3,800
- **GPS coordinates:** N 30° 04.952' W 097° 49.531'
- **Fact:** Cabela's second store in Texas; company's southernmost location

Lehi, Utah

- **Year opened:** August 2005
- **Square feet:** 170,000
- **Miles from Sidney:** 575
- **City population:** 34,500
- **GPS coordinates:** N 40° 26.227' W 111° 53.364'
- **Fact:** features displays of several trophy mule deer from Utah, including the No. 2 typical and non-typical Boone and Crockett records for the state

Rogers, Minnesota

- **Year opened:** October 2005
- **Square feet:** 185,000
- **Miles from Sidney:** 795
- **City population:** 6,000
- **GPS coordinates:** N 45° 11.234' W 93° 32.242'
- **Fact:** Cabela's third Minnesota store, which includes a bait shop with a convenient separate entrance

Cabela's

FORT WORTH, TEXAS

Fort Worth, Texas

- **Year opened:** May 2005
- **Square feet:** 234,000
- **Miles from Sidney:** 850
- **City population:** 534,700
- **GPS coordinates:** N 32° 57.694' W 97° 18.456'
- **Fact:** grounds feature a 5-acre lake; store features a 65,000-gallon aquarium

Glendale, Arizona

- **Year opened:** July 2006
- **Square feet:** 166,000
- **Miles from Sidney:** 1,110
- **City population:** 233,900
- **GPS coordinates:** N 33° 32.350' W 112° 15.704'
- **Fact:** features a unique "canyon country" museum; building across the street from the Arizona Cardinals' football stadium

Boise, Idaho

- **Year opened:** August 2006
- **Square feet:** 132,000
- **Miles from Sidney:** 840
- **City population:** 186,800
- **GPS coordinates:** N 43° 36.186' W 116° 17.099'
- **Fact:** home to the Elmer Keith Museum, which includes firearms, taxidermy, memorabilia and recorded interviews with the writer

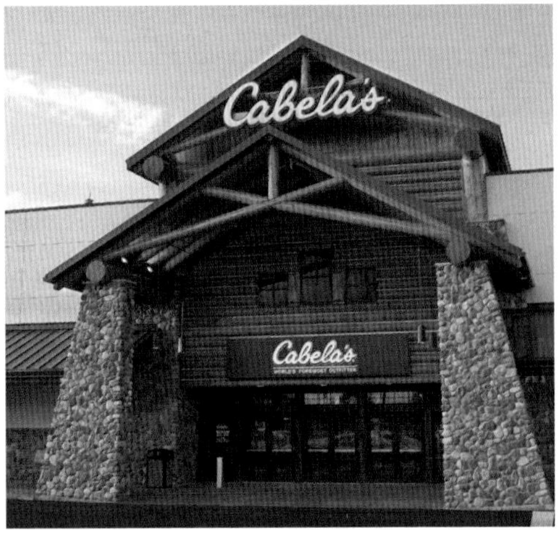

Richfield, Wisconsin

- **Year opened:** September 2006
- **Square Feet:** 166,000
- **Miles from Sidney:** 915
- **City Population:** 10,400
- **GPS coordinates:** N 43° 16.733' W 088° 11.294'
- **Fact:** Cabela's second Wisconsin store, which features a Northwoods wildlife museum

Hazelwood, Missouri

- **Year opened:** April 2007
- **Square feet:** 132,000
- **Miles from Sidney:** 770
- **City population:** 26,200
- **GPS coordinates:**
  N 38° 47.189'   W 090° 24.876'
- **Fact:** first Cabela's store to anchor a shopping mall, the St. Louis Mills

Hoffman Estates, Illinois

- **Year opened:** September 2007
- **Square feet:** 182,000
- **Miles from Sidney:** 855
- **City population:** 49,500
- **GPS coordinates:**
  N 42° 04.90'   W 88° 12.42'
- **Fact:** located within a few hundred miles of five other Cabela's stores

East Hartford, Connecticut

- **Year opened:** October 2007
- **Square feet:** 182,000
- **Miles from Sidney:** 1,745
- **City population:** 49,600
- **GPS coordinates:**
  N 41° 45.21'   W 72° 37.21'
- **Fact:** adjacent to Rentschler Field, home of the University of Connecticut Huskies football team

WORLD'S FOREMOST OUTFITTER
Cabela's
HUNTING, FISHING AND OUTDOOR GEAR
SINCE 1961
Cabela's
C1
Cabela's
Welcome
Special Guests
Private Sale

La Vista, Nebraska

- **Year opened:** November 2006
- **Square feet:** 129,000
- **Miles from Sidney:** 390
- **City population:** 1,700
- **GPS coordinates:**
  N 41° 10.770' W 96° 06.608'
- **Fact:** Cabela's third store in its home state of Nebraska

LA VISTA, NEBRASKA

Hammond, Indiana

- **Year opened:** October 2007
- **Square feet:** 189,000
- **Miles from Sidney:** 870
- **City population:** 72,500
- **GPS coordinates:**
  N 41° 34.15'   W 87° 28.57'
- **Fact:** the largest of eight Cabela's stores built in 2007, the company's busiest year in terms of retail expansion

Post Falls, Idaho

- **Year opened:** November 2007
- **Square feet:** 129,000
- **Miles from Sidney:** 1,080
- **City population:** 17,300
- **GPS coordinates:**
  N 47° 41.969'   W 117° 02.303'
- **Fact:** Cabela's second store in Idaho; includes display honoring writer Jack O'Connor

Reno, Nevada

- **Year opened:** November 2007
- **Square feet:** 129,000
- **Miles from Sidney:** 1,070
- **City population:** 205,500
- **GPS coordinates:**
  N 39° 30.45'   W 119° 57.57'
- **Fact:** includes a display featuring Africa's six most dangerous animals: elephant, rhino, lion, leopard, Cape buffalo and hippo

Lacey, Washington

- **Year opened:** November 2007
- **Square Feet:** 182,000
- **Miles from Sidney:** 1,375
- **City Population:** 31,200
- **GPS coordinates:**
  N 47° 03.762' W 122° 47.097'
- **Fact:** the store's Conservation Mountain features the only sea lion in a Cabela's store

Scarborough, Maine

- **Year opened:** May 2008
- **Square feet:** 129,000
- **Miles from Sidney:** 1,930
- **City population:** 3,900
- **GPS coordinates:**
  N 43° 36.157' W 070° 22.226'
- **Fact:** farthest Cabela's store from the company's world headquarters in Sidney, Nebraska

Winnipeg, Manitoba, Canada

- **Year opened:** May 2008
- **Square feet:** 41,000
- **Miles from Sidney:** 990
- **City population:** 700,000
- **GPS coordinates:**
  N 49° 53.628' W 097° 11.458'
- **Fact:** the company's first store located in Canada, converted from an S.I.R. Warehouse Sports Store after Cabela's acquired the outdoor gear retailer in 2007

Cabela's
Cabela's

GONZALES, LOUISIANA

Gonzales, Louisiana

- **Year opened:** October 2007
- **Square feet:** 167,000
- **Miles from Sidney:** 1,330
- **City population:** 10,000
- **GPS coordinates:**
  N 30° 12.33' W 90° 57.30'
- **Fact:** museum includes a display of a 13-foot alligator as well as an alligator snapping turtle

Rapid City, South Dakota

- **Year opened:** August 2008
- **Square feet:** 80,000
- **Miles from Sidney:** 230
- **City population:** 62,700
- **GPS coordinates:**
  N 44° 6.059' W 103° 9.74'
- **Fact:** second Cabela's store in South Dakota; a favorite stop for motorcycle riders and other tourists traveling through the scenic Black Hills

Billings, Montana

- **Year opened:** May 2009
- **Square feet:** 80,000
- **Miles from Sidney:** 560
- **City population:** 100,000
- **GPS coordinates:**
  N 45° 45.2063' W 108° 31.7925'
- **Fact:** the only Cabela's store built in 2009 and the first to reflect the company's efficient next-generation store format

Grand Junction, Colorado

- **Year opened:** May 2010
- **Square feet:** 76,000
- **Miles from Sidney:** 410
- **City population:** 53,700
- **GPS coordinates:**
  N 39° 5.4762' W 108° 36.172'
- **Fact:** Cabela's only store built in 2010; anchors Mesa Mall

That's our story. We hope you enjoyed it as much as we enjoyed reliving our history as we put this book together. Of course, Cabela's story is far from complete. This final-chapter tour through our stores is a work in progress. We plan to open three stores in 2011: Allen, Texas; Springfield, Oregon; and Edmonton, Alberta. We also announced plans to open a store in 2012 in Wichita, Kansas. But we're not stopping there. We'll let you know where we will be building next as soon as plans are finalized. Plus, we will continue to share information about our growth through World's Foremost Bank, our cabelas.com website and, where it all started, our catalogs. We are truly proud of all our stores, and the dedicated Outfitters who work so hard to help our customers find the gear they need to get the most out of the time they spend outdoors. We hope each of you has the opportunity to stop in and enjoy the Cabela's experience.

Thanks for joining us for this 50th Anniversary celebration.

Sincerely,

Dick Mary Jim Dennis

Fifty years ago, Dick Cabela stopped to
examine a small display of fishing flies.